Economies of English

Edited by
Martin Leer and Genoveva Puskás

SPELL
Swiss Papers in
English Language and Literature

Edited by
The Swiss Association of University Teachers of English
(SAUTE)

General Editor: Lukas Erne

Volume 33

Economies of English

Edited by
Martin Leer and Genoveva Puskás

Bibliografische Information der Deutschen Nationalbibliothek

Die Deutsche Nationalbibliothek verzeichnet diese Publikation in der Deutschen Nationalbibliografie;
detaillierte bibliografische Daten sind im Internet über http://dnb.dnb.de abrufbar.

Publiziert mit Unterstützung der Schweizerischen Akademie der Geistes- und Sozialwissenschaften.

© 2016 · Narr Francke Attempto Verlag GmbH + Co. KG
Dischingerweg 5 · D-72070 Tübingen

Das Werk einschließlich aller seiner Teile ist urheberrechtlich geschützt. Jede Verwertung außerhalb der engen Grenzen des Urheberrechtsgesetzes ist ohne Zustimmung des Verlages unzulässig und strafbar. Das gilt insbesondere für Vervielfältigungen, Übersetzungen, Mikroverfilmungen und die Einspeicherung und Verarbeitung in elektronischen Systemen.

Gedruckt auf säurefreiem und alterungsbeständigem Werkdruckpapier.

Internet: www.narr.de
E-Mail: info@narr.de

Printed in Germany

Umschlagabbildung und Einbandgestaltung: Martin Heusser, Zürich
Illustration: © Arnaud Barras

ISSN 0940-0478
ISBN 978-3-8233-8067-2

Table of Contents

Introduction   11

John E. Joseph (Edinburgh)
The Cerebral Closet: Language as *valeur* and *trésor* in Saussure   39

Claire-A. Forel (Geneva)
Value of and in Learning Foreign Languages   63

Eva Waltermann (Geneva) and Virág Csillagh (Geneva)
Teaching and Learning English in Geneva: Questions of Economy, Identity, Globality and Usefulness   75

Sarah Chevalier (Zurich)
The Value of English in Multilingual Families   97

Richard Waswo (Geneva)
Shakespeare and the Modern Economy   117

Indira Ghose (Fribourg)
Money, Morals, and Manners in Renaissance Courtesy Literature   129

Rahel Orgis (Neuchâtel)
"Father and son, I ha' done you simple service here":
The (Interrupted) Circulation of Money in Middleton and Dekker's *The Roaring Girl*   143

Barbara Straumann (Zurich)
"How to Live Well on Nothing a Year": Money, Credit and Debt in William Makepeace Thackeray's *Vanity Fair*   163

Sangam MacDuff (Geneva)
"Scrupulous Meanness," Joyce's Gift and the Symbolic Economy of *Dubliners*   181

Martin Mühlheim (Zurich)
Slippery Subjects: Intersecting Economies of Genre in Gay
Male Coming-Out Films, 1995-2015   199

Oran McKenzie (Geneva)
Spillage and Banditry: Anne Carson's Derivatives   225

Notes on Contributors   243

Index of Names   249

Acknowledgements

The essays of this volume form a selection of the contributions to the Swiss Association of University Teachers of English (SAUTE) 2015 Conference, held in Geneva on 24-25 April 2015. We wish to thank those who devoted so much of their time and energy to helping in the organization of this conference, Erzsi Kukorelly and Arnaud Barras. We are grateful to the Swiss Academy of Humanities and Social Sciences, the CUSO doctoral programs, the Faculty of Humanities and the English Department of the University of Geneva for their financial support, which made the organization of the conference possible. The variety and quality of the essays included in the present volume owe, in addition to their authors' expertise, also to the diligent and efficient work of anonymous peer reviewers, to whom we wish to address, without being able to name them individually, our warmest thanks. Many thanks also to Lukas Erne, General Editor, for his patient guidance and valuable advice in the preparation of the volume. We are grateful to Arnaud Barras for providing the cover picture and to Martin Heusser for designing the cover. Finally, we address our warmest thanks to Keith Hewlett for his help in the editing process, his minute and detailed comments and suggestions and, above all, his never failing patience.

General Editor's Preface

SPELL (Swiss Papers in English Language and Literature) is a publication of SAUTE, the Swiss Association of University Teachers of English. Established in 1984, it first appeared every second year, was published annually from 1994 to 2008, and now appears three times every two years. Every second year, SPELL publishes a selection of papers given at the biennial symposia organized by SAUTE. Non-symposium volumes usually have as their starting point papers given at other conferences organized by members of SAUTE, in particular conferences of SANAS, the Swiss Association for North American Studies and SAMEMES, the Swiss Association of Medieval and Early Modern English Studies. However, other proposals are also welcome. Decisions concerning topics and editors are made by the Annual General Meeting of SAUTE two years before the year of publication.

Volumes of SPELL contain carefully selected and edited papers devoted to a topic of literary, linguistic and – broadly – cultural interest. All contributions are original and are subjected to external evaluation by means of a full peer review process. Contributions are usually by participants at the conferences mentioned, but volume editors are free to solicit further contributions. Papers published in SPELL are documented in the *MLA International Bibliography*. SPELL is published with the financial support of the Swiss Academy of Humanities and Social Sciences.

Information on all aspects of SPELL, including volumes planned for the future, is available from the General Editor, Professor Lukas Erne, Département de langue et littérature anglaises, Faculté des Lettres, Université de Genève, CH-1211 Genève 4, Switzerland, e-mail: lukas.erne@unige.ch. Information about past volumes of SPELL and about SAUTE, in particular about how to become a member of the association, can be obtained from the SAUTE website at http://www.saute.ch.

Lukas Erne

Introduction

At the beginning of her book *Economy of the Unlost* the Canadian poet Anne Carson wonders:

> Humans value economy. Why? Whether we are commending a mathematician for her proof or a draughtsman for his use of line or a poet for furnishing us with nuggets of beauty and truth, economy is a trope of intellectual, aesthetic and moral value. How do we come to take comfort in this notion? It is arguable that the trope does not predate the invention of coinage. And certainly in a civilization as unconditionally committed to greed as ours is – no one questions any more the wisdom of saving money. But money is just a mediator for our greed. What does it mean to save time, or trouble, or face, or breath, or shoe leather? Or words? . . . What exactly is lost to us when words are wasted? And where is the human store to which such goods are gathered? (Carson 3)

The organizers of the SAUTE biennial conference at the University of Geneva in 2015 were motivated by a similar, if not even broader and more topical sense of wonder when we chose the theme "Economies of English." In the Call For Papers we took our point of departure in recent events:

> As the world still reels from the financial crisis of 2007-8, it seems timely to reflect on the connections between money and value embedded in all our discourses about economy, language and literature. Marxists and neoliberals have classically theorized this as reflecting the mechanisms of capitalism and the market. More recently, however, the literary theorist Marc Shell has seen the invention of coinage as underlying the whole of Western philosophy, while the anthropologist David Graeber has proposed that all the great religions and political ideologies are responses to the moral confusion of money. These are concerns that go to the heart of English studies, both because English is the global language of money, and because the discipline

and its language rest on a goldmine of unexamined economic metaphors: from literary debts to loanwords, from redemption to counterfeit and queer, from currency to exchange, from the economy of syntax to the economy of poetic expression.

As time goes on, after Brexit and other related shocks, the historical situation does appear apocalyptic in its original Greek sense of *revelatory*. The events that unfolded from the run on Northern Rock in October 2007 and the bankruptcy of Lehmann Brothers in September 2008 still seem, almost a decade later, to have been different from an ordinary "financial crisis" – even if as the conservative economists Carmen Reinhardt and Kenneth Rogoff pointed out in 2009, people at every financial crisis exclaim "This time is different!" The most centrally placed observer, Ben Bernanke, President of the US Federal Reserve at the time, has consistently argued that the potential consequences of "the Credit Crunch" (which seems to have become the most generally accepted term for the event) were far worse than the Wall Street Crash of 1929. Instead of a stock market collapse, there was a real possibility of a shutdown of the world monetary system, because the banks no longer trusted each other enough to lend to one another. Within days after Lehmann Brothers, according to many observers, all the major banks would have collapsed. And even before that ATMs would have run out of money. The "subprime mortgage" crisis in the US revealed the fragility, and insanity, of a period of economic history that had previously been dubbed "the Great Moderation."

A debate began which not only involved economists, bankers and politicians. In fact, these groups were reluctant participants. When Queen Elizabeth II visited the London School of Economics in the immediate aftermath and asked the hundreds of economics professors assembled, "Why did no one see this coming?" few clear answers were forthcoming (Martin). In fact there had been warning voices: Robert Shiller as one of the few major economists with an expertise in real estate, or the economic commentator Nouriel Roubini, who earned himself the nickname "Doctor Doom." Yet "subprime mortgage securitization," "Too Big to Fail Banks," the explosion of "shadow banking" (the unregulated activities of hedge-funds and, even more frequently, the major banks themselves) have somehow seemed too feeble explanations for the sheer scale of what had been revealed about the whole economic system and its social and political aftershocks, particularly in the Eurozone. Many economists have admitted to deep uncertainty, including the second most centrally placed observer, Sir Mervyn King, then Governor of the Bank of England, in his recent book *The End of Alchemy: Money,*

Banking and the Future of the Global Economy (2016), where he calls for a complete overhaul not only of banking regulations, but of mainstream economic analysis. But King's actual proposals seem curiously tame and even self-defeating, as Paul Krugman points out in his review in *The New York Review of Books*.

This is a long-established pattern. The maverick economist Paul Ormerod declared *The Death of Economics* in a book from 1995, arguing that the notorious failure of economic predictions about the future (performing at least 7 times worse than the toss of a coin) was an indication not just of uncertainty, but statistical proof that something in standard economic theory was basically wrong – yet at the end of the book he proposed greater attention to business profits as a major part of the solution: hardly a radical idea! Even Paul Krugman, sometimes described as "the world's leading economist," has seemed conceptually, if not linguistically, challenged in his commentary on events in the *New York Times*: his accounts of the wars between "saltwater" and "freshwater" economists (essentially the Neo-Keynesians in the great universities on the American coasts vs. the Chicago School) or his many coinages from "the confidence fairy" (the idea that "business confidence" is all that matters in "the Economy") to "zombie" and "cockroach ideas" (the misconceptions in economics that keep coming back, no matter how often you kill them or flush them down the toilet) have been illuminating as well as amusing. However, one does not have to disagree with Krugman's assertion that standard, textbook Keynesian macroeconomics have performed surprisingly well in this "Lesser Depression" with interest rates at the zero lower bound (even moving into negative) to be slightly puzzled by his insistence that the IS/LM model[1] is some kind of final truth about economics. Perhaps this is just Krugman's pugnacious defence of the whole intellectual framework of Post-War economics and the status of economists as the sages of our political system against what Krugman may be right to consider cranks and madmen with disastrously simple ideas about "the Economy." Nevertheless it is curiously blind to the questioning of the basis of economics, which has been gathering in strength.

---

[1] A mathematical representation, developed in 1936 by John Hicks and Alvin Hansen, of John Maynard Keynes' *General Theory of Employment, Interest and Money*, where an IS (interest rate/savings) curve crosses an LM (loans/ money supply) curve to define an equilibrium. In Krugman's defence, he is extolling the IS/LM model largely as an alternative to the Chicago School's DSGE (dynamic stochastic general equilibrium) model, which purports to *be* the economy as the sum of "micro-foundations," while IS/LM at least only purports to be a loose approximation.

Again this is a repeated pattern. The Great Depression produced three main lines of intellectual response: Keynes' *General Theory of Employment, Interest and Money*, which underlay economic policy in the Western world from the 1930s to the end of the 1970s and saw a limited revival with the economic stimulus of 2009; Friedrich von Hayek's *The Road to Serfdom*, which excoriated the tax-based welfare state and became the foundation of the Thatcher-Reagan revolution, which from the 1980s tried to reinvent society as a self-regulating market; and Karl Polanyi's *The Great Transformation*, which denied the foundational status of economics that Keynes and Hayek assumed, though much less dogmatically than their followers, and instead saw economics as the political ideology of industrialism, invented in the eighteenth century and implemented (by different political factions) with disastrous consequences ever since. Polanyi had some influence over the idea of the post-War welfare state and the removal of some aspects of society (health, education) outside the reach of "market forces," but he became the pet hate of economists and increasingly ignored by all sides of politics.

The more radical thinking after 2008 has come from outside of the economics profession, or by people looking outside it or beyond its usual models. The Czech economist Tomas Sedlacek in *The Economics of Good and Evil* has argued that economics never really escaped its origins in moral philosophy. This is especially noticeable in the case of Adam Smith's *The Wealth of Nations* (1776), which really invented the whole modern discourse of economics, but was written as a long footnote to his *Theory of Moral Sentiments*. Paul Ormerod in his later work, like *Why Things Fail*, or Nassim Nicholas Taleb in *The Black Swan* and *Fooled by Randomness* have argued that economics should rely on the mathematics of chaos, nonlinear feedbacks and improbability rather than stochastic equilibrium and Gaussian normal distribution (which did contribute in a major way to the subprime mortgage collapse). The Finnish-Danish econometrist Katarina Juselius describes herself as an "empirical economist," dispenses with models and looks hard at the statistics for major patterns of change and claims to have found two in her career: the increasing financialization of the economy after the 1980s and more recently, what looks like ecological limits to economic growth.

More important, for our purposes here, are scholars in the humanities (history, anthropology and linguistics) and imaginative literature, often at the borderlines between fiction and non-fiction. So much fiction has appeared about the crisis of 2008 that Katy Shaw has suggested the birth of a new genre in her book *Crunch Lit* (2015), where she relates works by John Lanchester, Jonathan Frantzen, Don DeLillo and others to the great nineteenth century representations of the world of finance like Dickens, Zola, Conrad and Trollope. The recent bestseller in economics, Thomas Piketty's *Capital in the Twenty-first Century* (2013) no doubt owes as much of its popularity to how Piketty uses nineteenth century French literature to describe the social effects of economic inequality as to his path-breaking use of historical statistics. These statistics show how after 1980, and with increasing strength after 2010, economic inequality, if you take into account the very richest 0.1 or 0.01 percent of the distribution (who are notoriously difficult to account for), has reached levels last seen during *la Belle Époque* in France or Gilded Age America – and exceeding the economic inequality of the *Ancien Régime*, before industrialization.

***

Literature seems to have stepped into the breach or vacuum which John Lanchester noted in an article called "Cityphobia" in the *London Review of Books* at the height of the panic in October 2008:

> The models and alternatives don't seem to be forthcoming . . . there is an ideological and theoretical vacuum where the challenge from the left used to be. Capitalism no longer has a global antagonist, just at the moment when it has never needed one more if only to clarify thinking and values, and to provide the chorus of jeering and Schadenfreude which at the moment is deeply appropriate. (Lanchester, "Cityphobia")

The world had turned upside down: "Wall Street turned socialist," *Le Monde Diplomatique* proclaimed on its October 2008 front page. Finance had turned into a business where gains were privatized, but losses socialized. But politically it was still the age of TINA, the Mother Goddess acronym for "There is no alternative," a phrase some have claimed, perhaps in a further attempt at myth-making, had first been popularized by Margaret Thatcher. The traditional anti-capitalist Left seemingly confirmed that it had disappeared "under the sea, like Atlantis" (as Svetlana Alexeievitch has said of the Soviet system), around two election cycles after the fall of the Berlin Wall – when the Italian Communist Party turned into Democrats and British Labour into New Labour. This is indeed one of the most under-explained phenomena of recent political history, its most important tectonic plate-shift alongside the gradual, but inexorable drift rightwards of the bulk of the old centre-right parties after the Thatcher-Reagan revolution. Rumours of the revival of this

Left, with Syriza in Greece, Jeremy Corbyn in Britain or Bernie Sanders in the US, seem somewhat exaggerated when their proposed economic policies are taken into account, which amount to little more than a return to old-fashioned centrist social democratic Keynesianism. New economic thinking (whether "Modern monetary theory" or Green "stable state" or "*décroissance*" economics") has had very little traction, perhaps so thoroughly suppressed by standard economic dogmas that the field is left open to the even more dangerous interventions of literature and humanities scholars.

Interestingly, Paul Krugman has been very perspicacious about the *literary foundations of economic thinking* in the case of his opponents, accusing the German government and especially Finance Minister Wolfgang Schäuble of seeing economics as "a *morality tale*" or the Republican Speaker of the House of Representatives Paul Ryan of getting his economic theory from Ayn Rand's novel *Atlas Shrugged*. But Krugman has also himself admitted to becoming an economist because economists most closely resembled the all-knowing "psychohistorians" of Isaac Asimov's *Foundations* trilogy.

What has gone on is perhaps most conveniently explained by a very short chapter in the Canadian novelist and political essayist John Ralston Saul's *The End of Globalism* (2005) entitled "A Short History of Economics Becoming a Religion." The role of Keynesian and neoclassical economists in the reconstruction and growth of the Western World in the decades after the Second World War seemed little short of miraculous – and that faith was transferred to economists of the monetarist and neoliberal-globalist schools in the subsequent generation (after 1980). Every aspect of society, culture and nature seemed to have a simple economic explanation, whether one asked vulgar Marxists or the authors of the *Freakonomics* books. And this was not just a fringe phenomenon: "New public management" attempted to create market efficiency in the public sector, only to end up with more hierarchical bureaucracy desperately trying to restructure the system to define the levels at which a fictional market "accountability" could set in – and equally desperate attempts among the groups affected to "game the system." But by the beginning of the twenty-first century that faith was wearing thin, to collapse almost completely after 2008. A fierce debate broke out, in moral philosophy as exemplified by Michael Sandel's *What Money Can't Buy: The Moral Limits of Markets* (2012) – and in higher education and the role of the humanities, as exemplified by Martha Nussbaum's *Not For Profit: Why Democracy Needs the Humanities* (2010) or Stefan Collini's *What Are Universities For?* (2012). Though they come from a long tradition going back at least to the nineteenth century, these defences of the humanities seem to demonstrate a new level of desperation, but perhaps also paradoxically, of hope. It seems to have become largely impossible to defend the existence of the humanities within the ruling discourse of economics, but the humanities continue to exist – and may even have a future, if the faith in economic discourse wanes.

Faith, belief and trust are central to economics, especially perhaps after the advent of modern European capitalism in the fifteenth and sixteenth centuries: it is what Richard Waswo in his contribution to this book calls "the *fiduciary* principle." This is particularly evident with what is known as *fiat* money: "paper money" which the state (or central bank) guarantees to have a certain value. An English 10 pound note still bears the inscription "I promise to pay the bearer on demand the sum of Ten pounds," signed by an official of the Bank of England (Scottish money is even closer to a simple IOU, as it is issued by private banks). This form of money is literally a speech act before it is anything else, especially as it is not specified what material substance (hardly "sterling" silver except in etymology) those ten pounds measure, as if to say "a litre litre." This is where the temptation of gold and silver standards come in, but it appears from history that even gold and silver coinage were never exactly (and often far from) the value of the metal on which they were stamped. Money is a measure of some shared (partly metaphysical) value, which involves faith, belief and trust, but also their opposites lying, mistrust and negotiation, though only in so far as they do not undermine the system. Waswo in his essay argues that it is a sign of Shakespeare's greatness how clearly he saw the human implications of this new economy in plays from *The Merchant of Venice* to *Troilus and Cressida*, long before economists theorized it.

A total systemic failure came close in 2008, partly because of the growth of *derivatives* markets after they were deregulated in the late 1990s. The proportions of financial markets to the "real economy" had turned on their head since the foundations of modern economics were theorized around 1800. At that time it is conventionally estimated that the "real economy" of the transaction of goods and services accounted for 95 percent of "the Economy," and financial transactions for 5 percent. By the late 1990s these figures were reversed, and by 2007 it was more like 1 or 2 to 99 percent. The November 2008 issue of *Le Monde diplomatique* estimated World Gross Domestic Product (GDP), or "the real economy," on an average day in 2007 at some 160 billion dollars, while the financial economy (stock exchanges, money and derivatives markets) on this average day was valued in excess of 5,500 billion dollars. It is hard for the uninitiated not to see this as a huge fictional bubble on a very small clay foot. Or not to think of the initiated as quite deranged when one popular derivative invented around that time was known as "end-of-the-world insurance," as if money would survive the end of the world.

At the time I wrote:

> For the literary critic observing the financial crisis of 2007-8, everything seems to turn on Coleridge's famous formula: "The willing suspension of disbelief." We have been engrossed in a fiction, a seemingly endless serial, which is now moving inexorably towards its *dénouement*. The media still treat it as a cliff-hanger: will it be recession or depression? The story will reveal its genre at last: comedy or tragedy, *Götterdämmerung* or history repeated as farce? Personally I am inclined towards Twilight of the Gods, though I can see the farcical aspects. The alternatives are not recession or depression, but depression or meltdown, of which the present "chaotic unwinding," in Ben Bernanke's phrase, is just the beginning. This is not the end of capitalism in any meaningful Marxian sense, but its Chernobyl. It is not in order to exaggerate that commentators are reaching for metaphor, but in order to reconnect with "reality." This "reality" had been conceded to economics and hedge-fund managers in an increasingly fictional "creative accountancy," where losses was registered as gains twice (as assets and future tax deductions). But now perhaps there is a brief chance for language to catch up, if only to express disbelief. (Leer 16)

Almost ten years later, little has changed. Any economic debate about basic principles has been stifled, even one so mild as my suggestion of replacing a (religious) belief in money markets with a more enlightened (literary) suspension of disbelief. Financial reform has barely happened, except very lightly in the US – and with a few international restrictions on "leverage": the proportion of equity to lending. The main policy intervention has been the pumping of credit into the system through *quantitative easing*, with debatable results.

Instead a picture seems to be emerging of a basic loss of faith in the liberal representative political system that was installed in the West after the Second World War and seemed set for universal expansion in the 1990s after the fall of the great Socialist adversary. This has been exemplified in various ways: by the EU treatment of the Greeks with its total disregard for elections and economic reality; the gathering collapse of a system of universal human rights extending to refugees; Brexit, Donald Trump; the increasing power of nationalist movements with strong anti-minority visions of "democracy." These phenomena are usually explained as the effects of growing economic inequality, the divide between "winners" and "losers" in "globalization" and a resulting xenophobia and racism; but it is in fact a much deeper loss of trust in the Post-War industrial social contract between workers, owners of capital and the professional middle classes. It is a crisis in representation: both in the political, the mediated and the linguistic sense. So of course were artistic modernism, postmodernism and postcolonialism. This is a further crunch, which may reveal the basis of the others.

The breach that emerged in 2007-8 was more radical than any of us thought at the time. Firstly it was *not just* a financial or an economic crisis, but a crisis of the whole *monetary system*, as the classicist turned banker Felix Martin points out in his *Money: The Unauthorised Biography* (2013): it raises the fundamental philosophical question of what money is, even beyond the classic tripartite definition of money as *store of value*, *measure of value* and *means of exchange*. These are often in conflict: the Gold Standard or any other system based on extreme "scarcity value" and thus a stable store of value often means that there is not enough money to go around to serve as a means of exchange; and if money is the only value (which often seems to be the case in the contemporary world), how does it measure itself? Can *value*, a monetary metaphor if ever there was one, even be separated from a monetary rationale? As such the "money crisis" has strong repercussions for our whole philosophical and moral system of representation and judgment, as the anthropologist David Graeber points out in his *Debt: The First 5000 Years* (2011), basing himself to a considerable extent on the work of the literary theorist Marc Shell and the scholar of classical Greek literature Richard Seaford.

Something has hit so deeply in our conceptual and linguistic way of making sense of the world that no authorized oppositional political discourse (Marxism being the obvious example) seems to strike the right note. Though a Marxist might quite accurately say "I told you so!" about "Capitalism," it is too generalized and evasive. Basically Marxist and so-called neoliberal assumptions about the world are too similar: "the Economy" is the bedrock of reality. Even economically literate discursive prose by excellent writers, like John Lanchester's brilliantly titled *Whoops! Why Everyone Owes Everyone and No One Can Pay* (2010), put too much effort into explaining the Crunch moment by (often comic) analogy to other spheres. To compare the 1973 publication of the Black and Scholes paper on "The Pricing of Options and Corporate Liabilities," which underlies modern derivatives, to Charlie Parker's saxophone break in a "A Night in Tunisia," strikes the wrong note, not just emotionally, as blasphemy for the jazz-lover; for if Parker's solo is "the arrival of modernism, right here, in real time" (Lanchester, *Whoops!* 33), the

Black-Scholes equations are surely the arrival of postmodernism. Keynes is a much better equivalent of "economic modernism," though he might have baulked at economics being an art form – and Keynes was a much better speculative investor than the Black-Scholes equations, which as Lanchester gleefully goes on to show led to the very fast implosion in 1998 of the Long Term Capital Investment hedge fund based on the Black-Scholes ideas about "rational investments in an irrational world" (Lanchester, *Whoops!* 41). Lanchester's account is an unsettling comedy, with an understated tragic background.

Postmodernism is too much the cultural arm of financialization (think of Jeff Koons or Damien Hirst's Golden Calf) to be any help in unmasking or criticizing it. Where literature succeeds, it is not in parodic anti-representationalism, but in sometimes much more conventional representational schemes where farce is parodied as – or suddenly gives way to – tragedy: in Kate Jennings' *Moral Hazard* (2002) or Michael Lewis' *The Big Short: Inside the Doomsday Machine* (2009). Jennings' novel tells the story of a writer, who in order to pay for her Alzheimer-struck husband's treatment and care, takes a job as a speechwriter at an investment bank. The language she learns to use comes over as almost a parody of Orwellian "doublespeak" in its transparent, self-serving, absurd predictability. But its basic assumptions so penetrate her own thinking that she begins to think of her husband in economic terms and in the end accedes to a kind of "mercy killing" because there is not enough return on her investment and her work at the bank is a living lie. At the same time the whole insane speculative circus at the bank implodes with impunity for everyone responsible because of a merger with another bank. In fact there turns out to be no responsibility behind the respectable conservative façade, while the narrator has to carry forever the responsibility of what she has done. "Moral hazard" has spread beyond its origins as an insurance term, where it refers to a situation in which a party to a contract can take extra risks because someone else bears the costs. Moral hazard has become the basic mode of functioning of society.

The Big Short tells the story of a group of very eccentric investors, who are the first to understand the subprime mortgage bubble and who, against the groupthink of the financial world, "short" or bet against these so-called "securitized investment vehicles," which one of them dubs instead "the doomsday machine." They make a lot of money when the market crashes, only to find that their opponents, who upheld the doomsday machine, have made almost as much. The morality of the market (the separation of winners and losers), in which they believed, is not working. The system is rigged. This may come as no surprise to the reader, or to Michael Lewis, who became a best-selling author with the book *Liar's Poker* (1989), a comic denunciation of his own career in Wall Street trading in the 1980s, straight out of university with an MA in Art History. In his preface to *The Big Short*, Lewis explains how after two decades, where a mad world he thought was doomed to extinction went from scandal to scandal, from hundreds-of-millions to billion-dollar losses caused by individual traders, he had basically given up writing with outrage about the corruption of Wall Street, until an obscure financial analyst called Meredith Whitney in 2007 predicted the near-collapse of Citibank and turned it into a general accusation: "This woman wasn't saying that Wall Street bankers were corrupt. She was saying that they were stupid" (Lewis, *The Big Short* xvii). She led Lewis to her mentor Steve Eisman and eventually the other strange heroes of his book. The genius of *The Big Short* lies in its combination of an engaging humanist characterization of a (real, not fictional) cast of misfits with a detective story plot that almost manages to explain to a lay readership the enigma, the fantastic fictions, at the heart of 21st century finance. But the moral resolution of the detective story remains elusive, the perpetrators unpunished, barely even unmasked. Lewis explains the unease that remains in the Afterword as the effect of an essentially comic writer having inadvertently written a tragedy.

The heart of it is what David Graeber terms "the moral confusion" of money, by which he means something more humane than what James Buchan, *Financial Times* journalist turned novelist, termed "the strangeness of money" in his study of the psychology of money *Frozen Desire* (1997). Buchan claims that the best index of the greatness of modern artists – whether Dostoevsky, Balzac, Dickens or Rembrandt – is their portrayal of the human relationship to money, which Buchan sees as the second-most important human invention, only exceeded by language, for instance in Rembrandt's portrait of Judas:

> What Rembrandt has understood, and portrayed as nobody before or since, is the strangeness of money: that it breaks the chain of desire and effect. Money provokes people to act, for the sake of payment, in a fashion that, if they knew how the action would turn out, they would not contemplate. Rembrandt seizes the moment when the veil of money is torn asunder and wish and consequence come explosively together: Judas realizes that he has assassinated the Son of Man. (Buchan 48)

Where Buchan sees the basis of the psychology of money in the storing of value ("frozen desire"), Graeber traces the origin of money to debt. It is impossible debt payments, rather than pecuniary greed which, in Graeber's history, has led to some of the most flagrant moral excesses: slavery, extreme patriarchy, anti-Semitism, the pillage of the New World by highly indebted conquistadors, or even the present crisis, which may have exploded in subprime mortgages in the US in 2008, and the sovereign debt crisis of Greece, but which connects with a longer history. Like many other commentators, Graeber traces the present debt crisis back through the Asian debt crisis of the 1990s to the Third World debt crises of the 1980s (still unresolved) to the point in 1971 when President Nixon abandoned the post-War Bretton Woods system of semi-fixed exchange rates by uncoupling the dollar from gold.

Graeber is most forceful and convincing, however, in puncturing the economists' *myth of barter* as the origin of economy and society; this is a myth which seems to originate with Adam Smith, but is repeated *ad nauseam* in every economics textbook. Graeber has much fun as a literary critic of the stories economists imagine about "primitive peoples", "amalgams of North American Indians and central Asian pastoral nomads" or "imaginary New England or Midwestern towns" (Graeber 25, 23), who live in societies and economies like the present, but without money. They have to barter potatoes for shoes and find it very inconvenient. Smith argued famously that economic life, and even social life, originated in a "certain propensity in human nature . . . the propensity to truck, barter and exchange one thing for another," which animals do not have. Graeber adds that in this scheme, central to the ideology of economic liberalism, "Even logic and conversation are really just forms of trading, and as in all things, humans will always seek their own best advantage, to seek the greatest profit they can from the exchange" (Graeber 25). A story emerges, which comes to be seen as the *history* of money and the economy, by which barter and the division of labour give way to the facilitation of trade by means of metal ingots and then coinage, guaranteed by the state, and then ever more sophisticated credit and debit systems.

> The story . . . has become the founding myth of our system of economic relations. It is so deeply established in common sense . . . that most people on earth couldn't imagine any other way that money could possibly have come about.
> The problem is there's no evidence that it ever happened, and an enormous amount of evidence suggesting that it did not. (Graeber 28)

Anthropology and ethnography since Smith's time have not been able to find a single society that relied on barter for its economic life, and the evidence of anthropology, archaeology and the study of ancient civilizations, especially the Sumerians, point to the reverse development of what economics teaches. The liberal Felix Martin (Martin 10) agrees with the anarchist Graeber: first came complex arrangements of credit and debt (including systems of derivatives in Sumeria 3000-2000 BC as complex as anything in the City of London or on Wall Street in the years after 2000 AD), then the introduction of coinage in the seventh century BC, and then, in situations where coined money is somehow absent or insufficient, barter.

This is enough to question many underlying assumptions not only in economics and politics, but in humanistic scholarship, linguistics and literature, though linguists and literary scholars have the advantage that our discipline is precisely to question the language we use. Martin and Graeber, however, go further, in sometimes diametrically opposite ways. Martin sees a *story of credit* and writes a largely progressive history, with a few setbacks, of how credit has been measured and meted out, beginning with the magnificent huge "stone money" of the remote Pacific Island of Yap, which was admired by both Keynes and his great monetarist opponent Milton Friedman, because "by its indifference to its physical currency it acknowledged so transparently that money is not a commodity, but a system of credit and clearing" (Martin 13). The heroes of Martin's book are the ancient Greeks for inventing a homogenous, individual and equalizing system of "economic value"; the great villain is the philosopher John Locke for trying to fix that value to a commodity, gold. The way out of the mess of 2008 is to imagine a new system of regulation and value, where to Martin "the boldest measures are the safest."

Graeber writes a *history of debt*, setting out not only to undermine the liberal economic vision of society as endless competitive exchange (from barter to communication), but also the conservative nationalist and social democratic welfare state notion of the "eternal debt" owed by the individual to "society." Graeber sees the last 5,000 years of history as dominated by two cycles: the "coinage-military-slavery complex" which imposes the rule of money as an easily measurable and portable means of exchange (such as marauding armies need: Alexander's and Rome's armies were the first organizations to expend enormous amounts of coined silver) – and the more metaphysical periods where money is part of a cosmic and socially rooted system of debt and credit. The latter dominates what Graeber calls the *"human economies"* before coinage and the state, where "money" in whatever form (Yap millstones, seashells, cattle) functions not as means of exchange for commodities, but for establishing connections between strangers (gifts) and other social exchanges that *cannot be measured*: whether bride wealth or blood money (the payments for marriage and the unlawful taking of human life). Debt and credit also dominate the early period of state civilization in Mesopotamia, where cuneiform writing seems largely to have been invented for the purposes of accountancy (literature might be seen as a mere spin-off, an *accountancy* of life, death and morality in *The Epic of Gilgamesh* and its followers). From Sumeria to Old Testament Israel the Middle East saw recurrent debt crises and the institution of debt relief to prevent social breakdown. Debt and credit return in "the Middle Ages," which Graeber does not see as a barbarian relapse into barter in Western Europe, but as a general Eurasian stabilization after the disruption of coinage and imperial expansionism in the ancient world, a stabilization which even creates more equitable versions of a market economy with or without state intervention in Buddhist China and the Islamic world, both of them less hostile to money than Confucianism or Christianity. These systems (which invented paper money, the check and other modern fiduciary tools) were stable at least as compared to the European capitalist empires, which developed out of the resurgence of coinage after the pillage of the gold and silver of the Americas, and which revived not just coinage, but global scale military expansion and chattel slavery. Finally a debt and credit system appears to be returning after Nixon abandoned gold in 1971, largely to pay for the debts accumulated by the Vietnam War. We are in a period of system change according to Graeber as well as Martin: we just have not created a new system yet, or become comfortable without "real money."

I have given such a detailed account of Martin and especially Graeber, because they seem to me to show a way for the humanities (and maybe humanity) out of our sense of having dwindled into uneconomic insignificance. In fact, significance, economy and value are inherently humanistic concerns, and redefining them may give new impetus to linguistics and literary studies. This may also pose a challenge to the foundations of our disciplines more profound than those of structuralism, phenomenology, Marxism, feminism, logical positivism or deconstruction in the twentieth century. When both Martin and Graeber see the introduction of coinage in the Greek kingdom of Lydia in the seventh century BC (hardly a great technological advance) as perhaps the most crucial event in world history, it has to do with its effect on the representation of "reality."

Martin sees the notion of economic value as the foundation of democracy: a universal measure of physical reality combines with a negotiable control over money (and thus social power) to allow for a flexible social order, whereas the aristocratic rejection of money with which Western literature begins in *The Iliad* is the last death-cramp of a dying rigid hierarchical order. Graeber on the other hand leads us back to the apparently outlandish idea of Marc Shell in *The Economy of Literature* (1978) that the introduction of coinage was the shock that led to the whole development of Western philosophy as a counter-measure, further developed by Richard Seaford in *Money and the Early Greek Mind* (2004) where this shock is extended beyond philosophy to both Homer and Greek tragedy.

Shell begins his essay "The Ring of Gyges" with the observation that for the ancient Greeks the Lydians were not only the inventors of coinage, but of tyranny:

> Many men pretend to dislike money and tyranny. Golden tyranny, though, may be the correspondent or foundation of much that we pretend to love. The myth of Gyges helps to reveal the origin of modern thought and to call that thought into question. (Shell 13)

In the version of the myth found in Herodotus' *Histories* Gyges is the King of Lydia's advisor, who is lured by the king to see the queen naked, an act of such shame and illegality that he has to kill the king and take his position, but to live his life as ruler in hiding. Shell interprets this as an "economic revolution" in Herodotus' play on the words *eidos* (visible form), *aidos* (shame), *oikos* (home, household) and *nomos* (law). The power of coinage is that it "turns invisibles into visibles and visibles into invisibles." Coins are *both* commodity (being made of gold) and the *symbolon* (the token, often a ring before the invention of coinage) of a contract, for example for turning real estate into money and back again, or money into real estate and back again.

In the version of the myth of Gyges in Plato's *Republic*, however, this becomes the foundation, and at the same time the negation, of how Socrates' version of dialectical thought operates. Shell quotes Marx in "Critique of the Hegelian Dialectic and Philosophy as a Whole": "Logic is the money of the mind, the speculative or thought-value of man and nature – their essence grown totally indifferent to all real determinateness, and hence their real essence" – and goes on to extend this to Plato:

> There is a ring of Gyges secretly at work within the minds of men: it is the money of the mind. Sometimes Plato studies that money by considering his original metaphor that the seal of a ring impresses the waxen or metallic minds of men. More often he studies the money of the mind directly, by

considering the thoughts of the sophists. Plato attacked sophists . . . because they changed money for wisdom (selling their wares and altering them according to the conditions of the market) and because, like the rhetoricians, they made convention, as exemplified in language and money, their universal measure. Gyges the tyrant had the power to make the unreal appear real. (Shell 36-7)

The Republic sets out "to prove the superiority of the life of the philosopher to that of the tyrant" (Shell 45) and the rich man. It does so by a heroic effort to remove the Ideas (and thus truth and wisdom) outside of the reach of money and market exchange and visibility into a realm of the intelligible (*to noeton*), which reflects but also stands in dialectical opposition to the visible (*to horaton*). While tyranny hides itself, "philosophy seeks to make the Idea visible" (Shell 43). Dialectic and hypothesis, the foundations of Socratic, Platonic and Aristotelian thought, introduce "a new kind of symbolization or relation between things and that which represents them (language or money for example)" (Shell 47). Here metaphor is crucial, the "tropic turn" as Shell explains it, quoting Plato, "The eye must be turned around from that which is coming into being . . . together with the whole soul until it is able to endure looking at that which is . . . and the brightest part of that which is" (Plato, *Republic* as quoted in Shell 50). In our usual sense of metaphor, deriving from Plato, the meaning of a metaphor is the higher invisible idea which is given expression in a visible trope. But Shell in the end prefers what he sees as the theory of metaphor of Heraclitus of Miletus in Fragment 90:

All things are an equal exchange for fire and fire for all things, as goods are for gold and gold for goods (quoted in Shell 52)

Miletus was the port for the land-locked kingdom of Lydia, where its coinage was exchanged for goods carried by the Phoenicians, who dominated Eastern Mediterranean trade at the time but did not accept coinage. Miletus was also the birthplace of Greek philosophy, where poet-thinkers like Anaximander and Heraclitus speculated on which physical substance the world was made of: Heraclitus favoured fire, the dynamic element of change, Anaximander the *apeiron*, whose exact physical substance nobody has been able to ascertain. Such thought, according to Shell, and confirmed by Seaford, only became possible with the introduction of coinage:

Gold has a universal nature that . . . can become something else and yet still remain itself. Gold minted into a coin, for example, is both homogenous with itself (as gold) and heterogenous with itself (as numismatic sculpture or money). (Shell 53-4)

Metaphor in the subsequent Western tradition and in subsequent Western thought has the same ambiguity of being both homogenous and heterogenous. This is why Western philosophy has never been able to resolve the dialectic between materialism and idealism: all because of coined money.

Seaford adds philological and historical depth to Shell's intuition: as with Western philosophy, so with Western literature. The epic world of Homer, far from rejecting money, is a critique of it, for undermining the sharing and just partitioning of animal sacrifice, which underlay both the tribal-heroic world to which Homer looks back and the *polis*, which was establishing itself as the model community of Greek culture at the time of composition of *The Iliad* and *The Odyssey*. Both begin with "a crisis of redistribution" and a rejection of monetary compensation (Achilles towards Agamemnon and the Trojans, Odysseus in refusing to pay for the entertainment of Penelope's suitors). Similarly tragedy, according to Seaford, begins in the conflict between the impersonality of money and individual identity:

> *Charakter* refers both to Orestes' distinguishing scar and to the mark on a coin. In other words the opposition between unique personal identity and *typical* value is exquisitely embodied in their each being recognised through a *charakter*. The ambiguity of *charakter* between scar and coin-mark represents the antithesis between the ancient uniqueness of the hero (marked here by a *charakter*) and a world in which the impersonal power of money has not only annihilated the uniqueness of the mythical hero but also provided a metaphor for the impersonal typicality of genuine worth. (Seaford 155)

If both metaphor and character are fatally flawed by money, it is perhaps not such a great leap to speculate, as David Graeber goes on to do (Graeber 223-51), that all the great Eurasian religions and moral systems to emerge in what Karl Jaspers called "the Axial Age" – the period from the great contemporaries Confucius, the Buddha and Pythagoras to Jesus and Muhammad – were in fact responses to the introduction of coinage. This seems to have led initially to the development of philosophies of such absolute materialism that there literally were no moral qualms about selling your mother as dog food or your daughter as a prostitute. The reaction of outrage led to systems that disparaged money almost out of existence (Confucianism or Christianity) and systems that separated out a higher spiritual realm from a low material realm (Buddhism and Pythagoreanism, which in turn gave rise to Platonism) and made almost impossible demands for disciplined transcendence into pure spirituality. No pre-coinage system seems to have this total separation of the material and the spiritual, physical and metaphysical – or imagines the world as being constituted purely of *material elements*. Maybe we need to return to the wisdom, practicality and pluralism of pre-coinage cultures.

The proliferation of local currencies in the last decade or *the shared economy* or *Zero Marginal Cost Society* prophesied by Jeremy Rifkin, among others, may bring us back there in a new global "Collaborative Commons." Bitcoin, the electronic money launched shortly after the collapse of Lehman Brothers, or at least the blockchain technology on which it is based, may be a universal unbreakable code of trust, as John Lanchester ("When Bitcoin Grows Up") has recently suggested, at least until the banks get their hands on it. "Connectivity" and sharing may even break with the *scarcity* that is often defined as the very basis of economics, as the Marxist Paul Mason argues in *Postcapitalism: A Guide to Our Future* (2015).

***

This, however, is not an exercise in futurology or a self-help book, nor is it, except in this framing introduction and perhaps the contributions of Richard Waswo and Oran McKenzie, a polemic with economics. It is a scholarly work with a very pluralistic conception of the economies of English. The contributions here also stem from a number of other intellectual traditions in the "economic humanities" that are not mentioned above, but some of which have a strong connection with Geneva. First come essays that deal with the notion of *linguistic value*, which is central to the thinking of Ferdinand de Saussure, the Genevese founder of structural linguistics and semiotics, including a version of Saussure's biographer Professor John Joseph's keynote address at the conference. Then follow essays which relate to the emerging discipline of *language economics*, one of whose foremost proponents is Professor François Grin of the University of Geneva, who kindly stepped in to replace the keynote of Marc Shell, when Shell had to cancel at the last moment. Language economics in Geneva has succeeded in putting actual monetary values to the acquisition of foreign languages for businesses and individuals. Third, but not least come essays that relate to the movement sometimes known as "The New Economic Criticism," which has revolutionized understanding of especially Early Modern literature, and one of whose founding figures is Richard Waswo, Emeritus professor in the English Department of the University of Geneva. Another founding figure, Professor Laura Brown of Cornell, gave a keynote at the conference on the circulation of money in the eighteenth century as a founding trope of the modern novel. The last keynote was given by Professor Stefan Collini of the University of Cambridge, who decided to forego his usual polemic style in discussing the monetization of university education and instead concentrated on the poetics of university study.

John Joseph's contribution "The Cerebral Closet: Language as *Valeur* and *Trésor in* Saussure" discusses Saussure's economic metaphor of *valeur* as it is presented in the *Cours de linguistique générale*. It places the notion of *valeur* in the innovative perspective of its relation to another economic metaphor, that of *trésor*, referring both to the object of Saussure's investigations, namely *la langue*, and to its location. Joseph shows that while the terms themselves may have been present in the teaching the future linguist and his colleagues received from their professors at the *Gymnase de Genève*, Saussure redefined such concepts as *langage, signe, langue, valeur* to fit them into the linguistic system he developed. Joseph raises the question of the source of inspiration which led to these reformulations. With carefully documented arguments, he shows that Henri Dameth's courses on political economy, which Saussure followed, were very likely inspirational in Saussure's reformulation of the notion of *valeur*. On the other hand, his notes on Victor Egger's thesis on *Inner Speech*, which he read while he was in Paris in the early 1880s, reveal his first encounter with the idea that language includes an *inner speech*, the location of which is necessarily in the brain (but the debate about whether there should be a specific location went well beyond the dispute Egger had launched against Alexander Bain's school). Joseph also dissects Saussure's references to the mind's closets (*casier*), which are not directly accessible (although the treasure, *langage*, is deposited there) but only via an externalization of language through *parole*. Here again, Joseph retraces the genealogy of the terms, and argues that Saussure had access to them via Egger, but also via Victor Henry and Henri Odier, two linguists Saussure knew and exchanged ideas with. Both the economist perspectives and the psychologically oriented perspectives are shown to have had an impact – whether as a source of inspiration or an argument of rejection – on Saussure's innovative conception of language as a system.

Claire Forel's article, "Value of and in Learning Foreign Languages," integrates the dual perspective of the value of language learning. On the one hand, the author notes that language policies build on the idea that there is a real economic benefit in learning foreign languages. Economy – here economy both as market value and non-market value, following François Grin's definitions – of language learning may be measured both at the level of individuals and of a society. The market value may be associated with individuals' well-being in terms of higher salaries or more interesting jobs. On the non-market side, as repeatedly emphasized by the Council of Europe, foreign language teaching contributes to unity through "mutual enrichment and understanding." But Forel also claims that foreign language teaching is central to what was already underlined by Ferdinand de Saussure, namely that linguistic diversity contributes to linguistic awareness. It is only through the prism of the differences that a coherent system can be built. Therefore, foreign languages have an intrinsic non-market value. Among other concrete implementations of foreign language learning, Forel examines the contributions of the EOLE *(Eveil au Langage et Ouverture aux Langues)* programme of the Suisse Romande schools to the notion of language awareness. The programme encourages teachers of young (primary school) pupils to explore the linguistic diversity of the class, comparing for example animal cries in different languages. It also focuses on the arbitrariness of the sign by encouraging the children to compare determiner+noun units and the gender they carry. The author shows that the various approaches to the notion of language are deeply rooted in Saussure's concept of language as a system of values.

In "Teaching and Learning English in Geneva: Questions of Economy, Identity, Globality and Usefulness," Eva Waltermann and Virág Csillagh propose new perspectives on English as a (new) foreign language in a multicultural and multilingual environment such as Switzerland. One side of the question considers the value of English as a foreign language from the learner/speaker's point of view. The authors show how the introduction of English as a foreign language in the teaching curricula, first at the secondary school level and, more recently, in primary schools has modified the perspective not only on English, but also on national languages. The growing emphasis on the economic advantage of English appears as a counterweight to the question of identity, of social cohesion associated with national languages. Using Grin's model of the economic weight of foreign languages, they show that knowledge of a second national language dramatically increases the income of a worker in Switzerland. However, in terms of personal motivations, a study carried out in Geneva reveals that English appears as the language which is the most positively perceived in terms of future self-vision. Moreover, the motivation for language learning is strongly shaped by contextual factors and by the importance of English as self-defined by local values. A complementary approach considers the point of view of foreign language teachers. The authors argue that teachers play a major role in the construction of foreign language perception and representation in the teaching/learning process. A large-scale study, carried out among more than a hundred secondary language schoolteachers in Geneva, reveals different perceptions about foreign languages. For example among the most cited word associations for English one finds "international," "Shakespeare" (!) or "useful." Compared to other foreign languages, the term "useful" is again ranked very high for English. But its relative value on the beautiful/ugly and the easy/difficult scales is also high. The authors conclude that in the language teachers' representations, the social value of English is very high, and is associated with more positive subjective connotations than (second) national languages.

Sarah Chevalier's contribution, "The Value of English in Multilingual Families," also examines the value of English in a multilingual environment. But her study targets language in the private sphere, in multilingual families. A study incorporating 35 families examines the motivations for choosing one or another of the available languages or even adding a new one to the linguistic environment of the family. The study, carried out on tri- and quadrilingual families with young and primary school age children, reveals that when a language which is not part of the linguistic background of either parent is added, the choice is, without exception, English. Given the background of the interviewed families, the author concludes that the choice of English reveals that it is valued as a language of global communication, which offers social and economic advantage to its speakers.

Richard Waswo begins his article "Shakespeare and the Modern Economy" with the incomprehension and ridicule that met Marco Polo when he reported on the use of paper money in China. Westerners have resisted paper money "until just yesterday" – in seventeenth and eighteenth century Europe and nineteenth century America – out of "the occidental fixation on value as something intrinsic to the object itself" rather than a social convention. Even today some bankers and economists seriously urge a return to the gold standard. Shakespeare, however, in the formative years of the modern capitalist economy in the sixteenth and seventeenth century, saw that money and words are homologous systems of exchange and dramatized the basic principles of this in a way only expressed by one or two other writers at the time, most clearly by the Florentine banker and man of letters Bernardo Davanzati. Shakespeare (in Waswo's words) explores how "neither money nor words need represent anything at all, but are social facts based on assent and trust, or credit – the fiduciary principle" and "that value is established in exchange and constituted by desire – the volitional corollary." This is evident in different ways in the action and argument of *The Merchant of Venice*, where value, credit and belief are issues both in the main plot that leads to the court argument between Shylock and the disguised Portia – and in the erotic and marital subplot. Law and not mercy, as Waswo sees it, carries the day "as it must in a state that lives by commerce." In a different but related way, the strange and infrequently performed *Troilus and Cressida* is seen to parody the conventions of epic and courtly love under the ruthlessness of the new economic principles.

Indira Ghose in "Money, Morals and Manners in Renaissance Courtesy Literature" looks at the nexus between wealth and noble status in the new genre created in Italy to redefine the role of the aristocracy as its military function waned in the early modern period. This genre was transmitted into English by translations of its masterpiece, Castiglione's *The Courtier* and many other lesser works, but also in books written by Englishmen like Sir Thomas Elyot in *The Boke Named the Governor* (1539). The debate in these books, often in dialogue form, purports to be about whether the essence of nobility is innate or acquired through virtue, as humanism maintained. But money (or wealth) plays a crucial role, often leading to contortions of argument, which Ghose chooses to see not just as blatant hypocrisy, but as a serious logical, moral (because it contravened Christian notions of virtue, which disparaged money) and practical problem, which led to some inventive solutions. Riches, Aristotle had argued in both his *Politics* and *Nichomachean Ethics*, were essential to enable the virtues of liberality, generosity and disdain for pettiness which were characteristic of the gentleman. The courtesy literature both served to defend aristocratic privilege and became highly profitable as manuals for those aspiring to join the ranks of the aristocracy. To fulfil this dual purpose, the genre turned wealth either into a precondition, in the case of Elyot, to allow the aristocracy to devote itself to public service, or in the case of Castiglione, a form of display of manners, a *sprezzatura*, which Ghose argues prefigures Pierre Bourdieu's concept of *cultural capital* by centuries.

Rahel Orgis in "'Father and Son, I ha' done you simple service here': The (Interrupted) Circulation of Money in Middleton and Dekker's *The Roaring Girl*" turns her attention to the surprising number of money transactions in the play. This despite the fact that, as Richard Waswo has pointed out, "money was in endemically short supply" in England in the period, and most trade, as the influential historian Craig Muldrew has shown, was based on pervasive debt and credit networks. The circulation of money thus, according to Orgis, emerges as an important theme in the play – with the protagonist Moll Frith, a high-ranking servant woman, functioning as a critic of self-interested money transactions and as an agent of the success or failure of the transactions. Moll, the "Roaring Girl," has been seen both as a cross-dressing proto-feminist and as an ultimately conservative figure who is reintegrated into patriarchal society. Orgis sees her as an ambivalent and transitional figure between a perhaps idealized economy of personal service, where foolhardy, but generous spendthrifts are saved, while parsimonious usurers are punished, and a "new economy" of self-interested financial transactions.

In "'How to Live Well on Nothing a Year': Money, Credit and Debt in William Makepeace Thackeray's *Vanity Fair*," Barbara Straumann takes us into a financial and fictive economy, where self-interest is well-established as the basic principle. Thackeray's novel from 1848 offers a satirical panorama of a society obsessed with acquisitiveness, wealth and status. The protagonist Rebecca Sharpe shows her great intelligence by using the vanities of others to gain both social and financial credit – without ever repaying her debts. Straumann argues that Becky Sharpe's ability to live off the credulousness of her creditors is an effect of what the German theorist or "theologian of markets" Jochen Hörisch has called the "autopoiesis" of money: the idea that money is backed by the belief in money. Money in Hörisch's definition, Straumann explains, "produces and reproduces itself in a self-referential system and, at the same time, requires our belief in order to work." Becky's self-fashioning as a character is of the same order – and commands the admiration even of people she has abused. There is even a sense in which Thackeray lays bare his fictional world as functioning according to these same principles, perhaps because he was among those Victorian novelists financially dependent on selling his fiction. What is unusual about *Vanity Fair* is not its exposure of an economy of "credit, debt, poverty, extreme wealth and economic extravagance," as Straumann puts it, but that its protagonist is a woman depicted as "an autonomous and independent economic agent" motivated by self-interest rather than domestic responsibility.

Sangam MacDuff in "'Scrupulous Meanness,' Joyce's Gift and the Symbolic Economy of *Dubliners*" takes the question of economy into the domain of literary style. "Scrupulous meanness" is Joyce's own description in a letter to his publisher of the style he intended to use in the book that would become *Dubliners*. The style of *Dubliners*, as MacDuff puts it, "is famously economical, if not miserly,, and Joyce's treatment of his characters and their role in what Joyce called "the moral history of Ireland" is harsh, but as MacDuff goes on to add, "the sparseness of the stories is complemented by richly symbolic passages in which Joyce's poetic gift shines through." As critics like Mark Osteen have pointed out, however, Joyce in his writing as in his life "reconciles spendthrift habits with bourgeois thrift to create an aesthetic economy of the gift, where loss is gain." The article demonstrates this in a close reading of the story "Two Gallants": a deceptively simple tale of "how two men, Lenehan and Corley, conspire to extract a gold sovereign from a young slavey, or maid of all work." In the course of his analysis MacDuff shows how an economy of circulation, which many critics have observed in Joyce's work, a circulation of information and gossip, of a rambling walk through Dublin, of the very elliptical story of the coin and the deceit of the "two gallants," is actually interrupted at various points, and it is at these points that lyricism, significance and epiphany break into the prose. This is where the meanness of moral judgment gives way to the gift economy (as Marcel Mauss or Anne Carson might have theorized it) of poetry, the *gnomon* of growth, which in the first paragraph of *Dubliners* is paired with two words of moral judgment: *paralysis* and *simony*, one which is famously supposed to sum up Joyce's judgment on Dublin and Ireland, the other of which refers to the selling of indulgences and preferments in the Church.

In "Slippery Subjects: Intersecting Economies of Genre in Gay Male Coming-Out Films, 1995-2015," Martin Mühlheim turns towards economy as a defining feature of genre, especially an emerging genre such as gay male coming-out films. Mühlheim has noticed the frequency of the motif of men or boys going swimming in the genre and employs a methodology borrowed from Franco Moretti's *distant reading*, which Mühlheim terms *distant viewing*, to try to get a sense of the statistical prevalence of the motif. The article explains the frequency of the motif through a set of intersecting reasons – aesthetic, legal and economic – which in the film industry give rise to generic conventions, and finally arrives at the conclusion that swimming scenes are particularly frequent in the sub-group of coming-out films which feature – or are targeted at – protagonists "still struggling to establish a non-heterosexual self-identity."

Finally, Oran McKenzie in "Spillage and Banditry: Anne Carson's Derivatives" returns us to the Canadian poet, who is quoted at the very beginning of this introduction. McKenzie's essay argues that new notions of literary value are needed to account for Carson's poetry, which is conceived for the age of financial derivatives. Not that Carson follows the American poet Kenneth Goldsmith into what he calls "uncreative writing," which "abandons traditional poetic practices in favour of activities such as databasing, recycling, appropriation and intentional plagiarism." Rather Carson's poetics in *The Economy of the Unlost* (1999) or her poetic practice in *Decreation* (2005) stem from a deep engagement, born out of her training as a classical philologist, with how the introduction of coinage in Lydia in the seventh century BC changed – or even created – subsequent ways of thinking in philosophy and poetry: the perception of reality and value, the notions of self, subject and object, the separation of form and matter. In her poetry Carson takes derivation (in both the literary and economic sense) beyond traditional forms of intertextuality, encouraging a "spillage" of sources within the text, which she observes already in Longinus' essay *On the Sublime*. Through her own practice of a form of "banditry" trading on this spillage, which makes the relationship between the original and the derivative ever more obscure, Carson explores the possibility of a poetical order grounded in a different kind of visibility and value from that of a coinage based culture. This new poetics, which Carson the classicist in effect traces back to Simonides of Keos at the very beginning of the Greek canon, does not deal in representations, illusionism and exchanges between an estranged self and an other, but strives for the *"withness" of a new form of gift economy*.

Martin Leer

References

Alexievitch, Svetlana. *La Fin de l'homme rouge – ou le Temps du désenchantement* (originally *Vremia second hand*). Paris: Actes Sud, 2013.

Bernanke, Ben. *The Courage to Act: A Memoir of a Crisis and its Aftermath.* New York: Norton, 2015.

Buchan, James. *Frozen Desire: An Enquiry into the Meaning of Money.* London: Picador, 1997.

Carson, Anne. *Economy of the Unlost: Reading Simonides of Keos with Paul Celan.* Princeton: Princeton University Press, 1999.

Collini, Stefan. *What Are Universities For?* London: Penguin, 2012.

Graeber, David. *Debt: The First 5000 Years.* New York: Melville House, 2011.

Hayek, Friedrich von. *The Road to Serfdom.* London: Routledge 1944.

Jennings, Kate. *Moral Hazard.* New York and London: Fourth Estate, 2002.

Juselius, Katarina: "Vi står foran store omvæltninger" ("We face great upheavals") interview with Jørgen Steen Nielsen. *Dagbladet Information.* Copenhagen: 2 December 2014.

Keynes, John Maynard. *The General Theory of Employment, Interest and Money.* London: Macmillan, 1936.

King, Mervyn. *The End of Alchemy: Money, Banking and the Future of the Global Economy.* New York: Norton, 2016.

Krugman, Paul. "How Did Economists Get it so Wrong?" New York: *New York Times Magazine*, 2 September 2009.

———. *The Conscience of a Liberal: Blog associated with* The New York Times.

———. "Money: The Brave New Uncertainty of Mervyn King." New York: *New York Review of Books*, 14 July 2016.

Lanchester, John. "Cityphobia." *London Review of Books*, vol. 30, no. 20, 23 October 2008, 3-5.

———. *Whoops! Why Everyone Owes Everyone and No One Can Pay.* London: Allen Lane, 2010.

———. "When Bitcoin Grows Up." *London Review of Books*, vol. 38, no. 8, April 2016, 3-12.

Leer, Martin. "Willing Suspension of Disbelief: A Literary Critic Looks at Financial Meltdown." *Planet: The Welsh Internationalist* 192, December 2008- January 2009, 16-22.

Lewis, Michael. *Liar's Poker: Rising through the Wreckage on Wall Street.* New York: Norton, 1989.

———. *The Big Short: Inside the Doomsday Machine.* New York: Norton, 2010.

Martin, Felix. *Money: The Unauthorised Biography*. London: Vintage, 2013.
Mason, Paul. *Postcapitalism: A Guide to Our Future*. London: Allen Lane, 2015.
Nussbaum, Martha. *Not for Profit: Why Democracy Needs the Humanities*. Princeton: Princeton University Press, 2010.
Ormerod, Paul. *The Death of Economics*. London: St Martin's Press, 1994.
———. *Why Most Things Fail: Evolution, Extinction and Economics*. London: John Wiley, 2007.
Piketty, Thomas. *Capital in the Twenty-First Century*. (Cambridge, Massachusetts: Harvard University Press, 2014.
Polanyi, Karl. *The Great Transformation: The Political and Economic Origins of Our Time*. Boston: Beacon Press, 2001 (originally 1944).
Reinhart, Carmen and Kenneth Rogoff. *This Time Is Different: Eight Centuries of Financial Folly*. Princeton: Princeton University Press, 2009.
Rifkin, Jeremy. *The Zero Marginal Cost Society: The Internet of Things, the Collaborative Commons and the Eclipse of Capitalism*. London and New York: St Martin's Press, 2015.
Sandel, Michael. *What Money Can't Buy: The Moral Limits of Markets*. London and New York: Penguin 2012.
Saul, John Ralston. *The Collapse of Globalism*. New York: Atlantic Books, 2005.
Seaford, Richard. *Money and the Early Greek Mind: Homer Philosophy Tragedy*. Cambridge: Cambridge University Press, 2004.
Sedlacek, Tomas. *Economics of Good and Evil: The Quest for Economic Meaning from Gilgamesh to Wall Street*. Oxford: Oxford University Press, 2011.
Shaw, Katy. *Crunch Lit*. London: Bloomsbury, 2015.
Shell, Marc. *The Economy of Literature*. Baltimore: Johns Hopkins University Press, 1978.
Smith, Adam. *The Wealth of Nations*. London: Penguin, 1982 (originally 1776).
Taleb, Nassim Nicholas. *The Black Swan: The Impact of the Highly Improbable*. New York: Random House, 2007.
———. *Fooled by Randomness: The Hidden Role of Chance in Life and in the Markets*. New York: Random House, 2001.

The Cerebral Closet: Language as *valeur* and *trésor* in Saussure

John E. Joseph

The economic metaphor of *valeur* plays a central role in the *Cours de linguistique générale* of Ferdinand de Saussure, which defines a language as a system of values. Much ink has been spilled in speculation over its possible sources, while relatively little attention has been given to another economic metaphor used by Saussure: that of language as a *trésor*, an ambiguous word which can refer either to valuables (in which *valeur* is stored) or to a container for valuables. Both meanings are apposite, since the metaphor arises in the context of discussing both what a language is and where it is located in the people who know it. In tnis study I examine work in political economics and psychology that Saussure had encountered, and show how the metaphors become more meaningful in the light of what his predecessors maintained about the nature of economic value, and about how knowledge of language is stored – within the nervous-muscular system involved in language production, or in what Alexander Bain scorned as a "cerebral closet." Also considered is Saussure's position on the negotiation of value in *parole* and in diachrony, and how his views on the *trésor* in multiple brains compares and contrasts with present-day views of extended cognition and distributed language.

1. The background to value in the *Cours de linguistique générale*

Two economic metaphors are especially striking in the *Cours de linguistique générale* (henceforth *CLG*), compiled posthumously from notes taken by students of Ferdinand de Saussure (1857-1913) in lectures he gave between 1907 and 1911. For Saussure, a language is a system of *va-*

leurs, values, in a sense that will be explored below; this word occurs many times in the book. In addition, in some passages it refers to a language as a *trésor*, an accumulation of valuables or the container for one.

Neither *valeur* nor *trésor* has an exclusively economic meaning: values can be moral, and a *trésor* can be a box or pouch which has never actually had money or valuables in it. Both meanings of *trésor* – as stored value (the contents meaning), and the location where values are stored (the container meaning) – are apposite in the context, since the *CLG* is discussing both what a language is and where it is located in the people who know it.[1]

Saussure's contribution to the understanding of language from the early 20th century onwards lay in no small part with his conceptual deployment of *valeur*. He envisaged a language as a collection of signs, each the conjunction of a signified, or mental concept, with a signifier, a mental sound pattern or sound-image. The term sound-image is deceptive, though, because a signifier is neither a sound nor an image, but a value. Nor is a signified a concept, exactly. The values that signifiers and signifieds consist of are nothing other than their difference from all the other signifiers and signifieds in the language system.

This modernist way of conceiving of a language was strikingly original to those who heard Saussure's lectures on general linguistics in Geneva from 1907 to 1911, and to the hundreds, and eventually millions, who read the *CLG*, the centenary of which we celebrate in 2016. It set linguistics on a new path, to be followed in time by ethnography, psychoanalysis, phenomenology, literary and cultural studies, sociology and other disciplines in which structuralism had an impact. Yet these concepts of sign and value were far from new. They had figured in Saussure's own education, before being abandoned as *passé*, and then forgotten until he unwittingly resurrected them.

As detailed in Joseph (*Saussure*), between his secondary education at the Collège de Genève and his university studies Saussure attended the Gymnase de Genève, which was located in the buildings of the Université de Genève, and where the teachers were men who also taught at the Collège or Université or both. The course given by the director of the Gymnase, Isaac-Antoine Verchère (1827-1916), may have had the most enduring impact on Saussure. One of his classmates wrote in his memoirs that Verchère "gave us an enjoyable logic course of extreme sim-

---

[1] Also meriting consideration are *dépôt*, which occurs at *CLG* 232 and can have the meaning of a financial deposit, and *somme*, which appears frequently in the book; but space limitations require me to set them aside, as it does the instances of all these words in the source materials that are not reflected in the published *Cours*.

plicity" (Lemaître 36);[2] another recalled that "I did not understand very much of it; the subject of his course was, I think, psychology" (David 110).[3] In fact the course was a comprehensive survey of philosophy from ancient to modern times, and it did cover psychology as well. It is interesting that Lemaître remembered it as a course in Logic, which was one of the main subdivisions and which included the section on language. The course notes taken by one student open:

> One of the great apanages of the human species is the ability to communicate intellectually. These communications are carried out by different means which generally take the name of *language* [langage]. The material processes are called *signs*. But if one gives a sign to an absent person it no longer has any value. Every time a collection of conventional or natural signs is made, this is called a language [langage]. There are several systems of signs: thus the sounds of the voice or *speech* [parole], which is language *par excellence* (*la langue*) (παραβολα [parabola], comparison, then language [langage]). (Claparède f. 426)[4]

Notes from a similar course that Saussure took as a university student, given by Henri-Frédéric Amiel (1821-1881), now remembered for his *Journal intime* (originally published in two volumes in 1882-4), likewise contain material on sign theory that links back to Amiel's and Verchère's own education of half a century earlier. Then the 17th-18th century *grammaire générale* tradition was still the core of Genevese education, unlike in France, where it had not survived Napoleonic reforms.[5] It is striking how many of the terms we associate with Saussure are present in this paragraph from Verchère: *langage, signe, langue, parole* and, of course, *valeur*. These terms were part of the academic air that Saussure grew up breathing; and when he began to lecture on general linguistics

---

[2] "Notre professeur de philosophie, M. Verchère, nous donnait un agréable cours de logique d'une extrême simplicité." This and all other translations are my own unless otherwise indicated.

[3] "Verchère enseignait la philosophie, à laquelle je ne comprenais pas grand-chose; la matière de son cours était, je crois, la pscychologie."

[4] "Un des grands appanages de l'espèce humaine c'est de pouvoir communiquer intellectuellement. Ces communications se font par différents moyens qui portent généralement le nom de langage. Les procédés matériels s'appellent signes. Mais si on fait un signe à une personne absente il n'a plus de valeur. Toutes les fois qu'on fait une collection de signes conventionnels ou naturels, cela s'appelle un langage. Il y a plusieurs systèmes de signes: ainsi les sons de la voix ou parole, c'est le langage par excellence (la langue) (παραβολα, comparaison, puis langage)."

[5] For more on Genevese education in the first half of the 19th century see Joseph, "Language Pedagogy."

in 1907 he may have been unaware that his students had grown up in a changed atmosphere. Saussure was in the one of the very last cohorts to be taught by these men of his grandparents' generation.

But the terms do not have the same *value* in Verchère's use of them as they will in Saussure's. He redefined all of them, making them into a system, where the value of each depends on its relation to the others. How did he come to conceive of them in this new way? Saussure mentions *économie politique* in his lectures on general linguistics, and many have speculated about economic theorists who may have influenced him. He never cites any. But the journal kept by one of his friends during their time as a student in the Université de Genève records that "De Saussure is taking an impossible load of courses, a bit of everything, theology, law, sciences; he's taking second-year courses where he understands nothing, since he didn't take the first year. In short, he's doing it as only he can" (Pictet).[6]

The Law Faculty had a course on political economy, taught by Henri Dameth (1812-1884), formerly a teacher in the prestigious Lycée Louis-le-Grand in Paris, until his Fourierist affiliations got him into trouble with the administration of Napoleon III (Busino and Stelling-Michaud 16). Dameth's *Introduction à l'étude de l'économie politique* was published in 1865, with a second edition in 1878, just three years after Saussure was attending lectures in his Faculty. It consists of a set of lectures, bound to be close, if not identical, to his university lectures. This is the nearest we have to a documented source for Saussure's comments on economics, and such is the oblivion into which Dameth has fallen that it was never explored prior to Joseph, "Saussure's Value(s)." In his second lecture Dameth asks:

So, has political economics discovered the great generating fact that plays such a decisive role in constituting a science? – Yes, it is the notion of *value*. To such a degree that a good many economists today propose defining political economics as *the science of value*. (Dameth 24, ^{2}30)[7]

---

[6] "De Saussure prend un tas de cours impossible, un peu de tout, il est autant en Théologie qu'en Droit, qu'en Sciences; il prend des cours de 2ème année où il ne comprend rien, vu que la Ière lui manque. Bref, il fait cela à sa manière lui."

[7] "Enfin, l'économie politique a-t-elle découvert ce grand fait générateur qui joue un rôle si décisif dans la constitution d'une science? – Oui, c'est la notion de la *valeur*. A telles enseignes que bon nombre d'économistes proposent aujourd'hui de définir l'économie politique la *science de la valeur*."

Saussure too will confront the question of whether linguistics is a science, and will argue that it is a science of values. When Dameth comes to explain *prix*, he again does so in terms that will have echoes in Saussure's discussion in the *CLG*:

> A rather intense degree of observation is needed to comprehend: (1) that price is only the monetary expression of the value of goods; (2) that, in the formation of price, money only plays the role of a term of comparison between goods; (3) that the value of the money itself depends on the ratio of the quantity of it available relative to the quantity of goods for which it serves as the means of exchange. (Dameth 41)[8]

Goods have a value, expressible in money, which is only a term of comparison – of difference – between goods. We have seen Verchère pointing out that the word *parole* derives from Greek *parabola*, comparison. At the same time, money itself has a value which depends on how much of it is available relative to the supply of goods. But what determines the value of particular goods?

Dameth says that economists recognize a "natural" or "real" value of goods, which represents their total cost of production, including raw materials, interest on capital, workers' salaries, taxes, transportation and the like. This he says gives the "essence" of the price of the goods; but not their market price. That follows the law of supply and demand, which "oscillates incessantly around the *natural price* and sometimes even strays distantly from it" (Dameth 41, ²52).[9] The *CLG* recalls this relationship: "through one of its sides a value is rooted in things and their natural relations (as is the case in economic science – for example the value of a plot of land is proportional to what it brings in" (*CLG* ²116).[10] But it then denies that this applies in the case of language, where there is no such natural basis, all being instead completely arbitrary. The system of a language is so complex that it is impossible to

---

[8] "[I]l faut un degré d'observation déjà assez intense pour comprendre: 1° que le prix n'est que l'expression monétaire de la valeur des marchandises; 2° que la monnaie ne joue, dans la formation du prix, que le rôle d'un terme de comparaison des marchandises entre elles; 3° que la valeur de l'argent lui-même dépend de son rapport de quantité présente avec celle des marchandises auxquelles il sert de moyen d'échange." Some changes were made to this passage in the 1878 edition.

[9] "oscille incessamment autour du prix *naturel* et s'en éloigne même parfois beaucoup."

[10] "par un de ses côtés une valeur a sa racine dans les choses et leurs rapports naturels (comme c'est le cas dans la science économique – par exemple un fonds de terre vaut en proportion de ce qu'il rapporte)."

study simultaneously the two axes which the *CLG* at this point christens synchronic and diachronic. They must be analyzed in sequence.

Dameth gives a potted history of the idea of value. First there was the mistaken identification of value with price. This the economists replaced with another concept, equating value with utility. This was progress, as it made value "internal, inherent to the object bought and sold" (77, ²95)[11] –but only by shifting the burden of definition from "What is value?" to "What is utility?" Nothing is more useful to man than air or light, yet because the supply of these is not limited, they have no 'value' in the economic sense. The utility-based concept of value fails to take supply and demand into account.

The next step was to place the origin of value in human work: this Dameth (80, ²99) attributes to Adam Smith's distinction between "*usage* value and *exchange* value,"[12] a necessary bridge out of pure utility. Ultimately though, the value of usage is individually based; it might apply to Robinson Crusoe on his island, but not to value in society. "The moment we leave this novelistic fiction, in order to reason about society, usage value too disappears, absorbed by exchange value" (81, ²100]).[13]

Dameth reduces his principle to a formula: "Value is the power of exchange that services possess relative to one another" (85, ²105-6).[14] He adds that "the chief meaning of this notion is that to man alone belongs the creation of value; that in reality he neither sells nor buys nor exchanges anything other than this [. . .]."[15] In other words, what can be owned, bought, sold or exchanged is not goods or property but *value alone*, and that is a human creation. "So conceived, the economic world appears to us as a vast market in which services are exchanged for services."[16] When the *CLG* revisits value at greater length, it takes this exchange-based approach, which helps us understand what Saussure meant in repeatedly calling a language a "social fact."

---

[11] "interne, inhérent à l'objet qui se vend et s'achète."

[12] "la valeur d'*usage* et la valeur d'*échange*."

[13] "Dès que nous sortons de cette fiction de roman, pour raisonner sur la société, la valeur d'usage disparaît à son tour, absorbée par la valeur d'échange."

[14] "La valeur est la puissance relative d'échange que possèdent les services entre eux."

[15] "le sens capital de cette notion, c'est qu'à l'homme seul appartient la création de la valeur; qu'il ne vend et n'achète ou n'échange en réalité que cela [...]."

[16] "Ainsi conçu, le monde économique nous apparaît comme un vaste marché où des services s'échangent contre des services."

> Even outside language, all values [. . .] are always constituted:
> (1) by a *dissimilar* thing susceptible to being *exchanged* for something of which the value is to be determined;
> (2) by *similar* things that can be *compared* with the one whose value is in question.
> [. . .] Hence for a five-franc piece, one needs to know: (1) that it can be exchanged for a determinate quantity of something different, for example bread; (2) that it can be compared with a similar value of the same system (a dollar, etc.). Likewise a word can be exchanged for something dissimilar: an idea; moreover, it can be compared with something of the same nature: another word. (*CLG* ²159-60])[17]

This is one of those instances where the *CLG*, for ease of exposition, keeps the vernacular terms word and idea, which it elsewhere replaces with signifier and signified.

2. From *parole* and diachrony to synchronic *langue*

For Saussure, *parole*, the production of utterances, is a free linguistic market. An individual brings his or her innovation to it, which may or may not "sell" to the broader speech community, in the sense that others hearing it may or may not start using it themselves. Most of the time they do not, but innovations are adopted often enough to ensure that no language stays unaltered over time. The market is free in the sense that changes from below, in social terms, are no less likely to occur than changes from above. If anything, the reverse is true (apart from cases where a strong-arm regime punishes disobedience of its linguistic diktats, and even that tends to spawn resistance).

What is it that determines whether a given innovation is adopted as a language-wide change? Saussure did not pretend to offer an answer; linguists can only give a *post hoc* rationale, based on the general assumption that an innovation that succeeds must offer something positive to the

---

[17] "[M]ême en dehors de la langue, toutes les valeurs [. . .] sont toujours constituées: 1° par une chose *dissemblable* susceptible d'être *échangée* contre celle dont la valeur est à déterminer; 2° par les choses *similaires* qu'on peut *comparer* avec celle dont la valeur est en cause. [. . .] Ainsi pour déterminer ce que vaut une pièce de cinq francs, il faut savoir: 1° qu'on peut l'échanger contre une quantité déterminée d'une chose différente, par exemple du pain; 2° qu'on peut la comparer avec une valeur similaire du même système, par exemple une pièce d'un franc, ou avec une monnaie d'un autre système: (un dollar, etc.). De même un mot peut être échangé contre quelque chose de dissemblable: une idée; en outre, il peut être comparé avec quelque chose de même nature: un autre mot."

languaging experience. Greater ease, perhaps – but this is tricky, because ease is not objectively measurable, and in many areas of language, as Gabelentz recognized, greater ease of articulation means that more effort has to be put into comprehension. Greater nuance, greater expressivity – again, all ultimately subjective. Joseph ("Iconicity") discusses cases in which Saussure applies what we might call iconicity or sound symbolism (he did not use either term) as an explanation for the development of certain seemingly exceptional forms in Latin and Greek. This is surprising, since Saussure is remembered for making the arbitrariness of linguistic signs the first principle of his synchronic linguistics. But how signs are *used* in *parole*, and how, consequently, they change in diachrony, is another matter: here the subjective reactions of *some* speakers might suffice to shift the balance in favour of a change, so that it becomes prevalent in *parole* and eventually in a new state of the language (*état de langue*).

Saussure ("Adjectifs") proposes that a particular set of sounds had a meaning or quasi-meaning in Indo-European. The "type" in question is a group of adjectives linked phonetically by having a diphthong that starts with /a/, and semantically by referring to some infirmity or deviation from the "right" or "straight." The diphthong could be /ai/ (as in Latin *caecus* "blind") or /au/, but also /ar/, /al/, /an/ or /am/, all of which are analyzed by Saussure, starting in his early *Mémoire*, as /a/ + sonant, hence as diphthongs in the same way that /a/ + /i/, or /a/ + /u/, form diphthongs. There is iconicity in the correlation between how the "straight" vowel /a/ "deviates" off into the sonant, and the meaning of deviance from the straight, the normal. Saussure points out that words with /a/ diphthongs, such as Latin *blaesus* "stammering," *claudus* "limping," *calvus* "bald," *mancus* "maimed," are few in number and are isolated within the language, being attached neither to any strong verb nor to an etymological family. The *a* diphthongs would be marked (to use a later terminology) for rarity and isolation, and being so marked they would correlate with meanings that likewise involve marginality or abnormality. It is through the regularity of this correlation that these apparently marginal elements are incorporated into the system where everything connects. But how does this happen? Saussure's explanation relies on another aspect of his general linguistic system, the relationship of synchrony to diachrony. He imagines

> a time when there existed perhaps only four or five adjectives of "infirmity" with the diphthongs *ai, au, an*, etc. Around this nucleus furnished by chance, ever more numerous formations will have come to fix themselves, where a

certain community of ideas favoured diphthongs with *a*. It would thus involve a fact of lexical analogy [. . .]. (Saussure, "Adjectifs" 206)[18]

Note that he attributes the *origin* of this "nucleus" not to iconicity, but to chance. Once the cryptotype was established, however, diphthongs with /a/ were "favoured" for words sharing this general idea of infirmity. The favouring would presumably take place in the competition amongst innovative forms that occurs within *parole*. For Saussure, the key question in language change is not "Why are new forms introduced?" In *parole* speakers are constantly introducing new forms, only a tiny proportion of which will find the social sanction that will make them part of *langue* (in a new *état de langue*). Rather, the question is "Why are certain forms sanctioned and not others?" (see Saussure, *Deuxième cours* 47; Joseph, "'La teinte'"). This is where the sort of analogy-driven favouring he refers to could make a difference.

The associative relations that are central to Saussure's conception of *langue* make it plausible that the analogy he proposes was synchronically real for speakers – again, for *some* speakers, enough of them for it to have left a recoverable diachronic trace, but perhaps not enough of them for the set of /a/ diphthongs to form a morpheme, a meaningful unit in the *langue* that all speakers share – the *trésor*, in the contents sense.

3. Language as *trésor*, value as difference, and the cerebral closet

On one occasion the *CLG* uses *trésor* to describe a language in a way that rather clearly means the contents:

> It is a *trésor* deposited by the practice of *parole* in the subjects belonging to one same community, a grammatical system existing virtually in each brain, or more exactly in the brains of an ensemble of individuals; for the language is not complete in any one, it exists perfectly only in the mass. (*CLG* 230)[19]

---

[18] "le temps où il n'existait peut-être que quatre ou cinq adjectifs 'd'infirmité' avec le vocalisme *ai, au, an,* etc. Autour de ce noyau fourni par le hasard seront venues se fixer des formations toujours plus nombreuses, où une certaine communauté de l'idée mettait en faveur les diphtongues par *a*. Il s'agirait donc d'un fait d'analogie lexicologique [. . .]."

[19] "C'est un trésor déposé par la pratique de la parole dans les sujets appartenant à une même communauté, un système grammatical existant virtuellement dans chaque cerveau, ou plus exactement dans les cerveaux d'un ensemble d'individus; car la langue n'est complète dans aucun, elle n'existe parfaitement que dans la masse."

Harris's translation (13) has "a fund accumulated" for *un trésor déposé*, while Baskin's (13) has "a storehouse filled." When ten years later Harris translated a student's notes from Saussure's third course in general linguistics (1910-11), in the passage corresponding to Saussure (*CLG* ²30) he rendered *trésor* as "hoard" (Saussure, *Troisième cours* 7a). If Baskin's "filled" is a stretch for *déposé*, it lets him translate *trésor* consistently as "storehouse" on its other occurrences (Baskin 123, 165):

> [T]hese coordinations [. . .] do not have an extension to support them; their seat is in the brain; they are part of this inner *trésor* that constitutes the language in each individual. We shall call them *associative relations*. (*CLG* ²171)[20]

> Every analogical creation must be preceded by an unconscious comparison of the materials deposited in the *trésor* of the *langue* where the generating forms are arranged according to their syntagmatic and associative relations. (*CLG* ²227)[21]

In the first passage, Harris (122) has "that accumulated store" for *ce trésor intérieur*, and again "store" for *trésor* in the second (164). The first passage comes from Saussure's second course in general linguistics (1908-9), the second from the first course (1907). Harris's student Wolf translated a set of student notes from each of these courses, rendering its occurrences of *trésor* as "treasury" (Saussure, *Deuxième cours* 119, 123) or "fund" (Saussure, *Premier cours* 63, 65, 66, 67). Before looking more closely at the student notes, which bring in other metaphors alongside *trésor*, some of them clearly of the container rather than contents type, it is worth considering the background to how the retention of knowledge was conceived.

Joseph (*Language, Mind and Body*) recounts the long history – as old as history itself – of arguments over what knowledge is and what form it takes in whoever or whatever has it. Through the middle ages and well into the modern period, medical and philosophical writers generally located memory in the posterior ventricle (or cell) of the brain, while the anterior ventricle was where sensory input and motor output were regulated by the common sense, and the middle ventricle was responsible

---

[20] "[C]es coordinations [. . .] n'ont pas pour support l'étendue; leur siège est dans le cerveau; elles font partie de ce trésor intérieur qui constitue la langue chez chaque individu. Nous les appellerons *rapports associatifs*."

[21] "Toute création doit être précédée d'une comparaison inconsciente des matériaux déposés dans le trésor de la langue où les formes génératrices sont rangées selon leurs rapports syntagmatiques et associatifs."

for reasoning. The rebirth of anatomical study in the early modern period brought improved understanding of the nervous system, and medical observation of reflexes showed that some nervous-muscular reactions involved only the spinal cord and not the brain. British philosophers starting with Thomas Hobbes (1588-1679) and John Locke (1632-1704) put forward a theory of "associations" as the source of knowledge, which David Hartley (1705-1757) would develop into an account of how knowledge is not only acquired but "stored" as vibrations in the nervous system. This associationism persisted in Britain, surviving periods in which rival theories were more to the fore.

In the second half of the 19th century, the work of Alexander Bain (1818-1903) put forward an up-to-date version of associationism that took account of contemporary medical science. It became the new modernism of the younger generation of French psychologists, thanks mainly to its being championed by Hippolyte Taine. Bain laid out a series of "general laws of alliance of body and mind," of which a central one was the Principle of Relativity, "the necessity of change in order to our being conscious," which he called "the groundwork of Thought, Intellect, or Knowledge, as well as of Feeling. We know heat only in the transition from cold, and *vice versâ;* up and down, long and short, red and not red – all are so many transitions, or changes of impression; and without transition we have no knowledge" (Bain, *Mind and Body* 81). He makes the strong claim that knowledge, in effect, equates with difference:

> Our knowledge begins, as it were, with difference; we do not know any one thing of itself, but only the difference between it and another thing; the present sensation of heat is, in fact, a difference from the preceding cold. (81)

The idea that "all consciousness is of difference" had been stated by Mill, crediting it to Hamilton. Spencer (324-7) contains a further elaboration of the steps leading from simple difference to "consciousness" in the full sense. Bain adds, as his predecessors did not do, that this principle applies to the sounds of language, and not just to concepts or ideas: "Our discrimination of *articulate* sounds is co-extensive with the combined alphabets of all the languages known to us" (Bain, *Mind and Body* 84).

Bain treats memory as a physical phenomenon, with a description that prefigures the "connectionism" of Rumelhart et al.: currents of force passing through nervous circuits create "specific growths in the cell junctions" (Bain, *Mind and Body* 91). The stronger the original force, the more vivid the impression left on the circuit, quite like the "weights" of connectionist analysis.

As for the mental recollection of language, it "is a suppressed articulation, ready to burst into speech. When the thought of an action excites us very much, we can hardly avoid the actual repetition, so completely are all the nervous circuits repossessed with the original currents of force" (90). But most remembered states or ideas are not so vivid, but of a "comparative feebleness" that is "an exact counterpart of the diminished force of the revived currents of the brain" (91), so suppressing our articulation of them is not difficult:

> [W]hen I see a written word and, as a result of my education, pronounce it orally, the power lies in a series of definite groupings or connexions of nerve-currents in the nerve and centres of the eye, with currents in motor nerves proceeding to the chest, larynx and mouth; and these groupings or connexions are effected by definite growths at certain proper or convenient cell crossings. (91)

Bain (*Senses and Intellect* 334) had already articulated this idea of a silent interior "nervous" speech. It challenges what he calls the "old notion" which "supposes that the brain is a sort of receptacle of the impressions of sense, where they lie stored up in a chamber quite apart from the recipient apparatus, to be manifested again to the mind when occasion calls." He contrasts this with "the modern theory of the brain," which "suggests a totally different view":

> We have seen that the brain is only one part of the course of nervous action; that the completed circles take in the nerves and the extremities of the body; that nervous action consists of a current passing through these complete circles, or to and fro between the ganglia and the organs of sense and motion; and that short of a completed course no nervous action exists. The idea of a cerebral closet is quite incompatible with the real manner of the working of nerve. Seeing then that a sensation in the first instance diffuses nerve currents through the interior of the brain outwards to the organs of expression and movement, the persistence of that sensation after the outward exciting cause is withdrawn, can only be a continuance of the same diffusive currents, perhaps less intense, but not otherwise different. (332)

The "cerebral closet" is the back ventricle of mediaeval cell theory, seat of the *virtus memorialis*. It is an uncharacteristically biting metaphor from Bain, whose alternative to it is essentially that offered by the connectionism that posed a powerful challenge to the Chomskyan mental closet in the 1980s.

After completing his doctorate at Leipzig in 1881, Saussure went to Paris with the intention of doing a second one. Early in his time there, Victor Egger (1848-1909) published his own doctoral thesis as a book entitled *La parole intérieure: Essai de psychologie descriptive* (Inner Speech: Essay in Descriptive Psychology). Saussure's notes on his reading of this book allow us to trace his reaction to it and to infer its impact on his subsequent thinking (see Joseph, *Saussure* 288-91). Egger begins his book by asserting that

> At every moment, the mind is speaking its thought internally. [. . .T]he series of inner words forms an almost continual series, in parallel with other series of psychic facts; it thus constitutes a considerable part of our consciousness. (Egger 1)[22]

Egger looked back mostly to French sources from the start of the century, following the Vicomte de Bonald (1754-1840) particularly closely, while blaming Maine de Biran (1766-1824) for a mistake that Bain repeated, and then transmitted to the younger generation of French psychologists: "much too great importance is attributed to muscular movement, which is only a means, and which, as such, is neglected by the attention, whereas all the mental effort bears upon the sound, which is the goal of the movement and the essential element of speech" (Egger 41).[23] Egger downplays the role of inner speech in Bain:

> in one of the rare passages he [Bain] devotes to it, inner speech becomes a muscular-tactile image. This latter idea, unfortunately, has caught on; for there is today, among psychologists, a *school of touch* or, more precisely, a *school of muscle*, which leads all the operations of the mind back willy-nilly to the active touch and the muscular sense. [. . .] Taine is among those who have accepted Bain's error without discussion, and he too accords only a brief mention to inner speech. (Egger 59)[24]

---

[22] "A tout instant, l'âme parle intérieurement sa pensée. [...L]a série des mots intérieurs forme une succession presque continue, parallele à la succession des autres faits psychiques; à elle seule, elle retient donc une partie considérable de la conscience de chacun de nous."

[23] "une importance beaucoup trop grande est attribuée au mouvement musculaire, qui n'est qu'un moyen, et qui, comme tel, est négligé par l'attention [...], tandis que tout l'effort mental se porte sur le son, qui est le but du mouvement et l'élément essentiel de la parole."

[24] "dans un des rares passages qu'il lui consacre, la parole intérieure devient une image musculaire-tactile. Cette dernière idée, malheureusement, a fait fortune: car il y a aujourd'hui, parmi les psychologues, une *école du toucher* ou, pour mieux dire, une *école du muscle*, qui ramène de gré ou de force toutes les opérations de l'âme au toucher actif et au

But Egger fails to consider the reasons behind Bain's nervous-muscular (not "tactile") location of inner speech: the fact that the alternative location is a "closet" in the brain in which is stored the "memory" of perceptions and productions, a memory that is a reflection transferred from the original mode of perception and production to something of an entirely different nature. Egger speaks of memory – particular *souvenirs* and the general capacity of *mémoire* – and above all of *images*, as in the preceding quote.

Further on, Egger makes it clearer that he does believe in an "image of buccal movement" that plays an essential role in producing outer speech, but none in inner speech, the essence of which is the sound image alone:

> Inner speech is a simple image, a purely sonorous image; in the same way, the outer speech of another heard by us is a simple sensation, purely sonorous; but it is otherwise with our own speech, perceived by our ear at the same time as it is produced by our vocal organs; this time it is a double sensation, simultaneously sonorous and tactile, or, more precisely, a couple of sensations. (Egger 75-6)[25]

Egger's view can be schematized thus:

inner speech   =   sound image

outer speech ⟨ speaker [experiences tactile sensation (in production) *plus*
              hearer [experiences sound sensation (in perception) ⟵

Presumably the speaker of outer speech is often experiencing inner speech at the same time, in which case another arrow should extend from *plus* upward to sound image. But Egger does not mention this; his aim at this point is to widen the gap between inner and outer speech, and to associate Bain's conception with the outer. As Egger goes on to specify where he differs from Bain, he acknowledges that an image of

---

sens musculaire. [. . .] M. Taine est de ceux qui ont accepté sans discussion l'erreur de Bain, et lui aussi n'accorde à la parole intérieure qu'une courte mention."

[25] "La parole intérieure est une image simple, une image purement sonore; de même, la parole extérieure d'autrui entendue par nous est une sensation simple, purement sonore; mais il en est autrement de notre propre parole, perçue par notre oreille en même temps qu'elle est produite par nos organes vocaux; celle-ci est une sensation double, à la fois sonore et tactile, ou, pour mieux dire, un couple de sensations."

the movement of the vocal organs *may* be present during inner speech — in fact the organs may actually move in a silent "sketch" — but he insists that this does not have the importance Bain accords to it:

> According to Bain and his school, on the contrary, the image of the buccal movement, or even an actual sketch of a laryngeal-buccal movement, always accompanies inner speech; moreover, if we take Bain literally, the phenomenon of inner speech would be essentially an interrupted movement or the simple image of this movement. [. . .] We know that, according to Bain, tactile-muscular sensation or its image is a necessary element of all intellectual facts; we fear that the systematic spirit has not led him, on the point we are dealing with, to any more rigorous observation. (Egger 76-7)[26]

The question remains of where inner speech takes place. Bain posited a stark choice between nervous-organic association and a mental "closet," while skewing the pitch by implying that only the former accords with scientific findings. Egger's response is one that he is not the first nor will be the last to give: that the "where" question does not apply to inner speech, because it assumes a spatiality and extension that belong only to what is external. "Exteriority is the reason for spatiality" (Egger 98).[27] When speech is exteriorized, it has an extension, hence a location, outside the speaker. Inner speech though is only "localized in a vague and indeterminate way in the head [. . .]. But this is not what were just calling *localization*, when we were speaking about outer speech; inner speech is not the object of a *special* localization in a *precise* place, that is to say a localization in the proper and ordinary sense of the word" (102).[28]

---

[26] "D'après Bain et son école, au contraire, l'image du mouvement buccal, ou même une ébauche de mouvement laryngo-buccal réel, accompagnerait toujours la parole intérieure; bien plus, à prendre à la lettre les expressions de Bain, le phénomène de la parole intérieure serait essentiellement un mouvement interrompu ou la simple image de ce mouvement. [. . .] On sait que, suivant Bain, la sensation tactile-musculaire ou son image est un élément nécessaire de tous les faits intellectuels; nous craignons que l'esprit de système ne l'ait entraîné, sur le point qui nous occupe, à une observation peu rigoureuse."

[27] "c'est l'extériorité qui est la raison de la spatialité."

[28] "est localisée d'une façon vague et indéterminée dans la tête [. . .]. Mais ce n'est pas là ce que nous appelions tout à l'heure *localisation*, quand nous parlions de la parole extérieure; la parole intérieure n'est pas l'objet d'une localisation *spéciale* dans un lieu *précis*, c'est-à-dire d'une localisation, au sens propre et ordinaire du mot."

4. *Trésor, casier, magasin*

The three *trésors* of the *CLG* come from the third, second and first courses in general linguistics respectively. The last of them (*CLG* 233, ²227), from the first course, is a passing reference to how the process of linguistic analogy requires "an unconscious comparison of materials deposited in the *trésor* of the *langue*."

The most complete set of notes from the third course, those by Émile Constantin, were not available to Bally and Sechehaye when they were compiling the *CLG*. Corresponding to the passage from *CLG* ²30, Constantin wrote: "One can say that the object to be studied is the *trésor* deposited in each of our brains, this *trésor*, without doubt, if taken from each individual, will nowhere be perfectly complete" (Saussure and Constantin 88; Saussure, *Troisième cours* 7).²⁹ This is what Harris translates as "hoard," which suggests a reading of *trésor* as contents rather than container.

The passage that appears at *CLG* ²171 is based mainly on the notes from the second course by Albert Riedlinger, the only one of the students whose collaboration is acknowledged on the title page of the *CLG*. Riedlinger recorded Saussure as referring to

> the inner *trésor* that is equivalent to the closet [*casier*] of memory [. . .]; there we have what can be called the storehouse [*magasin*]. It is in this *trésor* that is arranged everything that can enter into activity in the second location. And the second location is discourse, the chain of *parole*. (*CLG/E* [= Critical ed. of *CLG* by Engler] 281, II R 89¹⁹⁹⁸; Saussure, *Deuxième cours* 52).³⁰

The *casier* metaphor also makes an appearance in the third course: "In effect, we cannot explore the closets [*casiers*] existing inside our brains [We are] obliged to use an external means, supplied by *parole*" (Saussure and Constantin 224-5; Saussure, *Troisième cours* 80).³¹ The metaphor may

---

²⁹ "On peut dire que l'objet à étudier, c'est le trésor déposé dans notre cerveau à chacun, ce trésor, sans doute, si on le prend dans chaque individu, ne sera nulle part parfaitement complet." Komatsu (Saussure, *Troisième cours* 7) has *de* for the second *dans*. The other students' notes for this passage are similar, but more fragmented.

³⁰ "le trésor intérieur qui équivaut aux casiers de la mémoire; c'est là ce qu'on peut appeler le magasin [. . .]. C'est dans ce trésor qu'est rangé tout ce qui peut entrer en activité dans le second lieu. Et le second lieu, c'est le discours, c'est la chaîne de la *parole*."

³¹ "En effet, les casiers existant à l'intérieur de notre cerveau, nous ne pouvons les explorer. [Nous sommes] obligés d'employer un moyen extérieur, donné dans la parole." For an examination of the terms *trésor, casier* etc. in the context of the *langue/parole* distinction, see Béguelin.

have been chosen casually by Saussure, but it had a resonance with things he had read and that were in the *casiers* of his own memory. De Palo has noted Bréal's (555) comparison of intelligence to a *casier* in which ideas are arranged in order, and rightly points out that these metaphors were in regular use by psychologists of the late 19th century. Bourdieu (23) has also made a link between the use of *trésor* by Saussure and by Auguste Comte (1798-1857), who Bourdieu says "offers an exemplary expression of the illusion of linguistic communism that haunts the whole of linguistic theory."[32]

What has not been remarked upon previously is the central role this particular concept had in Egger, which predates Bréal's book and may have informed it, and which we know Saussure read carefully. It is also significant that Saussure uses the *casier* metaphor in conjunction with "associations," given that the immediate association that would call up for any French psychologist of the time would be the name of Bain. Following the preceding quote from Riedlinger's notes, he records Saussure as saying that

> In this mass of elements which we have at our disposal virtually but effectively, in this *trésor*, we make associations: each element makes us think of the other: all that is similar and dissimilar in some way presents itself around each word, otherwise the mechanism of the *langue* would be impossible. (*CLG/E* 281, II R 90-1[2038]; Saussure, *Deuxième cours* 52).[33]

It is true that 26 years would pass between Saussure's reading of Egger and the start of his lectures on general linguistics. In the interim however there had appeared Victor Henry's (1850-1907) *Antinomies linguistiques* (Linguistic antinomies; see Joseph, "'Undoubtedly a powerful influence'"). Saussure had known Henry since the start of the 1880s, when they both regularly attended meetings of the Société de linguistique de Paris, and Henry sent him an inscribed copy of his 1896 book, in which Egger figures strongly. In 1905, Henri Odier (1873-1938) published his doctoral thesis, which included the first account of Saussure's theory of

---

[32] "offre une expression exemplaire de l'illusion du communisme linguistique qui hante toute la théorie linguistique." Bourdieu bases this judgement on a citation from Comte (1929 [1852]: 254).

[33] "Dans cette masse d'éléments dont nous disposons virtuellement mais effectivement, dans ce trésor, nous faisons des associations: chaque élément nous fait penser à l'autre: tout ce qui est semblable et dissemblable en quelque sorte se présente autour de chaque mot, autrement le mécanisme de la langue serait impossible." Here again the other students' notes are similar in content.

the linguistic sign (see Joseph, "Centenary").[34] Odier's book too was in Saussure's library, and his copy of it contains underlining and notes showing that he read it carefully. The works specifically on language that Odier relies on most heavily are Egger and Henry. Yet Odier makes use of the concept of *valeur* in a way that surprisingly recalls Bain:

> The word has a common monetary exchange value. The effigy on it does not vary, but its intrinsic quality, its precise weight, its alloy varies. The particular value of the word, beyond the influence of its meaning, its form and its sonority resides in the mechanism of elocution itself. The muscular movements which are produced involuntarily in the speech organs, when we hear a word, contribute to the timbre of the emotion which the word produces [. . .]. (Odier 34)[35]

Odier makes it evident that he discussed language in depth with Saussure, but his interests tended toward psychology rather than linguistics, and he clearly departs from Saussure's views at several points. So when he writes that a word has an emotional value that "resides in the [. . .] muscular movements which are produced involuntarily in the speech organs, when we hear a word," we cannot assume that Saussure agreed. Still, Charles Bally's (1865-1947) book on *la stylistique*, defined as the study, not of style (as in later stylistics), but of "affective" language along the lines of what Odier is discussing here, bears a dedication to Saussure, who maintained that this should be included within the concerns of linguistics (see Joseph, *Saussure* 612-13).

---

[34] Odier was the youngest son of one of Geneva's top banking families, though he himself had no desire to go into the business, unlike his elder brothers, who had been friends of Saussure's since boyhood. Odier's grandson, the University of Toronto philosopher Ronald de Sousa, has told me that his grandfather was however the only one in the family to foresee the Crash of 1929, but was talked out of cashing in his stocks by his supposedly more economically astute brothers.

[35] "Le mot a une valeur monétaire d'échange commun. Son effigie ne varie pas, mais sa qualité intrinsèque, son millième, son alliage varie. La valeur particulière du mot, outre l'influence du sens, de la forme, de la sonorité réside dans le mécanisme même de l'élocution. Les mouvements musculaires qui se produisent involontairement dans les organes de la parole, lorsque nous entendons un mot, contribuent au timbre de l'émotion que produit le mot [. . .]."

5. Rereading *valeur* and *trésor*

Saussure's metaphors of *valeur* and *trésor* look less commonplace and offhand when read in the light of Dameth's economic views, and Bain's version of associationism together with Egger's rejection of it. Saussure's later remarks about political economy resonate closely enough with Dameth that either Saussure learned it from him, or else – a possibility I would not rule out – Dameth was simply teaching the common economic view current in middle and upper class Geneva in the second half of the 19th century. Value in language is exchange value, which is to say that it is defined by what it is not; a value determinable only through comparison with elements surrounding it with which it might be substituted. This is perfectly in line with Bain, and with Hamilton and Mill before him. The sum of the values, the system, constitutes a *trésor* in the contents sense.

Where it is kept – the *trésor* in the container sense – is where Saussure departs from Bain, as Egger did, but not in the same direction. Saussure refers at various times to Paul Broca's (1824-1880) paper of 1861 reporting his autopsy of a patient who had suffered damage to a specific part of his brain (now known as Broca's area) resulting in a kind of aphasia in which speech production was impaired. Saussure was far from alone in taking this as proof that, *contra* Bain, there is indeed a "cerebral closet" in which knowledge of language is kept, despite the fact that subsequent research has suggested that such a view is a vast oversimplification – even though Broca's identification of one particular area for one type of aphasia has held up, along with another such identification made by Carl Wernicke (1848-1905) in 1874 (see Eling and Whitaker; Joseph, *Language, Mind and Body*).

Recent years have seen a move away from attempts at localizing language functions in the brain, and toward rethinking how what we call the mind is "extended" throughout the body and beyond, at least to the blind person's white cane, possibly even to your iPhone – and how my mind may be "distributed," not just to my body but to yours. This is related to what Dameth was saying about Robinson Crusoe and the social nature of value, and to Egger's point about inner speech not having a location because it lacks extension. Perhaps it is also what Saussure was groping toward in his repeated insistences that a language is a "social fact," and was struggling to get across by saying that a language is a *trésor* deposited in the brain of each individual that is however actually complete only across the brains of all the individuals in a community. His retreat to what Bain rejected as a "cerebral closet" is ironic, given how closely Bain anticipated Saussure's contention that not only is the conceptual side of language a matter of pure difference, but the phonic side is as well.

To judge from Dameth's published lectures on political economy, if Saussure attended his course, as seems likely, he got a good education in the development of modern economics since the late 18th century. His reading of Egger at the start of the 1880s then gave him a solid grounding in the development of psychology over the same period. In both fields the key innovations had come from Britain – Adam Smith; the utilitarians Bentham, James Mill and John Stuart Mill; Ricardo; and for psychology, the tradition of Locke, which had its own branch in France, but where psychology was being re-Briticized under the influence of Bain. The modernity of economics was based on its becoming psychologized; the modernity of psychology was dependent in part on its becoming physicalized. They were, in this regard, moving in opposite directions: economics away from a theory of intrinsic value, to relocate the value of things in what people value, as realized through exchange; psychology away from a theory of intrinsic values, to relocate mind ultimately in mechanical operations in the body, whether in the brain alone or in the whole "sensorimotor apparatus."

Linguistics, by contrast, was in a relatively stable state – to Saussure's great frustration, because he could see that it rested on illogical premises and unsustainable assumptions. By the time of his lectures on general linguistics, his impending tragedy was that he had given up trying to write a book that would show this in a way that satisfied his self-imposed perfectionist demands. But he had a course to give, and his perfectionism was matched by his devotion to duty. He never dreamed that his colleagues and students would deal him the ultimate posthumous homage and betrayal that is the *Cours de linguistique générale* – a betrayal not because of any minor aspects of his teaching they got wrong, but because they set it down in print at all.

References

Bain, Alexander. *The Senses and the Intellect.* London: John W. Parker and Son, 1855.

———. *Mind and Body: The Theories of Their Relation.* New York: D. C. Appleton and Co., 1875. (Originally published 1872.)

Bally, Charles. *Traité de stylistique française.* 2 vols. Heidelberg: Carl Winter, 1909.

Béguelin, Marie-José. "Linguistique de la langue et linguistique de la parole." *Du système linguistique aux actions langagières: Mélanges en l'honneur d'Alain Berrendonner.* Ed. Gilles Corminboeuf and Marie-José Béguelin. Brussels: De Boeck-Duculot, 2011. 641-66.

Bourdieu, Pierre. *Ce que parler veut dire.* Paris: Fayard, 1982.

Bréal, Michel. "Comment les mots sont classés dans notre esprit." *Revue politique et littéraire: Revue des cours littéraires*, 3a s., 8 (1884): 552-5.

Broca, Paul. "Perte de la parole, ramollissement chronique de destruction partielle du lobe antérieur gauche du cerveau." *Bulletin de la Société d'Anthropologie de Paris*, (1861): 235-8.

Busino, Giovanni and Sven Stelling-Michaud. *Matériaux pour une histoire des sciences sociales à Genève: Lettres de Pareto, Pantaleoni, Einaudi, d'Adrien Naville et d'autres.* Cahiers Vilfredo Pareto: Revue Européenne d'Histoire des Sciences Sociales, 6. Geneva: Droz, 1965.

Claparède, Alexandre. Course Notes, I: Cours de Gymnase, 2e année, V: Cours de Philosophie, Mr le prof. Verchère, 1876. Bibliothèque de Genève, Département de Manuscrits, Cours univ. 578.

Comte, Auguste. *Système de politique positive, ou Traité de sociologie, instituant la religion de l'humanité*, t. IIe, *contenant la Statique sociale ou le Traité abstrait de l'ordre humain.* Paris: chez l'auteur, 1852. (5e éd. Paris: Siège de la société positiviste, 1929.)

Dameth, Henri. *Introduction à l'étude de l'économie politique. Cours public professé à Lyon pendant l'hiver 1864-1865 sous les auspices de la Chambre de Commerce.* Lyon: Méra; Paris: Guillaumin, 1865. (2nd ed. 1878.)

David, Jean-Élie. *Notes au crayon: Souvenirs d'un arpenteur genevois, 1855-1898.* Ed. by Marianne and Pierre Enckell. Lausanne: Éditions d'En-bas, 2004.

De Palo, Marina. "Memoria e significato: Linguistica e psicologia intorna a Saussure." *Cahiers Ferdinand de Saussure* 54 (2001): 359-83.

Egger, Victor. *La parole intérieure: Essai de psychologie descriptive.* Paris: Germer Baillière, 1881.

Eling, Paul and Harry Whitaker. "History of Aphasia: From Brain to Language." *Handbook of Clinical Neurology*, vol. 95: *History of Neurology*, Ed. S. Finger, F. Boller and K. L. Tyler. Amsterdam: Elsevier, 2010. 571-82.

Gabelentz, Georg von der. *Die Sprachwissenschaft: Ihre Aufgaben, Methoden und bisherigen Ergebnisse*. Leipzig: Weigel, 1891.

Hamilton, Sir William. *Lectures on Metaphysics and Logic*. Ed. Henry Longueville Mansel and John Veitch. 4 vols. Edinburgh and London: Blackwood, 1859-60.

Henry, Victor. *Antinomies linguistiques*. Paris: F. Alcan, 1896.

Joseph, John E. "'Undoubtedly a powerful influence': Victor Henry's *Antinomies linguistiques* (1896), with an annotated translation of the first chapter." *Language and Communication* 16 (1996): 117-44.

———. "The Centenary of the First Publication of Saussure's Sign Theory – Odier (1905)." *Historiographia Linguistica* 32/2-3 (2005): 309-24.

———. "'La teinte de tous les ciels': Divergence et nuance dans la conception saussurienne du changement linguistique." *Cahiers Ferdinand de Saussure* 64 (2010): 145-58.

———. *Saussure*. Oxford: Oxford University Press, 2012.

———. "Language Pedagogy and Political-Cognitive Autonomy in Mid-19th Century Geneva: The Latin Manuals of Louis Longchamp (1802-1874)." *Historiographia Linguistica* 39/2-3 (2012): 259-77.

———. "Iconicity in Saussure's Linguistic Work, and Why it Does Not Contradict the Arbitrariness of the Sign." *Historiographia Linguistica* 42/1 (2015): 85-105.

———. "Saussure's Value(s)." *Recherches sémiotiques/Canadian Journal of Semiotics*, in press for 2016.

———. *Language, Mind and Body: A Conceptual History*. Cambridge: Cambridge University Press, 2016.

Lemaître, Auguste. *En glanant dans mes souvenirs (Croquis et anecdotes)*. Neuchâtel and Geneva: Éditions Forum, s. d. [1922].

Mill, John Stuart. *An Examination of Sir William Hamilton's Philosophy, and of the Principal Philosophical Questions Discussed in his Writings*. 3rd ed. London: Longmans, Green, Reader and Dyer, 1867. (1st ed. 1865.)

Odier, Henri. *Essai d'analyse psychologique du mécanisme du langage dans la compréhension*. Inaugural-Dissertation der philosophischen Fakultät der Universität Bern zur Erlangung der Doktorwürde. Berne: Imprimerie Sheitlin Spring et Cie., 1905.

Pictet, Amé. Diary entry, 24 October 1875. Bibliothèque de Genève, Département des Manuscrits, Ms. fr. 1599, folder 25, Z. no. 9.

Rumelhart, D. E., J. L. McClelland and the PDP Research Group. *Parallel Distributed Processing: Explorations in the Microstructure of Cognition. Vol. 1: Foundations; Vol. 2: Psychological and Biological Models.* Cambridge, Massachusetts: MIT Press, 1986.

Saussure, Ferdinand de. *Mémoire sur le système primitif des voyelles dans les langues indo-européennes.* Leipzig: imprimé par B. G. Teubner, 1879.

———. "Adjectifs indo-européens du type *caecus* 'aveugle'." *Festschrift Vilhelm Thomsen zur Vollendung des siebzigsten Lebensjahres am 25. Januar 1912, dargebracht von Freunden und Schülern.* Leipzig: Otto Harrassowitz, 1912. 202-6. Repr. in *Recueil des publications scientifiques de Ferdinand de Saussure.* Geneva: Sonor; Lausanne: Payot; Heidelberg: C. Winter, 1922. 595-9.

———. *Cours de linguistique générale.* Ed. Charles Bally and Albert Sechehaye, with the collaboration of Albert Riedlinger. Lausanne and Paris: Payot, 1916. (2nd ed. 1922; further eds essentially unchanged. Critical ed. by Rudolf Engler, Wiesbaden: Otto Harrassowitz, 1968-74. English trans., *Course in General Linguistics,* by Wade Baskin, New York: Philosophical Library, 1959; another by Roy Harris, London: Duckworth; La Salle, Illinois: Open Court, 1983.)

———. *Troisième cours de linguistique générale (1910-1911), d'après les cahiers d'Émile Constantin / Saussure's Third Course of Lectures on General Linguistics (1910-1911), from the notebooks of Émile Constantin.* Ed. Eisuke Komatsu, trans. Roy Harris. Oxford and New York: Pergamon, 1993.

———. *Premier cours de linguistique générale (1907), d'après les cahiers d'Albert Riedlinger / Saussure's First Course of Lectures on General Linguistics (1907), from the notebooks of Albert Riedlinger.* Ed. Eisuke Komatsu, trans. George Wolf. Oxford and New York: Pergamon, 1996.

———. *Deuxième cours de linguistique générale (1908-1909), d'après les cahiers d'Albert Riedlinger et Charles Patois / Saussure's Second Course of Lectures on General Linguistics (1908-1909), from the notebooks of Albert Riedlinger and Charles Patois.* Ed. Eisuke Komatsu, trans. George Wolf. Oxford and New York: Pergamon, 1997.

——— and Émile Constantin. Saussure, "Notes préparatoires pour le cours de linguistique générale 1910-1911," Constantin, "Linguistique générale, cours de M. le professeur de Saussure 1910-1911." Ed. Daniele Gambarara and Claudia Mejía Quijano. *Cahiers Ferdinand de Saussure* 58 (2005): 71-290.

Spencer, Herbert. *The Principles of Psychology.* London: Longman, Brown, Green, and Longmans, 1855.

Taine, Hippolyte. *De l'intelligence.* 2 vols. Paris: Hachette, 1870.

Value of and in Learning Foreign Languages[1]

Claire-A. Forel

We are going to play on the meanings of the word *value* to discuss why there is value learning foreign languages, which is not very difficult to grasp, but also why understanding the fact that languages are systems of "values," a central Saussurean concept, can help overcoming some obstacles in learning foreign languages. We first shall look at two reasons why learning foreign languages is beneficial; we'll then examine the innovative concept of plurilingualism and show how this new competence broadens the perspectives of the language learner. We will then move to the concept of value as it is presented in Saussure's *Course in General Linguistics* (first published a hundred years ago) as well as in the students' notes the book is based on.[2] Finally we will see how it is used in raising learners' awareness of how languages work and therefore why it helps acquiring new languages.

1. Value of learning foreign languages
   1.1. Linguistic diversity as enrichment

The Council of Europe was founded in 1947 and its principal aim, as stated in the first article of its Statute, "is to achieve a greater unity between its members for the purpose of safeguarding and realizing the ideals and principles which are their common heritage and facilitating

---

[1] Special thanks to Eva Waltermann for her careful reading of this article and her precious advice.

[2] Saussure never wrote the book, his junior colleagues Ch. Bally et A. Sechehaye used the notes taken by the students who sat in the three courses given on the subject, and turned them into a book.

their economic and social progress." Of course one of the most salient aspects of this common heritage is the extraordinary variety of its languages. However, this diversity could also be seen as an obstacle which must then be overcome by education and notably linguistic education, as the Council of Europe goes on by saying: "the rich heritage of diverse languages and cultures in Europe is a valuable common resource to be protected and developed, and that a major educational effort is needed to convert that *diversity* from a barrier to communication into a source of *mutual enrichment* and understanding" (Recommendation R (82) 18 of the Committee of Ministers of the Council of Europe, emphasis mine).

The *diversity* mentioned by the Council of Europe however contributes to more than just unity. It is seen by the Swiss linguist Ferdinand de Saussure as the first step towards an *awareness* of what language is. "It is contact with foreign speakers which alerts people's minds to the existence of languages as such."[3] However this perception is to be placed in a larger context:

> Let us note that primitive peoples are disposed to recognize this diversity as a fact, and their conception is not without interest: for one thing, it is what distinguishes them most sharply from others, from their neighbours. This feature of their language, which they cannot help but notice, becomes one of the features they recognize as differentiating them from neighbouring people. And how do they conceive of this? As a different custom, comparable to different customs in clothing, hair styles, weaponry: and this is quite right. (Saussure, *Troisième cours* 11a-12a)

The starting point from which to understand what the concept of language is appears then to be the same both for the layman and for the linguist:

> As far as linguistics is concerned, the diversity of languages is indeed the fundamental act. There was no linguistics until attention focused on this diversity, which gradually led to comparison and step by step towards the general idea of linguistics. (Saussure, *Troisième cours* 11a-12a)

Hence the *linguistic education* that will help overcome the obstacle presented by the great diversity of languages in Europe can be understood not only as *learning foreign languages* but also, while doing so, *learning about what language is*. Offering language learners some insights into the nature

---

[3] However, translating Saussure's original *la langue* by "languages" as Harris does in this edition of Constantin's notebooks is rather unfortunate, because what Saussure meant was the abstraction, the linguistic phenomenon, rather than the multiplicity of languages.

in this specific tool of communication is what the language awareness approach is about and we will discuss it presently. But before, rather than concentrating only on the philosophical or educational value of language learning, one may also wish to consider its economic benefits.

1.2 The economic value of foreign language learning

The language economist F. Grin explains that the value of learning languages can be seen from four different perspectives:

> The benefits [of language learning] may be *market related*, such as higher earnings, access to more desirable jobs, etc.; other benefits are of the *non-market* kind, such as direct access, thanks to language competence, to other cultures and people carrying them. [. . .] whether of the market or of the non-market kind, the benefits and costs of education, [. . .] may be evaluated at the *private* or *social* level. The private level reflects the conditions confronting the typical or average person, whereas the social level concerns benefits and cost for society as a whole. (Grin 85-86)

A striking example of market value can be found in a study produced a number of years ago but which is both iconic and representative of how knowing languages can impact earnings. Comparing the relative "market value" of language knowledge in Switzerland, Grin showed that knowing French meant a potential increase in salary of 14.07 percent for Swiss German speakers, whereas being able to speak German meant 13.82 percent more wages for French speaking Swiss, thereby pointing at the very concrete "value" of language learning.

Among the aims and objectives of Council of Europe language policy as they are presented in the *Common European Framework of Reference for Languages* (referred to as *CEFR* below) we do find these various market and non-market values although they are not necessarily as neatly separated. For example, "to equip all Europeans for the challenges of intensified international mobility and closer cooperation not only in education, culture and science but also in trade and industry" can be read as yielding both non-market and market, as well as social and individual values. "To promote mutual understanding and tolerance, respect for identities and cultural diversity through more effective international communication" implies that great care is taken "to avert the dangers that might result from the marginalization of those lacking the skills necessary to communicate in an interactive Europe." Individuals who would not feel themselves to be members of a multilingual community become a social threat as "xenophobia and ultra-nationalist backlashes [constitute] a primary obstacle to European mobility and integration, and [. . .] a major threat to European stability and to the healthy functioning of democracy" (*CEFR* 3-4). Foreign language learning is thus seen as not only the means to get a good job, but also as an element of citizens' identity insofar as it allows them to feel they belong to a larger community than their own country, Europe, whose cultural wealth they are encouraged to enjoy.

It is therefore clear that the value and benefits of language learning are manifold. Although one could argue that these benefits have been recognized ever since languages have been taught, a European approach to the matter is fairly recent.

2. Value of plurilingualism
  2.1 *The Common European Framework of Reference for Languages* (*CEFR*)

In the period from 1989 to 1996, the Council of Europe put forward a project called "Language Learning for European Citizenship" and one of its key elements was the development of an instrument which would be a common framework of reference for all member states for the learning, teaching and assessment of foreign language learning. It is known today as *CEFR*. It describes "all the major aspects of language use and competence" (*CEFR* 43) and is an extraordinary overview on what knowing a language implies. It brought forward the concept of plurilingualism:

> Plurilingualism differs from multilingualism, which is the knowledge of a number of languages, or the co-existence of different languages in a given society. Multilingualism may be attained by simply diversifying the languages on offer in a particular school or educational system, or by encouraging pupils to learn more than one foreign language, or reducing the dominant position of English in international communication. (*CEFR* 4)

In fact, the authors of the *CEFR* postulated a language competence that did not add up the various languages learnt but rather used previous experience in learning one language for the acquisition of another and so worth building up a plurilingual competence:

> The fact that as an individual person's experience of language in its cultural contexts expands, from the language of the home to that of society at large and then to the languages of other peoples (whether learnt at school or col-

lege, or by direct experience), he or she does not keep these languages and cultures in strictly separated mental compartments, but rather builds up a communicative competence to which all knowledge and experience of language contributes and in which languages interrelate and interact. (*CEFR* 4)

In a way one could say that this competence aims at turning language learners into lay linguists, which seems very much in accordance with the programme Saussure sets for professional linguists at the beginning of his third course![4]

2.2 Understanding what languages are

To go into more detail, the *CEFR* describes a wealth of partial *language use* competences, such as those involved in sustaining a spoken monologue, or writing reports and essays, monitoring one's speech or listening to the radio, not to forget taking part in an informal conversation, etc. The learner should also grow specific *learner* competences among which a "language and communication awareness":

> Sensitivity to language and language use, *involving knowledge and understanding of the principles according to which languages are organised and used*, enables new experience to be assimilated into an ordered framework and welcomed as an enrichment. The associated new language may then be more readily learnt and used, rather than resisted as a threat to the learner's already established linguistic system, which is often believed to be normal and "natural."
> (*CEFR* 107, emphasis mine)

The question then is: how does one help learners develop this knowledge about languages?

---

[4] cf. "Languages constitute the concrete object that the linguist encounters on the earth's surface; 'the language' is the heading one can provide for whatever <generalizations> the linguist may be able to extract from all his observations across time and space." (Saussure, *Troisième cours* 11a). *The language* would be interpreted here as the counterpart of plurilingual competence.

2.3 Language awareness

We are now going to turn to language teaching/learning as such and we will discuss the contribution that Saussure's construct of "value" can make to that field. But first we need to look at a concept that is nowadays less fashionable but still as vital both in terms of acquiring new languages but also in understanding language at large. Eric Hawkins who promoted *language awareness* sums up the issue as "the foreign language as education, not simply instruction in a skill" (Hawkins 1999: 134). The aims of this approach foreshadow what will later be found in the *CEFR*:

> Language awareness was put forward, primarily by modern linguists, as a new "bridging" element in the UK school curriculum. It was viewed as a solution to several of the failures in UK schools: illiteracy in English, failure to learn foreign languages, and divisive prejudice. (Hawkins 124).

In order to promote linguistic tolerance and also skills in dealing with different languages, a team of researchers in the French speaking part of Switzerland led by Christiane Perregaux produced material for young children, very nicely nicknamed *EOLE* (*Aeolus*) which stands for *Eveil au Langage et Ouverture aux Langues*. Besides acknowledging and welcoming pupils' mother tongues it also aims at developing awareness of plurilingualism in close or distant environments and, at a more strictly linguistic level, structuring pupils' linguistic knowledge, increasing pupils' curiosity towards the functioning of other languages (but not forgetting their own!) as well as developing knowledge about languages.

Now activities like those that can found in *EOLE* certainly contribute to developing *knowledge and understanding* languages at large. However, in order to implement them in a satisfactory way teachers themselves should have a better understanding of what languages are before they start teaching any language, mother tongue or foreign languages. This is exactly what Eddy Roulet who inspired language awareness movements demanded:

> In order to guide learners in their discovery of what the system of a language is as well as what its use implies, it is not enough to have a good practical command of the language, nor a normative knowledge of its grammar rules, nor of the pedagogical understanding of how to impart these. One needs first to be fully aware of how it functions as a system – this is especially true for the spoken language – and to master the instruments which permit one to grasp this system. (119, my translation)

Let us then look at an instrument designed for children to understand some aspects of what a language is.

3. "Value" in plurilingual education

Besides arguing for the value of plurilinguistic language teaching, *EOLE* also raises another point as it deals with the Saussurean notion of *value* itself. Indeed, one of the first activities offered is about "the fact that languages are social constructs and the arbitrariness of the linguistic sign" (Perregaux 115, my translation) through the examination of onomatopoeia corresponding to animal cries. Children are confronted to the various ways the same animal cries are interpreted in different languages. Hence whereas the barking of a dog would be *Woof! Woof!* in English, *Ão! Ão!* in Portuguese and *Ouah! Ouah!* in French, the little resemblance between these disappears in Chinese *Wāng! Wāng!* (when the rooster's cry is *Wōwōwō!*) and even more so in Albanian *Hum! Hum!* "Can a dog bark 'in Portuguese' and a frog croak 'in Chinese'? That's strange!" is the title of a bingo game in which children have to recognize an animal through its cry as expressed in various languages.

A second activity is still about the arbitrariness of the linguistic sign but this time it deals with a morphological fact. The objective is to: "identify the gender of a noun by looking at its determiner; become aware of the arbitrariness of grammatical gender; notice construction similarities in simple noun phrases (determiner + noun) in various romance languages" (Perregaux 219, my translation). After observing that French, Portuguese Italian and Spanish all use the feminine gender for walnuts (*la noix, a noz, la noce, la nuez*) or for pears as well as for cherries, but use the masculine gender for lemons and radishes, pupils are presented the case of tomatoes whose gender varies according to the different languages, French being the only one to use the feminine *la tomate* where the other romance languages use the masculine: *o tomate, il pomodoro* and *el tomate*.

In the second volume of Perregaux et al we find yet another activity for slightly older children whose objectives are also about gender. However, this time gender is presented as a possible means of classifying nouns and is seen as both arbitrary and "cultural." Children are presented with a list of nouns in Swahili which they have to classify according to their suffixes. The criteria that define the various groups must seem very intriguing since they are for the first *"things"* and *nonliving entities*, the second, *human beings*, the third *parts of the body*, while the fourth is *abstract nouns* without a plural. Children are meant to "put their own systems of classification [of nouns] into perspective and imagine that there can be others" (Perregaux, Vol 2 206, my translation).

As we can see from these various activities, the *EOLE* project keeps its promises since Portuguese, Spanish or even Swahili are very likely to be some children's mother tongues that are thus highlighted; their classmates' curiosity for these languages they don't know will be aroused; linguistically speaking, the games makes pupils reflect about the different ways languages are organized which as in the case of the Swahili classification of nouns can be very different from the language used at school; these activities also sharpen their sense of observation and hence develop their skills as linguists in the making. However there is unfortunately an important flaw in the use that is made of the notion of *arbitrariness*.

4. "Value" in linguistics
   4.1 Arbitrariness and conventionality

Arbitrary is often seen as synonymous with *conventional* implying that there is no necessary link between the sequence of sounds used and what it indicates. The problem, as we shall see very shortly, lies with what we take *meaning* to be. If we decide that the *meaning* is the thing itself then language is seen as a kind of nomenclature, a list of labels for things. This is what the authors of *EOLE* seem to think when they explain in the teacher's book that *arbitrariness* is the "absence of 'physical' link between the signifier and the signified, between the object and the name that designates it". Saussure, who deems arbitrariness as "the organizing principle for the whole of linguistics" (*Cours de linguistique générale* 68), explains that not only is there no internal causality between the sign facets of the linguistic signs, signifier and signified, or to put it another way: the mental image of a sequence of sounds and the concept it refers to, but also reminds us that signs are "psychological entities" i.e. exist only in the minds of the speakers of a given language.

Onomatopoeias seem to challenge this definition. "Onomatopoeias are half way through the arbitrariness of the linguistic sign and an interpretation which is close to extra linguistic reality" (Perregaux 123, my translation) say the authors of *EOLE*, which seems to agree – even partly – with Saussure who explains that "onomatopoeic words might be held to show that a choice of signal is not always arbitrary" (*Cours de linguistique générale* 102). The variety of the representations of barking shows that phono-symbolism can be very diverse. Once these attempts have entered a language they become part of that language, they will for example conform to its sound system and, more importantly one may add, they will become linguistic signs, hence mental entities. In German, donkeys go *i-a*, in French we have almost the same sequence except that the second vowel is nasalized *hi han* [i ã]. Chinese on the other hand uses two of its five tones: neutral and falling in *yīang* and we may add that this version seems to really mimic the melody of braying! Finally, Saussure also reminds us that once in the language, onomatopoeias are submitted to the law of arbitrariness and can be altered: the word *pigeon* was once an onomatopoeic *pipio* supposed to reflect cooing! (*Cours de linguistique générale* 102).

Our next example will help us see more clearly the difference between *conventionality* and *arbitrariness*. EOLE explains very rightly that loan words are "words or expressions that [. . .] a community borrows from another language, which are not translated but generally adapted to the morphosyntactic or phonetic or prosodic rules of its own language" (Perregaux 255). It gives as an example the French word *la tomate*, a loan word from Spanish *el tomate*, which itself borrowed it from Aztec *tomatl*. However, giving as a didactic objective for children to "understand the arbitrary character of gender (by noticing that the gender of a *same noun* changes from one language to the next)" (Perregaux 222, my translation) contradicts what has just been said about borrowings. Once *el tomate* entered French as *la tomate*, it no longer was *the same word* because it fitted into another system with its own morphology, syntax, phonology and also lexicon. With either *el tomate* or *la tomate* one can refer to *the same object* but to speak of *a same word* would be tantamount to saying that languages are nomenclatures. What one can learn about languages with such an example is that they each have their own ways of speaking about the world.

4.2 Linguistic value

One of Saussure's great contributions to linguistics is precisely having stated that languages are systems of pure *values*. This means that the value of any of its members depends on the value of the other member of this same system. Saussure adds that values are "relative." Let us take an example:

The French word *mouton* may have the same meaning as the English word *sheep*; but it does not have the same value. There are various reasons for this but in particular the fact that the English word for the meat of this animal, as prepared and served for a meal, is not *sheep* but *mutton*. The difference in value between *sheep* and *mutton* hinges on the fact that in English there is also another word *mutton* for the meat, whereas *mouton* in French covers them both"(*Cours de linguistique générale* 114).

This brings us back to the arbitrariness of the linguistic sign. Nothing is given in advance nor is determined by some kind of relation to the world. In other words, values are determined by the system they are members of. This is yet another reason why *la tomate* and *el tomate* cannot be the *same word*: since they belong to two different systems, they necessarily have different values.

This brings us to our third example, the classification of nouns in Swahili. We can clearly see that the semantic features used to classify words in that language are very different from what we know in French or in English: "things and nonliving entities"; "human beings"; "parts of the body" and finally "abstract nouns" (without a plural) have little to do with, for example, the classification of nouns according to gender in French or into countable or uncountable in English. The objectives for this activity namely: "developing a better understanding of the idea of noun classification, by observing a language (Swahili) where they are classified very differently" as well as "putting one's own system of classification into perspective and imagining that there can be others" (Perregaux, Vol 2 207, my translation) clearly point towards languages being systems of values. Playing on words one could say that this realization also shows the value that can be found in knowing or knowing about foreign languages.

5. Conclusion

Of course Saussure's contribution to understanding what languages are goes far beyond what we discussed here. One should not stop at Saussure's *Course in General Linguistics* but it is a sound basis for any further developments: de Saussure's general linguistics and more specifically the concept of *value* in language can greatly contribute to help language learners and their teachers grasp what they need to understand, what languages are and how they function. Saussure's idea of languages being organized around systems of value, an idea incidentally based on economy, is a notion that can both help learners in a plurilinguistic approach in their insights on the linguistic phenomenon and also place language in the larger frame of economic systems.

References

Council of Europe. *Common European Framework of Reference Languages (CEFR)*. Cambridge: Cambridge University Press, 2011.

Council of Europe. *Language learning for European citizenship: final report of the Project.* Strasbourg: Council of Europe, 1997.

Forel, Claire-A. "La question: Entités linguistiques et réalités didactiques." *Atti del XLIV Congresso Internazionale di Studi della SLI, Vitterbo 27-29 Settembre.* Rome: Bulzoni, 2010.

———. "Pour une approche plurielle de la grammaire." *Babylonia* 02/14, 72-76.

Grin, François. *Compétences et récompenses: la valeur des langues en Suisse.* Fribourg: Éditions Universitaires, 1999.

Hawkins, E. "Foreign Language Study and Language Awareness." *Language Awareness*, Vol. 8, Nos 3 and 4 (1999).

Perregaux, C., De Pietro, J.-F., de Goumöens, C. and Jeannot, D., eds. *EOLE: Eveil au Langage et Ouverture aux langues.* Vols 1 and 2. Neuchâtel: CIIP, 2003.

Roulet, Eddy. *Langue maternelle et langues secondes, vers une pédagogie intégrée.* Paris: Hatier-Crédif, 1980.

Saussure, Ferdinand de. *Cours de linguistique générale.* Ed. T. de Mauro. Lausanne and Paris: Payot, 1967.

———. *Troisième cours de linguistique générale (1910-1911) d'après les cahiers d'Emile Constantin.* [Saussure's Third Course of Lectures on General Linguistics (1910-1911) from the notebooks of Emile Constantin]. edited and translated by E. Komatsu and R. Harris. Oxford: Pergamon, 1993.

Teaching and Learning English in Geneva: Questions of Economy, Identity, Globality and Usefulness

Eva Waltermann and Virág Csillagh

In multilingual and multicultural contexts such as Switzerland, language diversity is a core element of local culture, economy and language policies. However, the spread of English as a global language poses new challenges and raises questions of identity, equality and economic benefits, particularly when looking at policies of foreign language (FL) teaching. Consequently, national languages are frequently compared to English in terms of value, usefulness and necessity. But what does this evaluation of English truly represent? Is it based on economic reality, social values or urban legend? This essay addresses these questions from two perspectives. Learners, on the one hand, are faced with increasingly complicated choices and expectations, making the learning of English a complex matter of identity and self-expression, financial growth and social cohesion. On the other hand, these issues also resonate among FL teachers, who are those who face the learners in the end and transmit a certain representation of the English language. This study draws on the findings of two surveys carried out in Geneva to demonstrate the motivational power of Swiss national identity in relation to career prospects for learners, as well as the strength of socially constructed stereotypes on English among teachers.

Introduction

That the status of English is so often linked to questions of economy is no surprise, as the long-standing debate concerning the role of the language in current economic trends of empowerment and exclusion (see

Crystal; Graddol; Pennycook; Phillipson) also demonstrates. The importance of English in the realm of business and international trade – one of the many ways to look at *economy* – has become part of the everyday reality of a globalized world. Moreover, the spread of the language in the 20th century has been investigated in terms of economic growth or transnational relationships (e.g. Crystal) and, from a linguistic point of view, of establishing English as a *lingua franca* (e.g. Hülmbauer, Böhringer and Seidlhofer). Nevertheless, it is important to remember that introducing English in this new function in historically multilingual environments raises fundamental issues related to the existing balance of languages, linguistic identity and language learning policies. Switzerland is a particularly good example of this change, as the growth of English on the international level and its increasing momentum as a foreign language taught at Swiss schools have further complicated a linguistic landscape of long established complexity.

Foreign languages in Switzerland

Swiss plurilingualism dates back to the time of Napoleon (Elmiger and Forster), and encompasses a range of cultural values that point beyond the simple coexistence of languages. In fact, it makes Switzerland one of the few countries in the world where a range of official languages are accorded equal status. The four official languages, German, French, Italian and Romansh, form the basis of the country's multilingualism at the institutional level, as citizens can choose to communicate with authorities in any of the four languages. Moreover, as research indicates, individual plurilingual competence surpasses even these bounds.

According to the results of the 2013 census, where respondents were asked to name one language as their mother tongue, 63.5% of the population speak German, 22.5% French, 8.1% Italian and 0.5% Romansh, while the remaining 5.4% indicate another language as an L1 (Federal Statistical Office). Since these figures presuppose an essentially monolingual profile, the different languages are not represented equally. In addition, since the results do not take into account any form of individual plurilingualism, they conceal participants' skills as regards the other Swiss official languages. Nevertheless, as the Swiss Conference of Cantonal Ministers of Education (EDK-CDIP) warns, "the knowledge of a second national language is, for all citizens, of a great political and cultural importance" (*Recommandations du 30 octobre* 27, our translation); the particular linguistic situation of Switzerland is therefore all the more interesting to study (see also Lüdi and Werlen; Werlen).

In this context, the teaching of the other main official language (French or German) in the different linguistic regions started as early as the first half of the 19th century. However, the tradition was confronted when English emerged as an alternative to national languages and started challenging – in the 1970s – the undisputed primacy of the official languages. By 1975, the EDK-CDIP, which coordinates the teaching policies of the different cantons, therefore mentioned English in an official recommendation on the teaching of FLs in the Swiss obligatory curriculum that explicitly states as a pre-condition that:

> 1. [. . .] The teaching of a first foreign language is mandatory for all pupils. [. . .]
> 2. The first foreign language for the French-speaking part of Switzerland is German. The first foreign language for the German-speaking part of Switzerland is French. [. . .] The first foreign language for the Italian-speaking canton is French. [. . .]
> 3. The teaching of the first foreign language shall leave *no choice between a national language and English*.
> (EDK-CDIP, *Recommandations du 30 octobre* 27, our translation, our emphasis)

The pressure of English on political, economic and academic spheres and institutions however soon made its presence in the official curriculum unavoidable, which was also recorded in the *General concept on language teaching*, decided by the EDK-CDIP in 1998:

> 1. The recommendations of 1975 (obligatory teaching of a second national language from the 4th or 5th school year) remain applicable.
> 2. *English shall become obligatory from the 7th school year. Weak students may be exempted from its teaching.* [. . .] (1, our translation, our emphasis)

Despite recurring debates, general interest in the teaching of English has grown even more since then, and by 2004, the official position was even adapted to the following recommendation: "Two foreign languages at least are taught in Switzerland during the first school years, no later than from the 5th school year on, among which at least one is a national language" (EDK-CDIP, *Enseignement des langues* 4), leaving the freedom to each canton to decide which should come first and considering that English can be taught to *any* student – with no exception for weak students.

In fact, nowadays, English is present in every school curriculum and in some regions of the country it has even gained priority over national languages. While in the French-speaking part and in the cantons close to the linguistic border, the "other" main national language (French or German) is taught first (3rd school year) and English second (5th school year), the northeastern cantons give priority to English, placing further strain on the intricate system of federal and cantonal foreign language (FL) policies.

Each new political decision affecting this fragile balance however raises important questions regarding not only the role of financial considerations but also that of plurilingualism and national identity in FL teaching.

Conflicting representations

In fact, whenever one of the Swiss regions decides to change its local policy of FL teaching, promoting either the second national language or English, local and national media as well as stakeholders in teaching politics or economic sectors come to the front and issue sometimes conflicting statements about what solution should – or should not – be established, which are then sometimes heavily commented on by press readers. In this discourse, questions of economy, of importance, of usefulness or on the other hand of identity, of social cohesion and national strength (to name only a few) are often very vivid and push towards one choice or the other. Every time, strong beliefs about the value of a language or another are brought forward and bring up the predominance of the different representations that exist about the languages in conflict. These representations, as defined by social psychologists, are "forms of shared knowledge" (Jodelet 36) consisting both of descriptive and evaluative conceptions of languages that are underlying in social interactions and discourse.

These representations are particularly interesting because, as Castellotti and Moore point out, "it is precisely because representations and images of languages play a central role in language learning processes, and because they are malleable, that they are relevant to linguistic and educational policy" (7). In other words, these socially constructed images of given languages are not only bound to lay discourse but can heavily influence language learning and teaching – both in the classroom and in the offices of the policy makers.

The discussions around the choice the latter have to make hence regularly opposes national languages, which are most of the times associated with the cultural multilingual heritage of Switzerland and draw on ideas that go centuries back – favoring "mutual understanding" and "national cohesion" – to English, much more recently established but heavily linked to the "opening" of Switzerland to the rest of Europe and the world, to economic benefits and to the "international number 1 status" of the language.[1] In other words, based on this argument, one would have to choose between an official language on the one hand, an emblem of national history and identity, and a global language on the other, which carries some emotional value but is mostly characterized by its profitableness. However, as research shows, the distinction is far from clear-cut.

Languages and economic value

Indeed, when comparing the economic benefits of the main foreign languages taught in Switzerland, Grin (*Compétences*) found interesting patterns. His comparison was based on a classification of the different types of values a language carries. First, this model (Grin, "Language planning") distinguishes between market and non-market benefits and therefore separates emotional attachment, cultural enrichment or the enjoyment of speaking a particular language from financial advantages such as a higher salary or better job opportunities. Secondly, a distinction is made based on the level of impact, or in other words whether gains are reaped by society as a whole or by the individual proficient in the language. Table 1 displays the schematic structure of the model.

Individual market value	Individual non-market value
Social market value	Social non-market value

Table 1: Schematic representation of the four types of values (adapted from Grin, "Language planning")

---

[1] All the above mentioned quotes are translated from articles or readers' reactions to them issued in online newspapers on the decision of the Swiss canton of Thurgau, in 2014, to not only teach English before French at primary school but remove the latter from the primary curriculum

This classification renders computing the profitability of foreign language skills possible, with a few reservations. Grin (*Compétences*; "Language planning") discusses these difficulties in detail, but it is important to point out that what lies at the heart of the matter is that languages behave strikingly differently from other types of commodities. Therefore, estimating the actual value of a given language requires rigorous procedures and a wealth of information not often available to the researcher. Nevertheless, a large-scale study of Swiss residents of working age (Grin, *Compétences*) offers clear indications as to the individual market value of their language skills. Table 2 summarizes the results of the survey, showing that Swiss official languages were highly remunerated in all language regions.

% of salary increase	French	German	English
Men in French-speaking Switzerland	-	13.82	10.23
Men in German-speaking Switzerland	14.07	-	18.08
Men in Italian-speaking Switzerland	17.17	16.87	[11.78]
Women in French-speaking Switzerland	-	ns	[9.87]
Women in German-speaking Switzerland	ns	-	25.04
Women in Italian-speaking Switzerland	ns	11.46	ns

ns: results not significant
Brackets indicate that not all parameters were controlled for.

Table 2: Salary differentials per foreign language spoken
(adapted from Grin, *Compétences*)

While the figures for women are not conclusive due to a number of factors, it is clear that men tend to benefit considerably from their skills in foreign languages. Building on these and other findings, Csillagh considers Swiss plurilingualism as "the life blood of the country's economy" ("Global trends"). Research shows that official languages are used on a daily basis in corporate communication all around Switzerland (Grin et al.). In addition, if all Swiss residents who speak another, non-local, official language were to lose these skills from one day to the next, the financial loss would be equal to 10% of Swiss GDP (ibid.)

Love or money? A question of motivation

At the same time, little importance is attached to the motivational impact of these findings, although they can be surmised to play an important role in Swiss residents' attitudes to the languages in question. Csillagh ("Global trends") discusses this dimension in the light of current theories of motivation and concludes that economic aspects are inherent to many of the concepts used in mainstream L2 motivation research. Moreover, recent years have seen a shift in L2 motivation theory from a conceptualization of motivation as a personality trait to viewing it as part of the *complex dynamic systems* that surround individuals (Dörnyei, MacIntyre and Henry). These new approaches have great potential in investigating the role of contextual influences, of which economic factors form an integral component.

Building on decades of theoretical development on the one hand, and previous research conducted in a number of modern language learning contexts on the other, Dörnyei describes L2 motivation as an ongoing, dynamic process of identity creation and reinforcement. The three key elements of his model (ibid.) are the *ideal L2 self*, which refers to language-related facets of one's visions of one's ideal future self, the *ought-to L2 self*, which corresponds to perceived obligations and expectations as regards the language in question, and the *language learning experience*. Csillagh ("Global trends") argues that these components incorporate aspects of the economic milieu to different degrees and in different ways.

The ideal L2 self, generally measured as a variable of its own, includes questions of career prospects and the overall importance of the language as a means to one's coveted goals, many of which can be theorized to have economic implications. Quantitative studies (cf. Dörnyei and Ushioda) showed the ideal L2 self as key to predicting learners' motivation and performance. Often found to be an indirect or marginal motivational factor, the ought-to L2 self on the other hand reflects the values that society places in the language, economic concerns included, which thus become part of learners' socially influenced self. The same studies showed the L2 learning experience, assessed through language learning attitudes, to be influenced by both self-guides. Nevertheless, it is important to point out that since these concepts incorporate economic implications covertly, further research is needed to explore the direct impact of such factors.

A study of Swiss university students' L2 motivation and attitudes

Drawing on these quantitative traditions, in a survey study of university students in the multicultural, multilingual context of Geneva, Csillagh ("Global trends; *Attitudes*) found that factors related to the local economic and social milieu were strongly linked to participants' attitudes and motivation toward English. Investigating university students' attitudes and self-concept, the study furthermore revealed significant differences between Swiss and foreign respondents' profiles. Although a thorough analysis is beyond the scope of this essay, we briefly outline these results below, with special emphasis on the motivational role of the economic environment.

A total of 375 students completed the online questionnaire in fall 2013, and they pursued studies at four faculties of the University of Geneva, those of Law, Medicine, Science and Economic and Social Sciences (SES). Table 3 sums up their numbers as regards their gender and faculty. In addition, it displays where participants had completed their secondary education, which served as an indication of their origins, nationality being a delicate and unclear issue in Switzerland. Seven students attended several faculties and were thus excluded from the comparative analysis.

	Faculty				Place of upper secondary education		
	Law	Medicine	Science	SES	Geneva	Switzerland	Other countries
Male	27	20	52	23	62	83	41
Female	67	44	98	37	125	173	78
Total	94	64	150	60	187	256	119

Table 3: Participants in the motivation study per gender, faculty and place of secondary education.

In-depth analysis of the language data revealed high levels of plurilingualism among participants, as only 6.4% of them were completely monolingual. As many as 18.7% of students had skills in two languages, while 38.4% spoke three and 29.3% four languages and 7.2% reported competencies in five. Interestingly, a great majority (80%) marked only one of their languages as their mother tongue, indicating that they considered most of the languages they spoke as foreign languages. Indeed, many respondents spoke one (26.7%), two (37.1%) or three (24.3%) foreign languages, with an impressive 4% declaring proficiency in four. The analysis also showed that Swiss official languages played a central role in this diversity, both as L1s and as L2s.

Furthermore, overall mean values of the attitudinal variables included in the study (for details, see Csillagh ["Global trends"; "Love or money"]) demonstrated a remarkable trend. Whereas studies conducted in other contexts (cf. Dörnyei and Ushioda) revealed participants' future self-vision to be a key element, the aspect of the self-concept related to social obligations played only a marginal role, if any, in respondents' attitudes and motivation. The Geneva study, however, produced different results. The mean values of the attitudinal scales are compared in Figure 1.

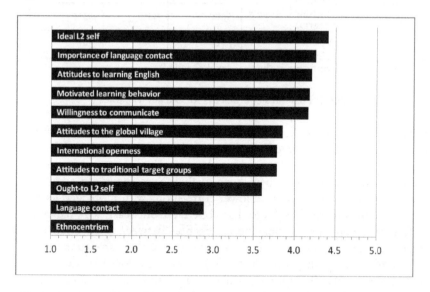

Figure 1: Mean values of the main variables included in the motivation study.
Note: Options ranged from 1 (complete disagreement) to 5 (complete agreement).

Interestingly, while the scale linking English to students' future self-vision was the strongest in the set, the socially influenced facet of their language-related self-concept also proved relevant. It is also important to point out that, as part of the former, the item on the role of English in participants' future career scored the highest of all. In addition, scales related to the global status of English also yielded high results.

Examining the links among these variables, Csillagh ("Global trends") concludes that the strongest relationships were found, on the one hand, between motivation to learn English and positive attitudes toward the learning process. This is perhaps not surprising, nevertheless, the strong correlation points to the importance of the learning context and educational practices. More interestingly, among the rest of the factors, the social aspects of the self showed the closest link to motivated learning behavior. Table 4 summarizes the correlation coefficients for three of the key variables, displaying the results for "Swiss" students and "foreigners" altogether as well as separately.

		Attitudes to learning English	Ought-to L2 self	Ideal L2 self
All students	Motivated learning behavior	.58**	.40**	.38**
Swiss students	Motivated learning behavior	.56**	.43**	.43**
Foreign students	Motivated learning behavior	.61**	.37**	.34**

**. Correlation is significant at the 0.01 level (2-tailed).

Table 4: Pearson's coefficients for the key variables

When compared, these figures are suggestive of some intriguing dissimilarities. Although the direction of the relationships is not known, it is clear that foreign students' attitudes to learning English are more closely linked to their motivation than those of their Swiss peers. In addition, both facets of the self achieved lower correlations with motivated learning behavior among foreigners. Last but far from least, a remarkable difference emerged regarding the connection between motivation and target cultures. In the case of Swiss participants, the correlations were moderate for English people ($r = .35, p < .01$) and low for Americans ($r = .29, p < .01$). By contrast, while foreign students' attitudes to the former showed a similar link to their motivation ($r = .32, p < .01$), their views of Americans correlated more with motivated learning behavior ($r = .47, p < .01$) than either element of their self-concept.

As international aspects of English, in the form of international openness and attitudes to the global village, were also only moderately related to motivation in both subsamples, it can be concluded that the results of the correlation analysis are indicative of the role of the local context in these relationships. Moreover, similar patterns can be observed in the connections between participants' attitudes to learning English and the variables mentioned above, as shown in Table 5.

		Ought-to L2 self	Ideal L2 self	Attitudes to English people	Attitudes to Americans	Attitudes to the global village	International openness
Swiss students	Attitudes to learning English	.37**	.32**	.55**	.44**	.34**	.24**
Foreign students	Attitudes to learning English	.37**	.40**	.51**	.43**	.48**	.21*

**. Correlation is significant at the 0.01 level (2-tailed).
*. Correlation is significant at the 0.05 level (2-tailed).

Table 5: Pearson's coefficients for learning attitudes and international aspects of English

When it comes to Swiss students' attitudes and motivation, these figures show the importance of the local context, on the one hand in influencing respondents' self-concept, but also in transmitting values related to target cultures and the international community. Moreover, students' views on target cultures might be suggestive of the role that teachers play in the development of these attitudes. In a study of Swiss teachers of English, Murray found their opinion of international varieties of the language very low, as survey participants preferred and valued standard dialects above all.

In sum, the results presented in this section are indicative of the impact of contextual factors on Genevan university students' attitudes and motivation to learn English. In contrast with research findings in other contexts, the Geneva study showed that socially influenced aspects of the self played an important role. Their connection to motivated learning behavior and learning attitudes equaled or even surpassed the relevance of ideal future self-images. The latter was especially true in the case of Swiss students, who showed a number of differences when compared with their foreign peers.

Despite the exceptional plurilingualism demonstrated by the whole sample, Swiss students consistently outperformed foreigners in the four foreign languages tested: French, German, Italian and English. Swiss official languages were at the heart of this phenomenon, their levels highest at the faculties of Law and Medicine, professions that offer coveted job opportunities locally (Csillagh, "Love or money"). Overall, these findings suggest that Swiss participants' language attitudes are linked to a socially defined self-concept, highly sensitive to the economic milieu. It is interesting to note that their perceived importance of English is more closely linked to locally defined values than to general international openness.

Nevertheless, Swiss students' positive attitudes to speakers from England, strongly related to their attitudes to learning English, raise questions concerning the impact of Swiss language teachers' views on traditional target language groups. Students' attraction to traditional target language groups seems to echo Murray's findings on teachers' opinion of international varieties of English. This, in turn, might be indicative of teachers' power in promoting plurilingual values on the one hand and motivating attitudes on the other. While in order to achieve the former it is essential to reconcile conflicting representations of English and Swiss official languages, the latter requires a reconceptualization of *target culture* to encompass global speaker communities, which might present many learners with a more immediate reality.

The role of teachers in the debate

Indeed, as we previously stated, teachers cannot be left out of this discussion, as they contribute to the spread of some of the representations and ideologies that lead to such distinctions. Although we will not address the question of University language teaching here, focusing on secondary school instruction, teachers play a fundamental role in the construction of the distinctions between national languages and English.

The position they hold is however quite an unstable one. On the one hand, they are not systematically taken into account – or at least not more than any other citizens – when it comes to redesigning the curriculum or to changing cantonal policies, and are thus at the mercy of governmental decisions that may regard as much the curriculum itself as the contents that are to be taught or even the methodology that should be used to do so. In other words, their own representations are not considered particularly relevant when FL teaching is reformed, or at most at a consultative level. However, on the other hand *they* are those who really enact the teaching curriculum within the schools and in front of the pupils, and who therefore impersonate some form of representation about the subject they teach. It has also long been established that "knowledge" is an essential part of any teaching situation – and we're referring to the *content knowledge* here and not the other forms of professional knowledge that are used, notably by Shulman – but it is essential at this point to remember that this knowledge is not homogeneous: teachers are not only educators and transmitters of a predefined form of content (i.e. grammar rules, speaking strategies, vocabulary and so on) but they also (and much more implicitly) convey a socio-cultural representational load about the language they teach. Whenever they consider a regularity / a rule as being "less important," whenever they focus on a certain domain of literature rather than another, whenever they comment on a language saying "you're going to need this for . . . ," they make explicit things *about* a language which are sometimes even stated as facts but pertain to the realm of representations, or, as Houdebine-Gravaud defines it, as "linguistic imaginaries":

> This relationship of the subject to the language [. . .], relationship which can be elicited in terms of images, part of social and subjective representations, in other words on one hand ideologies (social side) and on the other imaginaries (subjective side). (9)

Hence, the position of teachers is a crucial one when it comes to examining the importance of socially and individually constructed representations in the learning/teaching process.

Teachers' attitudes towards English: a study

It is therefore interesting to investigate the images that are vivid among language teachers: how far do they match the common message of the social importance of English? Do they correspond to the learners' motivational characteristics?

The following results are drawn from a larger-scale PhD study that was carried out among foreign language teachers in Geneva to analyze their attitudes and representations (i.e. both the descriptive and evaluative dimensions) of 7 of the most commonly used languages in the area (German, English, French, Italian, Spanish, Portuguese and Swiss-German), but we will restrain our presentation to the data concerning English for this paper, and keep to the elements that could enrich our discussion.

107 foreign language teachers in the Geneva area were submitted an internet questionnaire they voluntarily completed. All of them were foreign language teachers (70.7% of English, 33% of German, 11.3% of Italian, 11.3% of Spanish – 29.1% indicated teaching more than one of these languages) and taught at the level of secondary school (Secondary I or Secondary II schools, corresponding to learners aged respectively 11 to 15 or 15 to 19).

For each of the languages in the sample, they were asked to complete two tasks:

a. To write down the three first concepts that came to their mind when thinking about this language, through what is called a *Word Association Task*. This methodology, based on psychiatric processes, is one of the methods used in social psychology to uncover representations (see notably Doise et al.) These elicited concepts could be of any grammatical category, and could even be groups of words such as "difficult to read" or "too often left aside." Although the survey was carried out in French, answers in other languages were accepted. The concepts that were collected were examined both in a quantitative and a qualitative way, among which frequencies which we will present here.

b. To assess this language on 7 differential scales (based on the traditional Osgood *Semantic Differential*, cf. Osgood): easy-difficult, logical-illogical, melodious-rough, rich-poor, beautiful-ugly, useful-useless, and close-distant; these pairs were based on the most frequently cited adjectives when concerning a language, which were provided by another sample of 160 language teachers from a previous study. In this survey, the participants could indicate whether they assessed the language at the end of a scale, fairly on one side of it or whether they were neutral, for example:

	<<very		neutral		very>>	
Logical	☐	☐	☐	☐	☐	Illogical

Answers were therefore interpreted from a scale of -2 to +2 and compared both to other languages and to the other pairs.

The data collected from each of these two tasks were then compiled and analyzed, first globally and then according to individual variables such as experience or language level, on which we will not elaborate here.

The results of the Word Association Task proved very interesting. As we can see, simply by looking at the 11 most cited concepts (translated into English for this article) and without going into too much detail in the analysis, some of the common ideas re-emerge:

1. international (15 occurrences)
2. Shakespeare (12 occurrences)
3. beautiful (11 occurrences)
4. useful (9 occurrences)
5. culture (6 occurrences)
6. travel (6 occurrences)
7. "easy"[2] (5 occurrences)
8. easy (4 occurrences)
9. hello (4 occurrences)
10. literature (4 occurrences)
11. universal (4 occurrences)

We can for example see that the most frequently cited concept is "international," a word which directly places English on a very large scale, beyond the individual. Clearly, it seems to indicate that rather than personal subjective imaginaries (which are not absent from the list), it is a global picture that comes first when thinking about English, even if the representation of the language that can be understood here is much richer than this, notably through the words "Shakespeare," "useful," "travel" or "culture." The concept of *internationality* seems nevertheless to be the core element that characterizes English for the teachers interrogated here, which resonates with the social value placed on this language for learners that was stated previously.

We could however add, not far behind, a strong need to qualify the language and to take a personal stance (also pointing to these subjective representations), notably through the notions of beauty, usefulness and ease (adding "easy" and the French version "facile"), which characterize English both from a contextualized and an aesthetic point of view, but also from a learning perspective. Although the two last areas (represented by "beautiful" and "easy") are present in the most frequently cited terms for all of the languages in our sample (albeit not always positively, but sometimes rather through words such as "ugly," "complicated" or "difficult"...), the notion of usefulness is stronger for English than for the two other languages for which it's mentioned: Spanish (5 occurrences) and German (4 occurrences). It is thus clear that even if other languages share this representational feature with English, it is the one for which it is most apparent in the sample.

---

[2] Provided in English – the other one was translated from the French "facile."

This can also be verified when looking at the semantic differential scales:

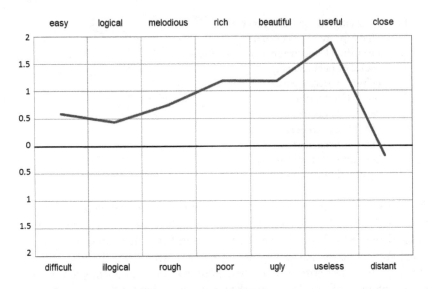

Figure 2: Semantic differential for English, all teachers (N=107)

Obviously, the idea that English is useful is predominant also in this form of evaluation the participants were asked to perform. Although almost all the adjectives (i.e. all except "close/distant") tend – here again – towards adjectives with positive connotations, the "peak" we can see for the adjective "useful" leaves no doubt that there is consensus on this idea, which is all the more interesting if the language is considered in the educational context, where disciplines are meant to be "useful," and still linked to the "international" level mentioned before. This was also the statement that was the most unanimous among all answers (i.e. all pairs of adjectives for each of the 7 languages), with an average of 1.92 and a standard deviation of 0.49.

This assessment is also interesting on the linguistic level because it shows that this characteristic of English is given more value, is more applicable than other more intrinsic characteristics conveyed by adjectives such as "logical," "beautiful" or even "easy." It is thus really the *use* of this language and not its personal value for the participants that seems to have priority in the shared representation of it. In other words, if we come back to the notion of *Linguistic Imaginary* developed by Houdebine-Gravaud, it appears that the factors that are maybe more "personal" or indicating a higher degree of personal involvement are less absolute than the form of social value brought by the term "useful." These results completely match the findings released by Araujo e Sá and Schmidt, who state when presenting their research carried out in Portuguese schools that

> [Their] results confirm the collective and homogeneous idea of English being a language of prestige. In concrete, the data obtained by means of the semantic differentials, reflects the image of an extremely useful language, politically and economically important. Moreover, this language seems to be considered rather beautiful and easy. (109)

This may confirm that the image conveyed by English goes further than the local area, some of the traits of representation being even internationally shared. It becomes however even more interesting when we realize that the opinions on German, which could maybe precisely differ between a Swiss audience and a Portuguese one due to the different status of the idiom in these two countries, also comes to the same conclusions. Indeed, we can read in the aforementioned article that

> As far as the German language is concerned, the scenario seems to be quite [different]: although it is considered to be relatively useful, this idiom is thought to be ugly and most definitely difficult. (10)

The same appears in our survey (see Figure 3 on next page). Indeed, we can see that – even if German is still considered fairly "useful" (albeit less than English), it is quite less "beautiful" and above all definitely "difficult." Even if for the majority of all these rankings, the average scores are rather positive, it is essential to point out that both for the pair "beautiful/ugly" as well as for the pair "easy/difficult," German is *last* of all the languages, and is followed only by the Swiss-German dialect which brings about even more negative attitudes.
It is thus interesting to see, in the light of all that has been written so far in this article, which representations and evaluations are underlying in the community of foreign language teachers in Geneva. More precisely, it is fascinating to realize that the social value of English seems to lead to much more positive connotations than the status of German which, albeit often publicly declared as indispensable for Swiss learners, reveals suffering from a much more severe reputation among teachers – who are apparently giving more credit to alleged market (economic or at least professional) advantages than to questions of non-market values.

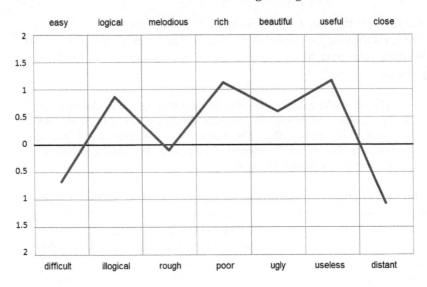

Figure 3: Semantic differential for German, all teachers (N=107)

Conclusion

In summary, the studies discussed in this paper demonstrate the complexity of the values that English represents in the multilingual setting of Geneva. Both individual market value and socially influenced non-market benefits played an important role in defining the status of the language in this particular local context. This marked lack of more personal orientations was manifest both in learners' attitudes and motivation and in teacher's ideologies. It can be concluded that these two studies revealed English as a language that is considered first and foremost as useful and even necessary in the local setting, much more so than as an individual aspiration or an attractive choice of genuine enthusiasm or international openness. Teachers value the usefulness of English above any other of its characteristics, and learners consider it as a skill they *need* to possess for their career and place in Swiss society rather than as a means of cultural enrichment and identity creation.

This view of English appears to be so strong among Swiss learners that it surpasses the influence of other representations that are also prevalent in the local context and loud in public discourse. By contrast, German, despite its high market value that exceeds even that of English on the Swiss market, seems to have the sole advantage of being an official language. Although this feature is important enough that it will continue to ensure the place of German in the curriculum, the question remains whether it will be enough to help counterbalance the socially constructed image of a difficult and fairly ugly language.

These conclusions testify to the strain that the emergence of English places not only on German and other local Swiss languages but also on the linguistic diversity of multilingual Europe. This pressure that a language of an undisputed reputation of usefulness in the economic and international field represents will only ease once the market value of local languages is recognized and added to their representations of cultural values and national identity. Breidbach argues that the benefits of the emergence of English as an "interlingual mediator" (22) in multilingual Europe can only be reaped if language policies continue to rest on fundamental European values of *both* mutual understanding among citizens as well as cultural and linguistic diversity. Only when the value of linguistic and cultural diversity is fully recognized can more positive representations and attitudes supersede the ideas of difficulty and limited importance that German has carried along the way ever since the economic contribution of English began playing a role in the Swiss language teaching context.

References

Araujo e Sá, Maria Helena and Alexandra Schmidt. "The Awareness of Language prestige: the representations of a Portuguese school community on important languages." *Conscience du plurilinguisme : pratiques, représentations et interventions*. Eds M. Candelier, G. Ioannitou, D. Omer and M.-T. Vasseur. Rennes: Presses Universitaires de Rennes, 2008: pp. 109-124.

Breidbach, Stephan. *Plurilingualism, democratic citizenship in Europe and the role of English*. Strasbourg: Council of Europe, 2003. http://theewc.org/uploads/content/archive/BreidbachEN.pdf. Last accessed on 29 February 2016.

Crystal, David. *English as a global language*. Cambridge: Cambridge University Press, 2003.

Csillagh, Virág. "Global trends and local realities: Lessons about economic benefits, selves and identity from a Swiss context." *Studies in Second Language Learning and Teaching*, 5 (2015).

———. "Love or money? Reinterpreting traditional motivational dimensions in modern social and economic contexts." *New directions in language learning psychology*. Eds. Christina Gkonou, Dietmar Tatzl, Sarah Mercer. Dördrecht: Springer, 2016.

———. *Attitudes toward English among students at the University of Geneva: a study of the social and economic status of the language* (Doctoral dissertation under completion). Geneva: University of Geneva.

Doise, William, Alain Clémence and Fabio Lorenzi-Cioldi. *The Quantitative Analysis of Social Representations*. Hemel Hempstead: Harvester Wheatsheaf, 1993.

Dörnyei, Zoltán. "The L2 motivational self system." *Motivation, language identity and the L2 self*. Eds. Zoltán Dörnyei and Ema Ushioda. Bristol: Multilingual Matters, 2009. 9-42.

———, MacIntyre, Peter, and Alistair Henry. "Introduction: Applying complex dynamic systems principles to empirical research on L2 motivation." *Motivational dynamics in language learning*. Eds. Zoltán Dörnyei, Alistair Henry, and Peter D. MacIntyre. Bristol: Multilingual Matters, 2015. 1-7.

——— and Ema Ushioda, eds. *Motivation, language identity and the L2 self*. Bristol: Multilingual Matters, 2009.

EDK-CDIP. "Recommandations et décisions concernant l'introduction, la réforme et la coordination de l'enseignement de la deuxième langue nationale pour tous les élèves pendant la scolarité obligatoire du 30 octobre 1975." *Recommandations et décisions*. Bern: CDIP, 1995

——. *Concept général pour l'enseignement des langues.* Bern: Assemblée plénière de la CDIP, 1998.

——. *Enseignement des langues à l'école obligatoire: stratégie de la CDIP et programme de travail pour la coordination à l'échelle nationale.* Bern: Assemblée plénière de la CDIP, 2004.

Elmiger, Daniel and Simone Forster. *La Suisse face à ses langues: Histoire et politique du plurilinguisme, situation actuelle de l'enseignement des langues.* Neuchâtel: Institut de recherche et de documentation pédagogique (IRDP), 2005.

Federal Statistical Office: *Languages and religions: Data, indicators,* 2013. http://www.bfs.admin.ch/bfs/portal/fr/index/themen/01/05/blank/key/sprachen.html. Last accessed on 29 February 2016.

Graddol, David. *English Next: Why Global English May Mean the End of "English as a Foreign Language."* London: British Council, 2006.

Grin, François. *Compétences et récompenses: La valeur des langues en Suisse.* Fribourg: Editions universitaires, 1999.

——. "Language planning and economics." *Current Issues in Language Planning,* 4 (2003): 1-66. doi: 10.1080/14664200308668048

——, Claudio Sfreddo and François Vaillancourt. *"Langues étrangères dans l'activité professionnelle: Rapport final de recherche."* Geneva: University of Geneva, 2009.

Houdebine-Gravaud, Anne-Marie, ed. *L'imaginaire linguistique.* Paris: L'Harmattan, 2002.

Hülmbauer, Cornelia, Heike Böhringer, and Barbara Seidlhofer. "Introducing English as a lingua franca (ELF): Precursor and partner in intercultural communication." *Synergies Europe* 3 (2008): 25-36.

Jodelet, D. *Les représentations sociales.* Paris: Presses Universitaires de France, 1989.

Lüdi, Georges and Iwar Werlen. "Le paysage linguistique en Suisse. Recensement fédéral de la population 2000." *Neuchâtel:* Federal Statistical Office, 2005.

Moore, Danièle and Véronique Castellotti. *Social Representations of Languages and Teaching.* Strasbourg: Council of Europe, 2002.

Murray, Heather. "Swiss English teachers and Euro-English: Attitudes to a non-native variety." *Bulletin Suisse de linguistique appliqué* 77 (2003): 147-65.

Osgood, Charles E., George J. Suci and Perci H. Tannenbaum. *The Measurement of Meaning.* Urbana, Chicago and London: University of Illinois Press, 1953.

Pennycook, Alastair. *The cultural politics of English as an international language.* London and New York: Routledge, 1994.

Phillipson, Robert. *Linguistic imperialism*. Oxford: Oxford University Press, 1992.

Shulman, L. "Knowledge and Teaching: Foundations for a new reform." *Harvard Educational Review*, vol. 57 No. 1 (1987): 1-21.

Werlen, I. *Schlussbericht: Sprachkompetenzen der erwachsenen Bevölkerung in der Schweiz*. Swiss National Science Foundation, National Research Programme 56, 2008.

The Value of English in Multilingual Families

Sarah Chevalier

In multilingual families, not all the languages available are necessarily spoken to the children. Some parents make the decision to not use one (or more) of their languages. Other families, by contrast, decide to add a language. This essay seeks to examine the motivations for such decisions. Specifically it asks: In multilingual families, which languages are cut, which ones are added, and why? The theoretical framework is based on Spolsky's tripartite model of language policy as consisting of language management, beliefs, and practices, as well as De Swaan's *global language system*, in which of all languages English has the highest value. The data consist of semi-structured interviews with 35 multilingual families in Switzerland. Results show that while parents do sometimes abandon languages, English is almost never one of those abandoned. Further, if a family adds a language, it is always English. Such language policy decisions are largely shown to be motivated by parents' belief in the opportunities available in a globalised world, opportunities for which English is felt to be the key.

1. Introduction

The present study is concerned with the status of various languages in multilingual families, and in particular the value of English. I would like to introduce the study via a description of one of the families who took part. This family consists of a Swiss mother, a Belgian father, and their daughter Lina.[1] The mother is a native speaker of Swiss German, and the family live in German-speaking Switzerland. The father, who grew up in Flanders, was raised bilingually from birth in Dutch and French. Lina's parents thus have three native languages among them. As such, a condition exists for a possible trilingual upbringing for Lina: potentially she could grow up exposed to Swiss German, French and Dutch. And Lina is indeed growing up with three languages; however, they are not precisely these three. Rather, Lina is growing up exposed to Swiss German, French, and English.

Two questions thus arise: Why English? And why not Dutch? With regard to the first question, Lina's parents use English between themselves as a couple language. It is the language they used when they first met on holidays in an English-speaking country, and it remains the strongest foreign language for both of them. Thus force of habit (see Barnes 91 on the difficulties a couple may have in changing their language of communication), as well as proficiency, play a role. But there is also another reason. Lina's parents made a conscious decision to keep English, and English only, as their couple language in order to provide their daughter with a "pure" model of English in the home. While they recognised that it would have been advantageous for Lina's father to practice his German with his wife (either the dialect or the standard variety) since they lived in German-speaking Switzerland, they decided to sacrifice this advantage in order to give their daughter the chance to be raised trilingually, with one of the languages being English. This presence of English in the home is reinforced by an American aunt (Lina's maternal uncle's partner), who lives nearby and visits often. Lina's aunt plays intensively with the child, insisting all the while that Lina speak English.

With regard to the question of why Dutch was abandoned, the parents explained that this language was not useful in Switzerland – and not useful generally. We can see clearly in the case just described the extent to which English is valued. In this family, English, which is not a native language of either parent, is given space, while Dutch, a native language, is not.

This case illustrates how in multilingual families not all the languages available are necessarily spoken to the children. Some parents make the decision to not use one (or more) of their languages. Other families, by contrast, decide to add a language, that is, to bring into their family a language which is not one of the parents' native languages, nor the lan-

---

[1] All names in this essay are pseudonyms.

guage of the community. Some families, like Lina's, even do both: abandoning one language, while adding another. This essay seeks to examine the motivations for such decisions. Specifically it asks: In multilingual families, which languages are cut, which ones are added, and why?

2. Theoretical frame

The theoretical framework relies on two complementary analytical approaches. First, language choices in multilingual families are examined according to Spolsky's tripartite model of language policy. One element of language policy is, according to Spolsky, *beliefs or ideologies* about language. Another is *language management*, which comprises concrete steps undertaken to promote a certain language or variety. Finally, Spolsky argues that *language practices* also form a part of language policy: what people actually do, whether consciously or unconsciously informs the policy. Describing separately beliefs, management and practices is one way to try and understand why some languages are valued and promoted in multilingual families and others are not, and, crucially, whether in fact the attempts work.

The second theoretical model used in this study is De Swaan's *global language system* (see *Words of the World*, chapter 1). In this framework, languages are considered as "collective goods" since they are available, in theory, to anyone, and they do not diminish in value as new users are added. In fact, in the case of languages, their value increases. De Swaan calculates the worth of a language according to its "prevalence" (number of native speakers) and its "centrality" (number of people knowing another language who can use it to communicate). He demonstrates that the centrality, and thus the worth, of English is continually increasing in a self-reinforcing dynamic: the more people there are who use English as a lingua franca, the greater incentive there is for yet more people to acquire it.

Behind this model is a conception of the languages of the world being connected by speakers. According to De Swaan, the worldwide constellation of languages comprises a system whereby mutually unintelligible languages are connected by multilingual speakers. This connection, however, is not random but hierarchical. The world's languages, De Swaan proposes, can be divided into three categories: peripheral, central and supercentral. Peripheral languages include most of the world's languages and are generally unwritten, for example, Swiss German. Central languages are the national or official languages of a ruling state, such as

Dutch. Finally, there are a dozen or so supercentral languages. These are languages which are widely spoken across national borders. Most have more than 100 million speakers, and they connect speakers of central languages. An example is French in francophone West Africa, connecting speakers of national languages. De Swaan further elaborates that among the supercentral languages, there is a single hypercentral language, namely English, connecting speakers of the supercentral languages. According to De Swaan, speakers who acquire a second language are far more likely to acquire one higher in the hierarchy than one lower in the hierarchy for reasons of wider communication. De Swaan's model is therefore useful for explaining language choices in multilingual families, and in particular choices concerning English.

3. Previous work on the value of English in multilingual families

While a huge body of research exists attesting to the global importance of English, from work on English as a second language (e.g. Kachru), to English as a lingua franca (e.g. Seidelhofer), to the role of English in a country's education policy (e.g. Ferguson *Language Planning*), to global English generally (e.g. Crystal), little work exists on the value of English in multilingual families. Two recent studies, however, do shed some light on this topic, namely research conducted by Braun and Cline ("Trilingual Families"), as well as by Barron-Hauwaert.

Braun and Cline studied 70 trilingual families living in mainly monolingual societies. Their data consist of parental interviews, 35 conducted in England and 35 in Germany. The families selected were those in which two non-community languages are spoken in the home. The 70 families could be categorised into the following three types (116–117):

Type I   Parent A and Parent B speak one different native language each. Neither of them speaks the community language natively. No common native language. (24 families)
Type II One or both parents speak two native languages (which may include the community language). (31 families)
Type III One or both parents speak three native languages (which may include the community language). (15 families)

While among the first two types of families there were not big differences between the families in England compared to those in Germany concerning language practices, the 15 Type III families displayed considerable differences. Of the nine families who lived in England, eight of them *only* spoke English at home. Thus, among these families, a potentially trilingual situation resulted in English monolingualism. In the six families in Germany, on the other hand, five actually used English as a third, non-native language in the home (118). Braun and Cline do point out that most parents in Type III families in England had English as a native language, while such parents in Germany did not have German as a native language, which may have led to these differing patterns (119-120). Nevertheless, the fact remains that English is favoured over other native languages in England, as well as being favoured by non-native speakers in Germany. Further, the value of English can clearly be seen in a different comparison in Braun and Cline's study, namely with regard to choice of school. Twenty out of 35 families in Germany enrolled their children in international schools, generally choosing the English section, while only two of the 35 families in England did so. The evidence from Braun and Cline's study clearly attests to the value of English compared to other languages in multilingual families.

In Barron-Hauwaert's survey, one aspect she considers is how languages with "high world status" (3) fare in trilingual families compared to languages without such status. Barron-Hauwaert gathered data via a survey on ten trilingual families in Belgium (3), Switzerland (3), Germany (1), France (1), the UK (1), and Nepal (1). These ten were among a number of families who had responded to advertisements for the study. The parents selected for participation had to fulfil two requirements, namely that they had children who were over two years of age (i.e. children who could talk), and that the parents spoke different native languages while living in a third language area (Braun and Cline's Type I family).

Barron-Hauwaert looked at which language was chosen as the parents' main language of communication, and compared languages with high world status to those without. She found that in six families one parent spoke a "prestigious" language (English, French or Italian), while the other parent spoke a language which, outside its own specific language area, carried no particular prestige (Swiss German, Polish, Catalan, Dutch and Czech). In each of these families, the parents used one of the former languages as their main communication language. Thus, she concludes that parental languages with high world status may threaten those parental languages with lower world status (3).

4. Data and method

The present study examines language choices among 35 tri- and quadrilingual families in Switzerland. One of the families actually lived in southern Germany but the mother worked in Switzerland, and the child attended day-care there as well. The informants were found mostly via an article I wrote for an English-language parenting magazine published in Switzerland, the *New Stork Times* (Chevalier, "Trilingual Tots"), plus an advertisement placed there. Since the magazine is aimed at parents with young or primary school age children, all of the families except three indeed had children in this age group. A few families were also found through personal connections, especially through university colleagues and students. Due to these methods of data collection, the parents who participated tended to be middle class, with at least one parent if not both working professionally. Further, the fact that many participants were recruited via a magazine written in English means that a bias towards the use of English in these families may exist. Semi-structured interviews were conducted by myself, usually in English (the language of the magazine in which most parents had heard of the study, and the author's native language). One interview was conducted in Italian (family 31 in Table 1, below), one in French (family 33), and one in German (family 34).

The interviews generally lasted a little under an hour (average length 52 minutes). Each interview was recorded and transcribed.[2] Attempts were made to interview both parents, as well as to meet and interact with the children in order to gain as full a picture of the family as possible in the time available. It was possible to interview both parents in 27 cases, while meeting the children was achieved in 32 cases. Having the children present made interviewing more strenuous since parents with younger children were often interrupted. On the other hand, being able to observe the multilingual family in action is clearly advantageous for the researcher.

Further data used in this study are derived from longitudinal case studies of two of the families (one being Lina's). Details on the data and methodology of these case studies can be found in Chevalier ("Mobile Parents," "Active Trilingualism," "Caregiver Responses," *Trilingual Language Acquisition*).

---

[2] I would like to acknowledge the University of Berne for providing me with funding for a research assistant for this project, as well the research assistant herself, Livia Gerber, for her meticulous transcription.

The method of enquiry is as follows: I give an overview of all the languages available to the families and compare these with the languages actually used by them; at the same time, I seek explanations for the parents' choices via a thematic analysis of the interviews; this analysis is, in turn, underpinned by the theoretical models of De Swaan and Spolsky.

5. Overview of the languages involved

The following table provides an overview both of the parental and community languages,[3] as well as the parental language choices. In columns 2, 3 and 4 the parents' native languages[4] and the community languages (CL) are listed. These are the languages which the families "automatically" had at their disposal for their children. Note that in the columns for parental native languages, the order of languages among those parents with more than one native language is given in order of dominance, if the parent stated that they felt dominant in a particular language. If this was not stated, the main language of the community in which the parent was raised is given first. Columns 5, 6 and 7 display the parents' language choices. Column 5 shows the language(s) the mother spoke to her child(ren), column 6 the language(s) the father spoke to his child(ren), and column 7 the language the couple used between themselves (which in two cases changed after the birth of the first child; see families 10 and 33). Finally, column 8 also lists to a large extent language choices parents made, since it shows any languages the children were exposed to via childminders or school if these were different from the community language.

While the table documents the parents' native languages and the community languages, it does not reveal the full extent of the languages actually available to the families interviewed, since in principle parents also have at their disposal any languages learnt later in life. However, when parents actually made use of this option, this information appears in the table. For example, in family 30, the bilingual Italian-Swiss German mother chose to speak English, a language she acquired formally via school, to her son. Further, if parents have the inclination and

---

[3] I use the term "community language" in the same way as Braun and Cline, namely to refer to "the language which is spoken in the wider community and neighbourhood" of the families in question (Braun and Cline, *Language Strategies* 3).

[4] The languages listed are those which the parents considered to be their native languages.

Fam	Mother's native language	Father's native language	CL	Language spoken by mother to child	Language spoken by father to child	Language spoken by parents to each other	School/caregiver's language when different from CL
1	English	Hebrew, English	SG	English	Hebrew	English	Hebrew
2	SG	Swedish, Arabic	SG	SG	Swedish (Arabic)	English	
3	Arabic	Spanish, German	SG	Arabic	Spanish	English	Spanish
4[5]	English	German	SG	English	German	English	
5	Arabic, French	SG	SG	Arabic (French)	SG	English	
6	Italian	SG	SG	Italian	SG	German	English
7	English	Arabic, French	SG	English	Arabic	English	
8	English	Swedish	SG	English	Swedish	English	
9	SG	Dutch,	SG	SG	French	English	

---

[5] Three families (4, 16, 24) living in Swiss German-speaking communities in which one parent came from Germany and the other from an English-speaking country expressed interest in taking part in this trilingualism research. They automatically considered themselves to be trilingual families. It is beyond the scope of this paper to discuss the diglossic situation in German-speaking Switzerland (see Ferguson, "Diglossia"); suffice to say that since Swiss German is not immediately intelligible to many native speakers of German German, it is quite justified for native speakers of the latter variety to feel they are dealing with a different language.

Value of English in Multilingual Families

		French					
10	French	German, English	SG	French	German	English, then German	
11	Danish	SG	SG	Danish	SG	English	English
12	Italian	Lingala, French, English	FR	Italian	English	French	
13	Persian	Italian	SG	Persian	Italian	German	
14	English, SG	Danish	SG	English	Danish	English	
15	English	French, English	SG	English	French	English	
16	English	German	SG	English	German	English, German	
17	French	English	SG	French	English	English	
18	English, Italian	Italian, SG	SG	English	Italian	Italian, English	
19	English	English	FR	English	English	English	Spanish, Swahili
20	Korean	German	SG	Korean	German	English	English
21	English	French	SG	English	French	English	
22	English, Italian	Italian, SG	SG	English	Italian	English, Italian	
23	English	SG	FR	English	SG	English	English
24	German	English	SG	German	English	German, English	English
25	Swedish	English	SG	Swedish	English	English	
26	Finnish	Ger-	SG	Finnish,	Ger-	German	Eng-

		man		English	man, English		lish
27	French	Dutch	SG	French	Dutch	English	
28	Basque	Spanish	SG	Basque	Spanish	Spanish	
29	Italian	Italian	SG	Italian	Italian	Italian	English
30	SG, Italian	SG, English	SG	English	English	SG	
31	Spanish	SG, French	IT	Italian, Spanish	Italian	Italian	
32	Polish, SG	Arabic	SG	English	English	English	
33	French	Italian	SG	Italian	Italian	French, then Italian	
34	German	French	SG	German	French	German	English
35	Greek, English	Danish	SG	Greek	Danish	English	

Key:
Fam: Family
CL: Community language
SG: Swiss German
FR: French
IT: Italian

Table 1: Languages available and languages used in 35 multilingual families in Switzerland

the means they may even choose to expose their children to other languages besides the ones they are able to speak themselves and the community languages; information concerning this option appears in the final column. For a number of couples interviewed, it was only the conscious decision to speak a third language which was not one of their native languages, or otherwise expose their child to a third language, which resulted in a multilingual rather than a bilingual situation. This brings us to the question: When is a language, which is not automatically available to a family, added?

6. When is a language added?

In the corpus of 35 interviews of multilingual families in Switzerland, we can see that when a language which is not automatically available (either as a parental or community language) is added, that language will be English. Three pieces of evidence attest to this.

The first piece of evidence concerns the use of English as a lingua franca between parents. Nine couples did not speak to each other in either partner's native language; instead they used a third language, a lingua franca (families 3, 5, 9, 11, 13, 20, 27, 31, 32 in Table 1). Of these nine families, two (families 13, 31) chose to speak the language of the community.[6] The other seven chose English.[7] It will be recalled that in Lina's family, for example, the mother's native language was Swiss German, the father's native languages were Dutch and French, and yet the couple communicated in English, their strongest non-native language. Dutch, according to De Swaan, is a central language. It is an official language, necessary for communication in Dutch-speaking regions. But it is not useful as a lingua franca outside of these regions. Thus, for this family living in Switzerland it did not have any communicative value and was therefore dropped from the family's linguistic repertoire. The other native language of the father, French, on the other hand, is a supercentral language. Further, it is one of the national languages of Switzerland (although not a language of their region). French, therefore, was maintained, as the father chose to speak this language to his daughter. However, it was hypercentral English, not a native language of either parent, nor the language of the community, which was added to the family repertoire. The decision in this family to maintain French over

---

[6] Italian in Italian-speaking Switzerland and Standard German in German-speaking Switzerland. Although the latter is not the spoken language of the German Swiss community, it is the variety taught in schools and to non-native speakers (see Ferguson "Diglossia").

[7] It is further of note that among those couples in which one parent *is* a native speaker of English (13 families), most communicate in English (11 families). The 13 families are 4, 7, 8, 10, 12, 14, 15, 16, 17, 21, 23, 24, 25. The exceptions are families 10 and 12. In family 10, the couple (mother French, father Indian-German, raised in Germany) had begun by speaking English. However, the father was dominant in German, and also wanted to give his wife practice in German, since they were living in German-speaking Switzerland. In family 12 (mother Italian, father Congolese), the couple also chose to speak the community language, in this case French. Families 16 and 24 communicated to each other in both languages of the couple (in each case English and German). In line with Barron-Hauwaert's findings (p. 3), only languages with high world status are used as couple languages in these families (English, French and German).

Dutch, and to add English conforms entirely to De Swaan's global language system theory, in which languages higher up in the hierarchy will be sought and used by speakers of languages which are lower in the hierarchy.

Let us now consider this example family's language choices through the prism of Spolsky's model of language policy. One element of language policy, it will be recalled, is *beliefs or ideologies* about language. In Lina's family, we can say that the parents are, on the one hand, ideologically committed to multilingualism, since they state that multilingualism is a good thing, and that it is advantageous for children to grow up speaking different languages. On the other hand, they also have a clear belief about the different values of languages, Dutch being less valuable than English. With regard to *language management* in Lina's family, this can be seen in the parents' efforts to keep up English as a lingua franca after Lina was born. Their using English as a couple language was intensified then, because after Lina's birth they became strict about not codeswitching. Once the father had become more and more proficient in Swiss German they said they had started to use also this language with each other before Lina was born. But after her birth, they consciously tried to employ English for her sake, in order to provide her with as good a language model for English as possible. Thus, in terms of language management they had defined clear strategies to follow, which, arguably, were more concerned with the promotion of English than the promotion of multilingualism.

The second piece of evidence showing that parents favour English is that parents in two families who were not native speakers of English spoke English to their children. In family 26, both parents spoke English to their children in addition to their native languages (Finnish and German), while in family 32, both parents spoke exclusively English to their son. In the first family, the use of English was a result of the family having lived for some time in the United States; this usage could be considered, in fact, the influence of the previous community language. In the other family, however, reasons are not so easily discernible, and in the following I shall try and explain this choice. The father, Ahmed, is from Egypt and is a native speaker of Arabic. The mother, Agnieszka, was born in Poland and moved to Switzerland at the age of seven; her native languages are Polish and Swiss German.

Ahmed had lived in Switzerland for twelve years at the time of the interview; he was conducting postdoctoral research and all of his work was done in English. He informed me that he had taken courses in German but hadn't actually managed to learn the language. Agnieszka spoke fluent English and no Arabic. Their lingua franca was by necessity English, and the couple did not seem to have any motivation to change this. The reasons for the parents speaking English to the child are less obvious. The father explained it by stating that "English is our family language." He had actually planned to introduce Arabic after the child had a "solid base in English." This strategy, however, did not work. After having been socialised into speaking English with his father, the child refused to respond not only in, but even to, Arabic. Although the father's answer only concerned the role of English in the family, I believe that the importance of English in the father's life more generally played a role in his choice to speak English to his son. The interview material shows that English is, for Ahmed, very much connected to education and professional life. He stated: "in the university it was everything, the study, was in English because I studied science." While with regard to his workplace in Switzerland he continued: "it's an international atmosphere and the main language is English so I didn't feel like I have to learn German so that's why I'm still speaking English." The importance of hypercentral English in these spheres adds to its value for the father generally, and is likely to have influenced his decision to speak English to his child.

I come now to the third piece of evidence which reveals that when a language is added, that language will be English. Six families, in which none of the parents spoke English natively, made English an integral part of their children's lives by sending them to an English-medium school or day care. Four families chose a bilingual day care, with the community language plus English (families 11, 20, 26 and 34), while the other two families (6 and 29) added English via their choice of school. In five of these families at least one of the parents had lived for some time in an English-speaking country. In family 6, for example, the mother, Marina, was Italian, the father, Jörg, was German Swiss and they had both studied in the United States. They lived there again in a later period for eighteen months, when they already had two children. They moved from the United States back to Switzerland when the children were aged two and five. When the family returned, the children could both speak English better than either Italian or Swiss German – and still can, despite having lived in Switzerland for eight years at the time of the interview. This is due to the fact that they attend an international, English-medium school. During the interview, I observed the children speaking English to each other, as well as sometimes to their mother – even though she addressed them in Italian. The motivations for the choice of the school and thus the upkeep of English are complex. On the one hand, the reason Marina gave was the quality of education. Her belief is that the Swiss primary school system is "not good." The children start late (age 7), and her daughter was told not to read and write in kindergarten. Moreover, according to Marina, Swiss German is spoken in the schools (author's note: the language of education is supposed to be Standard German from first grade on). Finally, Marina added, the children are forced to choose either an academic path or a trade path at a young age, when they might not be ready for it. At the international school, the opposite pertains in every case. Thus, the explicit ideology stated is that of a good school system (the international one) versus a poor one (the Swiss one). However, in a later part of interview, and not in response to the question of choice of school, we get a glimpse of a reason which is less about the quality of education than about the hope of being able to return to the United States. Marina stated "I mean for me it was a condition to come back to Switzerland to send them in international school and also with the hope to go back to the US one time." The school is thus certainly equally valued because it is English-medium, thus providing the mother with the (theoretical) possibility of mobility.

The question of mobility is an important one with regard to the decision to maintain or favour English. In the corpus, 16 of the families said that they were not sure whether they would be staying in Switzerland or not; 18 families said that they planned to stay, and one family said that they would have to leave. Of the six families whose parents were not native speakers of English and who chose to provide English via school or daycare, only one believed that they would stay in Switzerland. The other five, by contrast, were not sure. Thus, for these families, the value of English education may lie above all in the flexibility it allows the parents.

It should further be recalled that the participants in this study were self-selecting, many of whom (Marina included) had responded to an article in an English-medium magazine. Thus, an inherent predisposition towards favouring English cannot be excluded.

In this section I have provided evidence of the importance of English in multilingual families, and claim that, overall, it is the most valued language. However, it is essential to also seek negative cases in order to check the strength of this claim. Thus, it is also important to ask: Is a language ever added which is not English? Only one negative case could be found. An American family (family 19) living in French-speaking Switzerland had enrolled their children in French-Spanish bilingual daycare. In addition, for a certain period they employed a nanny who spoke

Swahili to the children. Thus two languages, Swahili and Spanish, were added in this family which were not automatically available, and which were not English. However, this family of course already spoke English. Therefore, while this is formally a negative case it is not a counter example.

7. When is a language cut?

The interviews revealed considerable enthusiasm for multilingualism, and several times it was called a "gift." Yet not all parents made use of all the languages available to them. One question which arises in this context is therefore: Which potentially multilingual families feel three languages are too much and intentionally choose a bilingual upbringing for this reason?

The conscious decision to opt for bilingualism rather than trilingualism (or quadrilingualism) occurred in only two of the 35 families. In one of the families (family 33) the mother came from the French-speaking part of Switzerland, the father from the Italian-speaking part, and the language of the environment in which they brought up their children was Swiss German. When their first child was born they chose to make Italian the home language and addressed each other and the children in Italian (previously the couple had spoken together in French). Thus, rather than a trilingual upbringing they opted for a bilingual upbringing with one home language. The other family (family 31) cut two of the four languages available. What is striking is that both families in question are a generation older than all the other families interviewed. They both had adult children, whereas the other families had young or school-aged children. The decisions of these two families who chose to cut a language match the mindset of the times, when many educators and doctors were sceptical even of bilingualism, let alone trilingualism. In the interview, the parents in family 33 comment that their decision back then to cut a language may not have been the right one:

> Father: *A ce moment-là on a dit, il faut choisir une langue, on peut pas parler deux langues. Peut-être c'était faux.*
> [At that moment we said, we have to choose one language, we can't speak two languages. Perhaps it was wrong.]
> Mother: *Bien sûr ! Moi je pense.*
> [Surely! I think so.]

All the families a generation younger were, by contrast, enthusiastic about raising their children multilingually. Nevertheless, even among the younger families, decisions were made not to use all the languages available. This could be seen among the parents who were raised bi- or trilingually themselves. There were 19 such parents and all of them chose to speak (or at least to try and speak) just one language to their child, hence dropping their other language. The only slight exception to this pattern was the Swedish-Arabic bilingual father in family 2, who generally spoke Swedish to his baby but thought he might try some songs or games in Arabic. Generally, though, the data from this 21st century corpus attest to the enduring popularity of the "one person, one language" principle, first described over a century ago by Ronjat (3, paraphrasing advice given to him by the linguist Grammont).

As to the choice of language, three factors played a role. The first was dominance in one of the languages. Nine parents stated that the reason for choosing one native language over another was that they felt dominant in the one chosen (families 2, 5, 7, 10, 35; both bilingual parents in 18 and 22). The only example in the corpus of interviews of when English is cut from an entire family repertoire is for this reason. In family 10, the Indian-German father raised bilingually with English and German in Germany, chose to speak his dominant language, German, to his son.

A different reason for not speaking one native language actually had the aim of providing children with the possibility of an extra language (families 3, 12, 14, 15, the father in family 30). For example in family 15, the mother was a native speaker of English, the father a native speaker of both English and French (born and raised in England with French parents) and the community language was Swiss German. The father chose to cut English and only speak French to his daughter precisely in order to give her an "extra language," since English was already available from the mother. (Thus, in this case the bilingual parent cuts out one of their own languages in speaking to the child, but this does mean the language is cut from the family.)

The third reason given was how useful a language was. Usefulness, however, appeared to be conceived of in terms of global usefulness rather than, for example, the ability to communicate with grandparents. Thus, when this reason was given, a supercentral (or hypercentral) language was always chosen over a more localised one (families 9, 12, 32; the mother in family 30). We have already seen how in Lina's family (family 9), the bilingual Belgian father chose to speak the "more useful" French with his daughter over Dutch. In families 30 and 32, the bilingual mothers chose to speak neither of their native languages to their children but opted for hypercentral English instead. Finally, in family 12, the preference for a supercentral language is combined with the aim of an extra language. Here, the trilingual father grew up in the Democratic Republic of Congo with Lingala, French and English. He began by speaking French to his daughter, but since the family lived in Geneva he switched to English in order to give her an extra language. Lingala, the local language of the area in which he grew up, was not considered as an option.

8. Conclusion

The overview of languages available and languages used, and the reasons for the choice of languages in multilingual families in Switzerland are in line with De Swaan's conception of a hierarchical global language system. The choices reveal that while multilingualism generally is viewed positively, not all languages are equally valued and promoted. English is overwhelmingly favoured, whether as a couple language, as a foreign language which parents decide to speak to their children, or as the medium for daycare or school. We have seen that the majority of couples who do not communicate in either parent's native language(s) use English as a lingua franca (7/9 couples), while among those couples in which one parent is a native speaker of English, most communicate in English (11/13 couples). A particularly salient finding in this study is that among the non-native speakers of English, if an extra language is added to the family repertoire it is *always and only English*. This result must however be considered in the light of the methodology: since the recruitment of families was mainly via an English-language magazine, a favourable disposition to English was likely to be a given.

The interviews suggest that English is valued in this way due to the personal experience of the parents. The parents comprise a group of mainly middle-class, professional, mobile adults, many of whom have studied or worked in English-speaking countries, or currently work in English-speaking institutions. For them, the value of English comes from it being part of their professional lives, and their academic and social background. This global generation appears to have quite naturally appropriated the global language. They place a high value on the ability to communicate globally – and recognise the need for English in order to achieve this. That their children should acquire English seems obvious and takes precedence over, for example, fostering the ability of their children to communicate with their grandparents in their grandparents' native language. Thus, although these parents have an overall positive view of multilingualism, this does not, in practice, extend to all languages equally. To return to Spolsky's model, the parents' belief in multilingualism is not matched by language management or practices which support all the languages available. The present study has thus revealed a kind of selective multilingualism in favour of the highly-valued, hypercentral English.

References

Barnes, Julia. *Early Trilingualism. A Focus on Questions*. Clevedon: Multilingual Matters, 2006.

Barron-Hauwaert, Suzanne. "Issues Surrounding Trilingual Families: Children with Simultaneous Exposure to Three Languages." *Zeitschrift für Interkulturellen Fremdsprachenunterricht* 5/1 (2000): 1-13. http://zif.spz.tu-darmstadt.de/jg-05-1/beitrag/-barron.htm

Braun, Andreas and Tony Cline. "Trilingual Families in Mainly Monolingual Societies: Working Towards a Typology." *International Journal of Multilingualism* 7/2 (2010): 110-127. DOI: 10.1080/14790710903414323

———. *Language Strategies for Trilingual Families: Parents' Perspectives*. Bristol: Multilingual Matters, 2014.

Chevalier, Sarah. "Trilingual Tots." *The New Stork Times: The Parenting Source for Switzerland* 14/4 (2006): 12-13.

———. "Mobile Parents, Multilingual Children." Ed. Annette Kern-Staehler and David Britain. *On the Move: Mobilities in English Language and Literature*. SPELL, Swiss Papers in English Language and Literature 27. Tübingen: Narr, 2012. 99-115.

———. "Active Trilingualism in Early Childhood: The Motivating Role of Caregivers in Interaction." *International Journal of Multilingualism, Special Issue: Social and Affective Factors in Multilingualism Research* 9/4 (2012): 437-454.

———. "Caregiver Responses to the Language Mixing of a Young Trilingual." *Multilingua. Journal of Cross-Cultural and Interlanguage Communication* 32/1 (2013): 1-32.

———. *Trilingual Language Acquisition: Contextual Factors Influencing Ac-tive Trilingualism in Early Childhood*. Trends in Language Acquisition Research (2015). Amsterdam: Benjamins.

Crystal, David. *English As a Global Language*. Cambridge: Cambridge University Press, 2003.

De Swaan, Abram. *Words of the World: The Global Language System*. Cambridge: Polity Press, 2001.

Ferguson, Charles. "Diglossia." *Sociolinguistics: The Essential Readings*. Ed. Christina Bratt Paulston and Richard Tucker. Malden, Massachusetts: Blackwell, [1959] 2003. 345-358.

Ferguson, Gibson. *Language Planning and Education*. Edinburgh: Edinburgh University Press, 2006.

Kachru, Braj B. "Models for Non-Native Englishes." *The Other Tongue: English Across Cultures*. Ed. Braj B. Kachru. Chicago: University of Illinois Press, [1982] 1992. 48-74.

Ronjat, Jules. *Le développement du langage observé chez un enfant bilingue*. Paris: Champion, 1913.

Seidlhofer, Barbara. *Understanding English as a Lingua Franca*. Oxford: Oxford University Press, 2011.

Spolsky, Bernard. *Language Policy*. Cambridge: Cambridge University Press, 2004.

Shakespeare and the Modern Economy

Richard Waswo

Describing money and words as homologous systems of exchange that function to embody, formulate, and transmit values, this essay will explore the formative period of the modern economy, when sixteenth-century writers were struggling to conceptualize it*, and Shakespeare was dramatizing its basic principles. These are 1) that neither money nor words need "represent" anything at all (precious metal or reality), but are social facts based on assent and trust, or credit – the fiduciary principle – and 2) that value is established in exchange and constituted by desire – the volitional corollary. Economic theorists of the period (quite like most mainstream economists yesterday and today) did not quite grasp these principles, which are nonetheless evident in the action and arguments of *The Merchant of Venice* and *Troilus and Cressida*.

One of the most astonishing things Marco Polo reported to Europe at the end of the thirteenth century when he returned from his 17-year sojourn at the court of Kublai Khan was the use there made of paper money. Polo himself is amazed by this practice: that throughout the Great Khan's realm, even those objects thought to possess supreme value in the west – jewels, gold, and silver – are themselves purchased by paper. The paper, made from mulberry bark, was black and stamped with some heraldic device of the Khan's. Polo marvels that such intrinsically worthless stuff, so much lighter and insubstantial than all

---

*A fuller analysis of the sixteenth-century accounts may be found at www.pum.umontreal.ca/revues/surfaces/vol6/waswo.html

Economies of English. SPELL: Swiss Papers in English Language and Literature 33. Ed. Martin Leer and Genoveva Puskás. Tübingen: Narr, 2016. 117-127.

the things it can buy, is nonetheless gratefully accepted by all the merchants in the kingdom. The Khan himself keeps a great store of gold and silver (hence his fabulous wealth), and prints, says Polo, as much of the paper "as he pleases." But since everyone accepts it, Polo concludes, "the value is the same to them as if it were of gold or of silver" (238-40).

The value certainly isn't the same to him, however, for he shares the occidental fixation on value as something intrinsic to the object itself. A fixation that continues to be powerful in our culture until just yesterday – as witnessed by the massive resistance to the idea of paper money in the west: from the introduction of banknotes in seventeenth- and eighteenth-century Europe to the protest and ridicule of the greenback in nineteenth-century America. Until the Bretton Woods agreement of 1946, paper money was acceptable to us only because the government had promised that it was convertible to a certain amount of gold or silver. And even after this pretense was abandoned, the dollar was still officially pegged – that is, said to represent or correspond – to some fixed amount of precious metal, in order to stabilize exchange rates among currencies. And only in 1971 was this pretense abandoned, when President Nixon unpegged the dollar from gold though still permitting its use as a fixed standard for other currencies. And this situation has in turn reawakened the archaic nostalgia for the supposed stability of currencies redeemable in precious metal. Even some contemporary politicians and bankers have seriously urged a return to the convertible gold standard for the dollar that existed *before* Bretton Woods (e.g. Lehrman).

So after seven centuries, some people are still failing to understand, as Polo did, the real source of the value of money. This is neither the material it's made of, nor any putatively precious material that it is said to represent. As Karl Marx observed, the "purely symbolic character" of money, and of credit, arises from its function (126-27). Today's coinages function perfectly well without containing, or representing, any precious substance at all. Money today has in fact become what Georg Simmel suggested in 1907 was its ineluctable nature: "a pure token" or symbol, detached from any substantive value, not something that *has* a function, but *is* one (165). Simmel's prophecy has been amply confirmed by two of the most ambitious analyses of the new millennium: Graeber's *Debt* and Martin's *Money*. The value of money is constituted quite simply by the fact of its use; it's established in circulation by social assent. If you can spend it, it's money; and it's worth whatever it will buy. Whatever it's made of – mulberry bark or linen fiber, or leather or seashells or anything else – makes no difference at all. Except, of course, when it comes to the financing of large-scale long-distance commerce. For this purpose, precious metals are especially unsuitable: the difficulty and danger of hauling around bags of gold and silver was what led late medieval merchants to develop paper instruments of credit and debt assignment that were the functional equivalents of money. Thereby they invented the modern economy, which was operational long before it became conceptual – that is, before the principle of its operation was recognized and formulated. And it took until 1973 for the logic of the principle to be fully enacted, when President Nixon unpegged the dollar from any fixed exchange rate with other currencies, allowing them to float, as now they do. Thus tenacious is our western fixation on value as something intrinsic to an object, instead of, as it is, wholly dependent on the use of the object, which is determined merely by the social agreement so to use it.

I call this principle – the conferring of value by social use – the fiduciary principle. From the Latin *fides*, or faith, the term well evokes all the paper exchanges in which we must believe, and which therefore public laws must somehow enforce, in order that the modern economy may function. It is this principle that underlies the necessary and essential role of credit in the economy – another word whose Latin origin (*credo*) implies the social nexus of shared belief as the sine qua non of monetary and commercial activity. And other terms imply the same: the "trusts" that are both legal arrangements and the institutions that make them; the "confidence" that investors have or lack in a company, commodity, currency, or market. Along with the fiduciary principle- that value results from socially agreed-upon use – goes what I shall call the volitional corollary – that what is thus valuable because useful is also, naturally enough, desirable. The modern economic system functions because we believe what others believe and want what others want; values are consequently constituted by the ever-fluctuating relations and conflicts among our mutual beliefs and desires.

I shall try to show that Shakespearean drama presents, far in advance of its time, the operation of both the principle and the corollary. The former is dramatized as the necessity of observing an acknowledgement of debt in *The Merchant of Venice*; the latter as a justification for continuing to fight the Trojan war in *Troilus and Cressida*. Before looking at the plays, though, I must briefly review the received opinions about money, value, and credit in the sixteenth century.

These subjects, along with the economy as a whole, were then of newly crucial concern because of the galloping inflation set off in Europe by the massive influx of gold and silver from the new world. Both French and English observers diagnosed this at the time, but could find no way to deal with it other than by fulminating against governments that persisted in devaluing or debasing their currencies. Theorists were obsessed with the content of precious metal that they thought gave money its value. All their efforts were to stabilize this, even though they were aware that the value of gold and silver was itself unstable. The English in particular were horrified at the very existence of a money market and the ability of bankers "or money merchantes," who deal in no tangible goods, to "use the Exchange onely for gayne by marchandisynge of money, who lye watching to take advantage of the tyme and occasyone to falle or Raiese the Exchange to their moste proffyte" (Tawney and Power 3.356). Even those who understood how to manipulate this market, like Sir Thomas Gresham, the ablest of Queen Elizabeth's financial advisors, desperately sought to control it by establishing once and for all the precious metal content of the pound.

Almost none of the sixteenth-century theorists of money was able to conceive of it as a pure instrumentality, whose value is determined by what it can perform, and not by what it is or contains as an object. They see only that it now performs less, and seek to restore its power by adjusting its content. Consequently, they wholly ignore the crucial role of credit, the way in which fiduciary paper functions and circulates as money. Such practices as payment orders on banks of deposit (the ancestors of cheques), letters obligatory (promissory notes or acknowledgements of debt), and most importantly, bills of exchange – had made possible what one economic historian calls the "commercial revolution" of the thirteenth century (Spufford 240-63). Bills (or letters) of exchange were contractual agreements among a minimum of four people in two different countries recording a payment in one currency in one place, and requiring its repayment in the other place and currency some time later (see de Roover). They were initially devised (in twelfth-century Genoa) as ways to transfer currency and enable international trading of commodities without having to haul bags of silver around. Such paper transfers alone did more to expand trade than any individual currency (Spufford 262) and made bills of exchange the functional equivalent of money (de Roover 117). But by the late Middle Ages they were being used for more purposes than simply to secure foreign exchange to pay for goods; they had become (disguised) ways of obtaining loans, as well as ways of speculating in the fluctuating rates of exchange between foreign currencies (Spufford 395-96). Finally, they became, by the much-contested practice of endorsement, fully negotiable commercial paper. In a famous English lawsuit of 1437, the bearer (not one of its four principals) of a bill of exchange successfully sued for its repayment

(Holden 23-24). Such negotiability was not invariably honored in lawcourts, but was widely practiced. Another historian calculates that in the course of the sixteenth century the volume of credit in circulation must have expanded enormously in order to account for the economic growth observable during the period (*Dawn* 286).

Yet it occurs to almost no contemporary writer on money ever to consider the central role that paper credit instruments actually performed in making possible the global traffic of commodities. I know of only two partial exceptions: a Mexican Dominican, Thomas de Mercado, and a Florentine banker and man of letters, Bernardo Davanzati (1529-1606). Both accept, even if they can't entirely approve, that credit, currency transfers, and even currency speculation are essential to the operation of the economy. Davanzati, who delivered orations to the Florentine Academy on money and credit in 1558 and 1581, is well aware that money is an arbitrary social convention, that gold and silver are the "measure of all things because men have so agreed, and not because these metals are worth so much by nature" (445). And he is above all aware that the real motor of the economy is the exchange of fiduciary paper. Davanzati describes Lyon as a purely financial market "because," he says, "people do not go there to buy merchandise, but only fifty or sixty exchangers, with paper notebooks, to settle the accounts of exchanges made in almost all of Europe" (432). Davanzati even allows that most of these exchanges may be purely speculative profit-making on differential rates between currencies, and hence motivated by the greed of individuals. He then justifies the aggregate result of these transactions in what seems to be the first statement of classical economic liberalism as it would be preached by Adam Smith: "so that if indeed the intention of individual exchangers is not a good thing, the general effect that follows is itself good; and even nature permits many small evils for the sake of one great good, like the death of base animals for the life of the nobler" (429).

If Davanzati is unique in the sixteenth century as a prophet of capitalism, Shakespeare is unique in describing the implications of the fiduciary principle that Davanzati managed to articulate. For if paper agreements move goods more efficiently than pocketsful of coins, then it becomes a primary function of the state to see that such agreements are honored. The new economic order is based on the validity, the trustworthiness, of the written contract. This situation provides Shakespeare with the main plot of *The Merchant of Venice*. The broke young aristocrat Bassanio, you will recall, needs 3,000 ducats to make a flashy courtship of the rich young heiress, Portia. He seeks the money from his best friend, the merchant Antonio, who acquires it for him only by borrowing it from the Jew Shylock. Antonio signs a bond, which is duly notarized, that failure to repay on the date due will result in his forfeiting a pound of flesh. The forfeit is agreed to as a kind of bitter joke, in lieu of the interest that Shylock usually demands. The lady is wooed and won; but Antonio's ventures miscarry; he can't pay back the loan at the stipulated time, so Shylock has him arrested and brought to a trial which occupies the fourth act of the play.

In the course of this action, the issue at stake is made explicit no fewer than six times. First, when Antonio is arrested, a friend of his tries to console him: "I am sure the Duke / Will never grant this forfeiture to hold." But Antonio, the merchant, knows better. "The Duke cannot deny the course of law," he explains,

> For the commodity that strangers have
> With us in Venice, if it be denied,
> Will much impeach the justice of the state,
> Since that the trade and profit of the city
> Consisteth of all nations. (3.3.24)

Second, Shylock petitions the Duke at the trial

> To have the due and forfeit of my bond.
> If you deny it, let the danger light
> Upon your charter and your city's freedom. (4.1.57)

Third, Shylock rejects all pleas that he relent, and repeats the point: "if you deny me, fie upon your law! / There is no force in the decrees of Venice" (4.1.101). Fourth, Portia, come to court in disguise as an erudite young judge, admits to Shylock:

> Of a strange nature is the suit you follow;
> Yet in such rule that the Venetian law
> Cannot impugn you as you do proceed. (4.1.172)

Fifth, Portia concludes her famous speech begging Shylock to show mercy with the same admission:

> I have spoke thus much
> To mitigate the justice of thy plea,
> Which if thou follow, this strict court of Venice
> Must needs give sentence 'gainst the merchant there. (4.1.197)

Sixth, Bassanio beseeches the supposed judge to "Wrest once the law to your authority; / To do a great right do a little wrong." But Portia replies exactly as Antonio had first replied to the same suggestion:

> It must not be; there is no power in Venice
> Can alter a decree establishèd;
> 'Twill be recorded for a precedent,
> And many an error, by the same example,
> Will rush into the state; it cannot be. (4.1.210)

Shakespeare has clearly taken some pains to make the issue perfectly clear: if written contracts are not honored, there is no credibility in Venice, which exists by trade among all nations, and must therefore uphold agreements with no respect to person, nationality, race, or creed. If contracts are not enforced, there can be no economy. The law of contracts is absolute; no individual will, learned or monarchical, can alter it. Mercy is supremely irrelevant here. And it is law, not mercy, that of course solves the problem. Portia discovers in the bond no mention of blood, and so awards Shylock his pound of flesh on condition that he shed no drop of blood. This being impossible, Shylock offers to settle for the money; but Portia rubs his nose in the "justice" he has demanded, insisting he have his forfeit or nothing, and finally convicting him of the attempted murder of a Venetian citizen. The legal system triumphs in every sense, as it must in a state that lives by commerce. It is this political consequence of the fiduciary principle of the modern economy that Shakespeare has so presciently dramatized – a rule of law that upholds contractual agreements among any and all persons: in short, the modern state as opposed to both the feudal oligarchy and the Renaissance monarchy, in which laws vary in application according to social rank, and can be abrogated by the will of the ruler. It is the kind of state that the first world now has, made necessary by our need to believe in the pieces of paper that we agree to value.

In *The Merchant of Venice*, the issues of value, credit, and belief are not confined to the main plot – the contracting of the bond and its climactic trial – but also link that plot to the erotic and marital one. Here, the aristocrats must learn that a new form of marriage accompanies the new economic order, that wives too are to be valued differently. But this matter is treated, in this play, primarily in terms of social class. A more general, even philosophical, analysis of the volitional corollary – that value established by use is ultimately constituted by desire – is presented in the Trojan council scene of *Troilus and Cressida*. This rather strange, and infrequently performed, play is a corrosive satire on both its titular story of idealized "courtly" love, inherited from Chaucer, and its whole context, inherited from Homer, of the most heroic legend in the west: that of the fall of Troy. Shakespeare simply trashes the traditionally supreme values of love and war, reducing the culture's grandest epic to an affair, as Thersites puts it, between a "whore and a cuckold" (2.3.68). The whore is Helen, stolen by Paris from Menelaus, the cause of the war.

In the second scene of the second act, Priam, the king of Troy, holds a council with his sons to consider the latest offer of the Greeks to end the siege and the war if Helen is returned. Hector proposes letting her go because she costs too many lives:

> If we have lost so many tenths of ours
> To guard a thing not ours nor worth to us,
> Had it our name, the value of one ten,
> What merit's in that reason which denies
> The yielding of her up? (2.2.21)

Hector is claiming that the Trojans would not have sacrificed a tenth of the lives already lost for Helen even in defense of one of their own citizens – which Helen is not. Troilus responds with passionate indignation, saying that the calculation of reasons is irrelevant to the "infinite" honor of their royal house, which is at stake. Hector insists, "Brother, she is not worth what she doth cost / The keeping." Troilus asks, "What's aught but as 'tis valued?" And Hector replies,

> But value dwells not in particular will,
> It holds his estimate and dignity
> As well wherein 'tis precious of itself
> As in the prizer. 'Tis mad idolatry
> To make the service greater than the god. (2.2.51)

Hector thus articulates the ancient conviction that worth must be intrinsic to the object, and goes on to attack the younger hotheads who prize things only according to their own individual passions. Troilus then reminds Hector at length that the value of Helen was something they all agreed on: when Paris went to ravish her,

> Your breath with full consent bellied his sails . . .
> Is she worth keeping? Why, she is a pearl
> Whose price hath launched above a thousand ships
> And turned crowned kings to merchants.
> If you'll avouch 'twas wisdom Paris went–

As you must needs, for you all cried, "Go, go"—
If you'll confess he brought home worthy prize—
As you must needs, for you all clapped your hands,
And cried, "Inestimable!"—why do you now
The issue of your proper wisdoms rate,
And do a deed that never Fortune did,
Beggar the estimation which you prized
Richer than sea and land? O theft most base,
That we have stol'n what we do fear to keep! (2.2.74)

After other issues are raised and disposed of, among them the morality of wife-stealing, Troilus will win this argument about value. Hector agrees to keep fighting for Helen, "For 'tis a cause that hath no mean dependence / Upon our joint and several dignities." And Troilus celebrates the decision as the achievement of the traditional aim of all heroic endeavor, "glory." But Troilus describes glory in terms, both religious and economic, that make clear the volitional corollary of the fiduciary principle: value is what others accept, think, and desire. It resides neither in individual desire, as Hector rightly said, nor in the qualities of any object, as Troilus rightly denied. Helen (whom the play depicts as lewd, silly, and superficial) is a pretext, a repository, an occasion; she is, says Troilus,

... a theme of honor and renown,
A spur to valiant and magnanimous deeds,
Whose present courage may beat down our foes
And fame in time to come canonize us;
For I presume brave Hector would not lose
So rich advantage of a promised glory
As smiles upon the forehead of this action
For the wide world's revenue. (2.2.192)

Fame, or glory, is what everyone else will think of us; and it is worth more than the GNP of the entire planet.

The satirical events of the rest of the play (which concludes with Achilles' gang murder of the unarmed Hector) make a concerted effort to destroy the glory of this action, to change our opinion of it, to make it worthless. For Shakespeare's understanding of the modern world and the economic basis of the modern state is ruthless, and requires the rewriting of more than one of western culture's cherished myths. Those of heroism in particular, along with those of kingship and of love, receive radical revision in many of his tragedies, histories, and comedies.

But I must conclude here simply by stressing the extent to which Shakespeare grasped, as did no other writer in the sixteenth century, the central principle of the new economic order that had been developing for three centuries. It is the fiduciary and volitional character of a market economy ruled by the social, mutual, general desires of supply and demand, the world where nothing is anything "but as 'tis valued." Paper money, bills of exchange, bonds of debt, Helen of Troy, are what we credit them to be; nothing in themselves, and everything in terms of what we may use and exchange them for. Political and legal and literary systems exist to maintain that credit and make possible those exchanges. The genius of Shakespeare has been often praised as universal—"not of an age, but for all time," as Ben Jonson put it. But even after four hundred years, it's a little too early to tell. For his age is still ours. Since his own lifetime, Shakespeare has passed for universal easily enough because he described so accurately the world in which we still live.

References

Davanzati, Bernardo. *Opere*. Ed. Enrico Bindi. Florence: F. Le Monnier, 1852.

The Dawn of Modern Banking. Papers from the Center for Medieval and Renaissance Studies, UCLA. New Haven: Yale University Press, 1979.

de Roover, Raymond. *L'Evolution de la Lettre de Change XIVe-XVIIIe siècles*. Paris: Armand Colin, 1953.

Graeber, David. *Debt: the First 5,000 Years*. Brooklyn: Melville House, 2012.

Holden, J. Milnes. *The History of Negotiable Instruments in English Law*. London: Athlone, 1955.

Lehrman, Lewis E. "The Curse of the Paper Dollar." *The Wall Street Journal Europe*, 8 November 1990.

Martin, Felix. *Money: the Unauthorised Biography*. London: Vintage, 2014.

Marx, Karl. *Capital*. Vol I. Tr. Samuel Moore and Edward Aveling [from 3rd ed., 1883]. Ed. Friedrich Engels. New York: International Publishers, 1967.

Mercado, Thomas de. *De' Negotii, et contratti de mercanti*. Brescia: Marchetti, 1591.

Polo, Marco. *The Description of the World*. Tr. Moule and Pelliot. London: George Routledge, 1938.

Simmel, Georg. *The Philosophy of Money*. Tr. Bottomore and Frisby [from 2nd ed., 1907]. London: Routledge and Kegan Paul, 1978.

Spufford, Peter. *Money and its Use in Medieval Europe*. Cambridge: Cambridge University Press, 1988.

Tawney, R. H. and Eileen Power, eds. *Tudor Economic Documents*. 3 vols. London: Longmans Green, 1924.

Money, Morals, and Manners in Renaissance Courtesy Literature

Indira Ghose

This essay looks at the way the nexus between wealth and noble status is represented in Renaissance courtesy literature. For an elite whose pre-eminent position was under threat, it became imperative to find new modes of legitimation for its privileged status. The courtesy books discussed in detail use various strategies to justify the wealth of the elite. What they reveal are the social tensions in an age when money increasingly served as a catalyst for social mobility. Ironically, the texts that sought to shore up the position of the elite were drawn on as manuals for those aspiring to join the ranks.

"Let me tell you about the very rich. The rich are different from you and me." The opening lines of F. Scott Fitzgerald's short story, "The Rich Boy" (1926), describe a world in which the rich are the aristocracy. In an earlier era, it was the aristocracy who were the rich. The distinction, it would appear, is significant. What is striking, however, is the common assumption that undergirds the position of the elite in both societies: the notion that the wealthy possessed a unique set of attributes. This essay is concerned with the nexus between nobility and wealth in the English Renaissance and how the relations between the two are debated in courtesy literature of the sixteenth century. Treatises on manners articulate key ideas of the age. In doing so, they often reflect contemporary tensions in social relations, and they play a role in shaping cultural developments whose legacy remains influential to the present. At a closer look, it emerges that early modern society prefigured pervasive strategies to legitimate the wealth of the social elite – by attempting to demonstrate that they were different from the rest of society.

Economies of English. SPELL: Swiss Papers in English Language and Literature 33. Ed. Martin Leer and Genoveva Puskás. Tübingen: Narr, 2016. 129-141.

The Renaissance saw the emergence of a distinctive body of texts that discussed an aristocratic code of ethics from a humanist point of view, marking a departure from the predominantly Christian ideals of chivalric culture (Watson 38-75). The spate of Renaissance courtesy literature was a reflection of the deep crisis the aristocracy was undergoing during this period (Elias; Stone). The crisis of the aristocracy, like the Renaissance itself, had its roots in Italy. The invasion of the French in 1496 had precipitated a process of fragmentation that shaped the political fate of Italy well into the age of Garibaldi. The Italian aristocracy, formerly defined predominantly through their military function, found their status eroded and their self-justification undermined. Their decisive military humiliation made it apparent that the days of cavalry and man-to-man combat were counted – new technological developments in warfare had made them obsolete. Throughout Europe, the process of state formation meant that local aristocratic power bases were increasingly weakened by a centralised polity dominated, to a greater or lesser degree, by an absolutist ruler. The aristocracy were under pressure to redefine themselves and find new sources of legitimation for their role as political and social elite.

One of the solutions mooted in social theory was the idea that the gentry define itself through public duty and service to the Commonwealth. This was the concept promoted in Sir Thomas Elyot's *The Boke of the Governour* (1531), which became one of the foundational works for the English concept of the gentleman.[1] Concomitantly, a culture of aristocratic self-cultivation emerged, launched by Baldassare Castiglione and reiterated by legions of writers of courtesy manuals in his wake. Castiglione's *Book of the Courtier* (1528) became a bestselling work both in the original and in translation, and its influence was felt in aristocratic circles throughout Europe. What Castiglione suggested was that what distinguished the wellborn from lesser mortals was their style – their refinement in matters of speech, demeanour and presentation, their superior knowledge of the finer points of social comportment. A vital element in the legitimation strategy of the elite was the glamour surrounding them in the public eye. Castiglione's treatise furnishes a gamut of strategies as to how to manipulate public opinion in favour of the aristocracy. Crucial in this respect was how outward appearance could project an image of innate superiority. As the scholar and diplomat Sir Thomas Smith puts it, "As for their outward shewe, a gentleman (if hee will be so ac-

---

[1] In the sixteenth century the terms nobility and gentility were used interchangeably. See Kelso 18-19.

counted) must goe like a Gentleman" (38). Wealth played an important role in the self-definition of the nobility. Traditionally, the aristocratic ethos had been bound up with a suspicion of commerce and a disdain for making money (Thomas 112-13). However, in an age that according to some historians saw the birth of consumer society, conspicuous consumption of luxury commodities, clothes, fashion, housing, hospitality and servants were a requisite badge of nobility (Peck).

Lawrence Stone sums up, "Money was the means of acquiring and retaining status, but it was not the essence of it: the acid test was the mode of life, a concept that involved many factors. Living on a private income was one, but more important was spending liberally, dressing elegantly, and entertainingly lavishly. Another was having sufficient education to display a reasonable knowledge of public affairs, and to be able to perform gracefully on the dance floor and on horseback, in the tennis-court and the fencing school" (27).

Courtesy books spell out the necessity to display one's gentility in an appropriate manner. Stephano Guazzo in his *Civil Conversation* puts it in a nutshell: "Absolute gentlemen are those who to their gentrie by birth and vertue have great riches joined, which serve greatly to the maintenance of gentrie" (1.186). As Castiglione affirmed, it was imperative to demonstrate noble status in deportment and style of life. Furthermore, the aristocracy were expected to demonstrate munificence and generosity in their behaviour at all times. Riches, as Aristotle had argued, were essential to enable the virtue of liberality (*Politics* 1263b), which both Aristotle (*Nicomachean Ethics* 1119b-1123a) and Cicero (1.42-60) list among the attributes befitting a gentleman. The ideal of magnanimity as set out by Aristotle in the *Nicomachean Ethics* (1123b-1125a), which encompassed aspects such as courage, generosity, and a deep contempt for pettiness, was decisive in shaping the ethos of Renaissance nobility. The elite was defined by a distinctive set of moral standards, which, though premised on disdain towards the money motive, were in reality underpinned by economic relations.

In his *Courtiers Academie* (1585), translated into English by John Keepers in 1598, Annibale Romei sets out to imitate the pattern of Castiglione's *Book of the Courtier*. His literary dialogue is set at the Court of Ferrara, not Urbino, and traces the course of a seven days' discussion about the ideal courtier. As at Urbino, the handful of elegant courtiers while away the hours playing parlour games: amongst the ladies a different queen is selected every night, and she selects a courtier to discourse on a topic of common interest. The seven chosen topics evoke the standard topoi of courtesy books of the time: beauty, love, honour, single combat, nobility, riches, arms and letters. While the desire to emulate Castiglione is clear, Romei's prose lacks the panache of its model. His text is of interest mainly as an attempt to fortify the embattled status of the aristocracy.

When it is his turn to discourse on nobility, the chosen speaker, one Signior Hercules Varano, makes it clear that nobility is to be defined through birth. As he declares, "Nobilitie is for no other respect, by all men had in price and estimation, but only because he noble seemeth borne with a better inclination, and disposition unto vertue than a plebeyan, or one extracted from the common sorte" (187). Furthermore, he takes care to draw attention to the fact that only those whose noble descent can be traced back four generations count as noble, by which time the taint of commonness will no doubt have worn off. Varano's definition is aimed at excluding even the most affluent upstarts who ape the lifestyle of the gentry. He is at pains to point out that "neither riches, nor sumptuous vestimentes make a man noble, but further it is necessarie, that the renowne of his progenie [ancestry] thereunto concurre: for hee borne of mechanicall parentes, although never so rich, cannot come within the compasse of this definition" (187). Varano refutes as "vaine and sophisticall" (190) the views of philosophers such as the Stoics who claim that since we are all created by God, we share the same blood and that therefore it is ability alone that makes the gentleman.

In response to a question as to whether riches, even riches begotten by avarice, conferred nobility in equal measure with "virtue, honour, magistracie, and glory" (196), Varano declares categorically that virtue is not possible without wealth. He attempts to exclude riches which are "not the companions of vertue" (197), such as those amassed by usurers and the like. His insistent interlocutor presents him with a list of classical figures who were virtuous but poor, culminating in Socrates. Varano dismisses this interjection, and announces: "Nobilitie cannot be nourished, nor brought to her perfection, without riches" (199). The reason is that the gentleman is expected to cultivate the liberal arts, "for as the practice of mechanicall and vile trade, is proper to him [who is] ignoble, so belongeth to him noble, to use freely liberall artes" (199). By the liberal arts Varano means above all the art of war and the study of law, both of which need to be exercised for their own sake, not for the sake of profit. He then cites Aristotle to buttress the statement that "the life of mechanicall artificers is base, degenerating from vertue, and unworthy a civill man" (199). Quiet and leisure are preconditions for the acquisition of virtue.[2] To practise the liberal arts is impossible without affluence. Varano goes even further. Loss of wealth entails the loss of nobility, since impoverished gentry frequently "applie themselves to base courses, and mechanicall arts" to earn a living, and thus their nobility is tainted (200). In short, Varano asserts that riches are indispensable for nobility.

A further member of the circle reminds Varano of the Venetian aristocracy who are also merchants, famously mocked by Machiavelli. Here Varano draws on the distinction Cicero makes in *De Officiis* (1.151) between retail trade and trade with commodities "brought out of farre countries" (205), which, it seems, is undertaken mainly for the benefit of the commonwealth. Varano ties himself into knots to stress that trade practised "with Decorum" is perfectly acceptable, defining the decorous businessman as the merchant managing his business "by the hand of his agents," without abandoning his study of the liberal arts, as is the case with the Venetian colleagues (205). These noblemen practise trade for largely altruistic reasons, to help their country and also many other neighbouring provinces. Varano's rejoinder to the question as to whether heaping up treasure can be considered noble is that this is perfectly fine so long as the nobleman accumulate wealth for a "good & honest end" and with "decorum," endeavouring each year to increase his revenues rather than the contrary, so that he "fal not into some distresse." There is nothing more pernicious for nobility than to be in want. This, he blandly maintains, is the honest purpose of "gathering wealth." In a remarkable contribution to Christian thought, Varano alleges that since one is heaping up riches for one's children, this aim is even sanctioned by evangelical law (206).

The courtier selected to discourse on riches is Signior Tassone, who shares Varano's views on the close relation between virtue and wealth. Riches, he insists, are "the principall instrument wherewith to exercise vertue" (243). He is challenged by another nobleman, Signior Antonio, who cites the standard Christian arguments against riches: that the source of material wealth is covetousness or worse, that its influence is corrupting, inducing arrogance, pride, envy, greed, and furthermore it breeds evils such as contention and war. Instead, a stoic indifference to prosperity is advisable. Tassone dismisses these arguments as rooted in envy. He draws an analogy to the commonwealth, which is made up of

---

[2] In the *Nicomachean Ethics* (10.7) Aristotle states that the highest form of fulfilment, namely mental activity and philosophical contemplation, is only available to an elite possessing the necessary leisure and education.

different professions; it follows that not all members of the state can be affluent. Those who pursue the liberal arts deserve riches to uphold their lives of virtue; as for those exercising arts mechanical, "their sordide lives requireth it not" (249). Aristotle is wheeled out to support the view that "nobilitie, rather accompanie the rich, then poore" (249). The poor often commit evil deeds to gain money, which is a fate spared the wealthy. The rich, it might be concluded, are not only different: they are more virtuous.

The Courtiers Academie might be a particularly blatant assertion of aristocratic privilege, complete with a Neoplatonic gloss. A variation on the nobility debate is provided by Giovanni Battista Nenna of Bari in his *Nennio, Or A Treatise of Nobility* (1542), translated into English by William Jones in 1598. The frame narrative is slightly different, and gestures towards the *Decameron*: a party of the *beau monde* take refuge from the plague in a country estate, where a mysterious lady appears, promises the noblest of two gentlemen a precious ring, and then disappears. The dialogue consists of three parts – the first gentleman, Possidonio, lays out the case for deserving the ring on the basis on his lineage and his affluence. The second contender, Fabricio, stakes his own claim on the grounds of his acquired virtue. The final part of the book consists of the judgement delivered by a third member of the party, Nennio.

The opposed arguments are not new. Possidonio rehearses the usual reasons why riches are an inseparable part of nobility. Without wealth a gentleman would be hard put to sustain the virtues of magnanimity and charity. Fabricio's counterstatement consists of a disquisition on the theme that true nobility consists in the virtues of the mind. The genealogical argument is contemptuously rejected as pertaining to animal husbandry and not of relevance for humans. Riches, he insists, do not make us better people, but are at the root of all evil. Nennio's judgement speech is carefully balanced and reconciles both sides: both birth *and* virtue are desirable qualities. Riches are not a precondition for nobility, "yet doe they bring some aide thereunto" (96). More interesting are the devastating sideswipes against the elite that spice up the somewhat anodyne narrative. Take, for instance, the tongue in cheek allusion to jokes in the *Cortegiano* that readers at the time would have enjoyed:

> As it happened the other day, that being in companie with certaine Lordes (with some of you that are here present) where there were men of greatlearning, and skill: and amongst them some of those who bragge so greatly of their Nobilitie, wee discoursed a great while both of hautie, and meane matters; and intending to passe the middle of the day, in iestes and disportes, we set abroche certaine tales, which seemed so much the more

pleasing unto us, as they were farre from the trueth: but these noble men did marvellously wonder at them: As the tale of the ape of India, that plaid so well at chesse, & this other, that in the midst of the river Tabor mens words do freese, & afterwards thawe when they come to the fire. (77-8)

While the members of the group Nennio belongs to chortle happily, the doltish noble lords stand amazed. But the joke takes a more savage twist:

Truely the ignorance of them is so great and grosse, that it depriveth them of their understanding, that it maketh them like unto brute beasts: as by an example which happened the other day, I will give you better to understand. For comming to church with certaine of my friends to heare masse, one of these worthy lords (whose name for some respect I will not utter) sate next unto me, even at the very instant when they lifted uppe that which they cal the body of Christ, and he hearing that I saide *Adoramus te Christe*, he demanded of me what these words *duramus te Christo* signified . . . afterwardes hee asked mee what the sacrament which the priest lifted up with his two handes, and the chalice did signify. (78-9)

While the otherwise conciliatory Nennio takes care to exclude all present members of the select society from the charges of palpable ignorance, obscenity and blasphemy, and to draw them into complicity with him, he makes no bones of his boundless contempt for the lords. The elite do not cut a pretty figure elsewhere in the text either:

Turne your eies (if you so please) upon every town and every place of the world, inhabited by noble men and those of the common sort; and you shall finde no place exempt, where there is not rooted amongst noble men one with another, amongst the nobilitie & the comminaltie, hatred, persecution, envy, ambition, ignorance, and pride. These are the fruites which nobilitie of bloud doe give to the mind. (82)

Far from being exemplars of virtue, the well-born practise every vice in the book. The alternative myth of origins that he cites is deeply cynical: "Nobilitie beganne in the first age, to be noted in those (and they were esteemed Noble) who either by force or fraude, did surmount others" (83). Instead of the tale of noblemen singled out for virtue, the narrative he offers is that of a vicious struggle for power. The first nobleman was the Biblical murderer Cain, who passed on the worthy tradition; "others, who descending from Cain (that proud murtherer and usurper of other mens goods, & so consequently noble) they were likewise esteemed noble" (83). Although the treatise punctiliously fulfils the norms of the literary dialogue by treating its theme in an ostensibly even-handed manner (Cox), it smuggles a vitriolic attack on the ruling class into the discourse of Nennio, the arbiter of the debate.

As for Castiglione, he is far too sophisticated to allow even the shadow of partiality to fall across his polished prose. In Book 1 of the *Courtier* he briefly treats the question of how to define a gentleman. When enumerating the traits the ideal courtier should possess, Count Ludovico begins by naming gentle birth. The usual reasons are arrayed: the essence of nobility is a "hidden seed" (1.14; 21) planted by nature, which is passed on to one's scions; the deeds of one's forebears act as a spur to emulation. The eternal naysayer in the book, Gaspar Pallavicino, immediately objects by pointing to the innumerable cases of noblemen who are anything but paragons of virtue. Gifts of nature, Pallavicino maintains, are distributed quite randomly across humankind. The Count elegantly sidesteps the issue. He fully concedes that the lowborn might be richly endowed with gifts of nature. But what is decisive is public opinion. Merely by being well-born the courtier garners esteem; society is invariably prejudiced in his favour. The real point the Count wants to make is about the importance of first impressions: "anyone who aspires to have the rank and name of good Courtier must strive from the beginning to make a good impression" (1.16; 24). Indeed, beside his noble birth, he would wish the Courtier "endowed by nature not only with talent and with beauty of countenance and person, but with that certain grace which we call an 'air,' which shall make him at first sight pleasing and lovable to all who see him . . . giving the promise outwardly that such a one is worth of the company and the favor of every great lord" (1.14; 22). Much of the book turns on how precisely to achieve this intangible quality of graceful style.

Castiglione elides the question of riches entirely. He has no need to discuss them as a condition of nobility. The text has moved on – to a different form of capital entirely. The ideal courtier should be fully aware of the fact that he will be judged on the basis of his external appearance, by the impression he creates. Not only will his clothes speak volumes, his "ways and manners, as well as deeds and words, are all an indication of the qualities of the man in whom they are seen" (2.28; 90). Indeed, his very gestures and habits of "walking, laughing, looking, or the like" are an index of his worth. To be sure, his ultimate purpose is to serve his prince, but in order to win the favour of the prince and steer him onto the path of virtue, it was imperative that the courtier charm him with his accomplishments and graceful conduct.

Several centuries before Bourdieu, Castiglione offered a theory of social distinction based on *habitus*, the often trivial forms of manners and behaviour that demonstrate one's membership in a certain social class. Material wealth needed to be turned into cultural capital to signify nobility. The elite justified its position at the apex of society on the grounds of its superior taste, its command of a body of knowledge that, amongst other things, encompassed how to behave, how to dress, how to converse, how to jest, and how to make love. Carefully cultivated style and taste were the new key to status and needed to be perpetually displayed to a world of peers in competition for precisely the same goods and qualities. One might argue that Castiglione undermined the idea of essential nobility far more decisively than did Nenna – but so elegantly that very few noticed. For if nobility was a matter of performance, a quality that needed to be ceaselessly demonstrated to the world in one's taste and lifestyle, how could it be innate? Perhaps the mystique surrounding the nobility was precisely that, a shimmering mirage that disappeared at a closer look.

At the end of *Nennio*, the eponymous arbiter needs to bestow the prize for greater nobility on one of the two contestants. With a passing nod to the rich boy, Possidonio, Nennio awards the ring to Fabricio, whose claims to nobility on the basis of virtue rather than birth are deemed to be more convincing. For his part, Fabricio makes a gift of the prize to his opponent, which the latter attempts to refuse, but in the face of overwhelming pressure from the surrounding company, reluctantly accepts. With his graceful gesture, the social upstart Fabricio demonstrates his skill in the discipline Castiglione defines as the true mark of the gentleman: *sprezzatura*, a nonchalant ease in concealing the effort one invests in any act or form of behaviour. Style and manners in the arena of cultural consumption defined you as noble. *Sprezzatura*, however, was premised on having the material means to acquire the requisite skills.

As numerous writers point out, the preserve of the nobility was increasingly being encroached upon by social climbers. In 1568 in the anonymous English treatise, *Institucion of a Gentleman*, the author laments the large numbers of upstarts creeping into the strongholds of the gentry. His manual is a self-proclaimed attempt to shore up the position of the gentry and rebuild the house of nobility, which is threatened by invasion: "these base sorte of men have easelye entred therin, & at this day do beare those armes which wer geven unto old gentry" (sig. *iii^r). Admittedly, the nobility themselves are to blame, and he blames their crumbling conditions upon their decadence: "such corruption of maners hath taken place, that almost the name of gentry is quenched, and handycraft men have obtayned the tytle of honour, thoughe (in dede) of themselves they can chalenge no greater worthynes then the spade brought unto their late fathers" (sig. *ii^v-iii^r). Nevertheless, as he stresses, noble status cannot be bought (sig. B6^v). Half a century later Henry Peacham published *The Complete Gentleman* (1622), one of the best known courtesy books written by an Englishman. Peacham rehearses the standard ideas about nobility circulating in the early modern period, and grounds his argument firmly in the idea of a universal, hierarchical order. With regard to riches, he reiterates the standard line that money alone cannot buy nobility. Peacham even begrudges the leading families of cities like Venice, Genoa, and Florence the rank of aristocracy, and sniffs that what foreigners agree to accept in their native countries is all very well, but in England other rules would apply (22). Unfortunately, he concedes, England, and indeed, the entire continent, is in the grip of a pandemic: "every undeserving and base peasant aiming at nobility" (25). Above all, what he roundly condemns is the sordid reality outside the magic circle of social theory: "the most common and worst of all is in all places the purchasing of arms and honors for money" (26). In truth, as the writers of courtesy books knew all too well, money was the main agent of social mobility. It was the chief means to buy status. Money and nobility were so closely entwined that they were impossible to untangle. As Robert Greene scoffs in his pamphlet, *Greenes Groats-Worth of witte* (1592), "what is gentry if welth be wanting, but bace servile beggerie" (sig. B2^r).

Ironically, courtesy literature itself was inextricably bound up with money. Originally written to shore up the precarious position of the aristocracy, the books were avidly read as how-to manuals by those segments of society aspiring to rise in status (Whigham). The texts became highly marketable and cornered a significant section of the print market, which it shared with other "self-help texts" ranging from epistolary guides to books of compliments, purporting to teach their readers polite discourse. Courtesy itself was purveyed in a variety of forms: in manuals, in the academies for manners that burgeoned in the early seventeenth century, and in the theatre, where plays afforded their spectators a glimpse of a world of gentility, sophistication, and wealth, peopled with well-born characters as glamorous and elegant as in the golden world conjured up by Castiglione. And yet: not everybody was hoodwinked by Castiglione's dazzling performance of nobility. Lord Burghley, in his own conduct book, a set of precepts intended for his son, drily notes, "Gentilitie is nothing but aunctient Riches" (10), dropping the Aristotelian reference to virtue entirely. Hemingway, in his riposte to F. Scott Fitzgerald, put it more drastically. In response to the statement that the rich are different, he remarked laconically, "Yes, they have more money" (Trilling 183).

References

Aristotle. *Nicomachean Ethics*. Trans. Terence Irwin. Second edition. Indianapolis, Indiana: Hackett, 1999.

———. *Politics*. Trans. H. Rackam. Cambridge, Massachusetts: Harvard University Press, 1932.

Bourdieu, Pierre. *Distinction: A Social Critique of the Judgement of Taste*. Trans. Richard Nice. 1979. Cambridge, Massachusetts: Harvard University Press, 1984.

[Braham, Humfrey.] *The Institucion of a Gentleman*. London, 1555.

Burghley, William Cecil, Baron. *Certaine preceptes or directions, for the well ordering and carriage of a mans life*. London, 1618.

Castiglione, Baldesar. *The Book of the Courtier*. 1528. Trans. Charles S. Singleton. Ed. Daniel Javitch. New York: Norton, 2002.

Cicero, *On Obligations*. Trans. P. G. Walsh. Oxford: Oxford University Press, 2000.

Elias, Norbert. *The Civilising Process: The History of Manners and State Formation and Civilization*. 1939. Trans. Edmund Jephcott. Oxford: Blackwell, 1994.

Elyot, Sir Thomas. *The Boke named the Governour*. 1531. Ed. Donald W. Rude. New York: Garland, 1992.

Fitzgerald, F. Scott. "The Rich Boy." *Red Book*, January and February 1926. Web. Accessed 10 September 2015.

Greene, Robert. *Greenes Groats-Worth of witte, bought with a million of Repentence*. 1592.

———. *A Quip for an Upstart Courtier*. London, 1592.

Guazzo, Stefano. *The Civile Conversation of M. Steeven Guazzo*. Trans. George Pettie and Bartholomew Young. London, 1581, 1586.

Kelso, Ruth. *The Doctrine of the English Gentleman in the Sixteenth Century*. 1929. Gloucester, Massachusetts: Peter Smith, 1964.

Nenna, Giovanni Battista. *Nennio, or A Treatise of Nobilitie*. Trans. William Jones. London, 1595.

Peacham, Henry. *The Complete Gentleman, The Truth of Our Times, and The Art of Living in London*. 1622. Ed. Virgil B. Heltzel. Ithaca, New York: Cornell University Press, 1962.

Peck, Linda Levy. *Consuming Splendor: Society and Culture in Seventeenth-Century England*. Cambridge: Cambridge University Press, 2005.

Romei, Hannibale. *The Courtiers Academie*. Trans. I. K. London, 1598.

Smith, Sir Thomas. *The common-wealth of England and maner of government thereof*. London, 1594.

Stone, Lawrence. *The Crisis of the Aristocracy 1558-1641*. Oxford: Oxford University Press, 1967.
Thomas, Keith. *The Ends of Life: Roads to Fulfilment in Early Modern England*. Oxford: Oxford University Press, 2009.
Trilling, Lionel. Review of *The Crack-Up*, by F. Scott Fitzgerald. *The Nation*, 25 August 1945: 182-84.
Watson, Curtis Brown. *Shakespeare and the Renaissance Concept of Honour*. Westport, Connecticut: Greenwood Press, 1976.
Whigham, Frank. *Ambition and Privilege: The Social Tropes of Elizabethan Courtesy Theory*. Berkeley: University of California Press, 1984.

"Father and son, I ha' done you simple service here": The (Interrupted) Circulation of Money in Middleton and Dekker's *The Roaring Girl*

Rahel Orgis

Thomas Middleton and Thomas Dekker's *The Roaring Girl* features a surprising number of money transactions considering the historical and economic context of the period where hard currency was scarce and trade based on pervasive debt and credit networks. The circulation of money thus emerges as one of the themes of the play, with the protagonist Moll Frith determining the failure or success and, by extension, the acceptability of many of the financial transactions. Through Moll's character and actions the play engages in a critique of self-interested money transactions that may damage or even destroy others and their social standing. This critique is further sustained by parallel episodes on different plot levels and characters that contrast with or mirror Moll and her actions. The occasionally cross-dressed figure of Moll has been analysed as a subversive proto-feminist character, as a projection of cultural and economic fears and fantasies or as an ultimately conservative figure who is reintegrated into patriarchal society. My own reading proposes that Moll stands for an idealistic society and economy but that the ending of the play leaves it open whether Moll is finally assimilated into a society where "simple," disinterested, service is superseded by self-interested financial transactions.

"[M]oney," as Richard Waswo points out in his discussion of "Monetary and Erotic Economies in the Jacobean Theatre," "was in endemically short supply . . . in Britain throughout the late sixteenth and early seventeenth centuries" (57).[1] Yet, this does not seem to be the case in Tho-

---

[1] Waswo's assertion is based on Craig Muldrew's influential study *Economy of Obligation*; see especially the section "Money and Credit" (98-103).

Economies of English. SPELL: Swiss Papers in English Language and Literature 33. Ed. Martin Leer and Genoveva Puskás. Tübingen: Narr, 2016. 143-162.

mas Middleton and Thomas Dekker's city comedy *The Roaring Girl*, which refers to or stages more than a dozen money transactions. This is a surprisingly high number given that at the time "full and direct payment in cash was unusual except in the smallest transactions, or in cases where the buyer's credit was weak or unknown," as Craig Muldrew notes ("Interpreting" 171). Interestingly, however, many of these transactions fail to achieve their purpose, and this is often due to the eccentric heroine of the play, Mary or Moll Frith, the roaring girl of the title. Thus, while some of the more obvious themes of *The Roaring Girl* are reputation and slander, marriage, cross-dressing and propriety, the circulation of money emerges as a further concern. Indeed, the play investigates the acceptability of different types of money transactions and repeatedly brings to the fore how these underpin issues of reputation, propriety and marriage negotiations. Through the figure of Moll and her actions, I would argue, the play engages in a critique of self-interested financial transactions that may damage or even destroy others and their social standing and that undermine the prevalent "market relations" in early modern England based, according to Muldrew, "on trust, or credit" ("Interpreting" 169). This critique is further sustained by parallel episodes on different plot levels and characters that contrast with or mirror Moll and her interventions. Hence, Moll gradually comes to stand for an idealistic and utopian social and economic code of conduct. Furthermore, the question of whether Moll loses her potentially subversive exceptionality at the end of the play and becomes assimilated into society depends not solely on her attitude towards marriage and gender roles,[2] but essentially hinges, I contend, on how her reaction to the money transaction proposed in Sir Alexander's very last speech is staged.

The play opens with a thwarted financial transaction: because the "covetous" Sir Alexander is unwilling to pay his part, that is, sign over part of his lands to his son, he prevents the marriage between his son Sebastian and Mary Fitz-Allard despite Mary's substantial dowry (I.i.80-

---

[2] See, for instance, Jane Baston or Mary Beth Rose, as discussed below. Natasha Korda challenges the idea of Moll as an exceptional figure, qualifying her "status as a worker within the networks of commerce surrounding early modern London's public theaters" as "unexceptional," given that "women appear to have worked within these networks in significant numbers" (71). My use of the term exceptional refers primarily to the perception suggested by the play itself of Moll as markedly different and therefore potentially threatening to the established social order.

92).³ Contrary to many of the following money transactions, this bargain finally comes to fruition in the last scene of the play thanks to Moll's support of the young couple. While Jane Baston has pointed out the contradiction between Moll's refusal of marriage for herself and her support of the marriage plot (328),⁴ Moll's actions can also be interpreted as supporting a certain type of financial transaction, i.e. legal inheritance, the passing on of capital and land from fathers to children. In other words, Moll's intervention might be interpreted not so much as condoning the subjection of women in marriage, but as upholding children's right to the financial support of their parents.

In this respect, Moll's rescue of the simple-minded but harmless prodigal Jack Dapper from his father's scheme to have him imprisoned on false charges in order to teach him a lesson can be seen as a parallel to her intervention on behalf of the young couple.⁵ Jack Dapper certainly has "profligate habits" (181), as Jonathan Gil Harris puts it, buying extravagant feathers (II.i) and spending money on food (II.i, V.i), drink and dice (III.iii). Yet, unlike the gallants Laxton or Goshawk, Jack Dapper does not seem capable of intentionally harming someone – losing his money at dice even when he has "false dice of [his] own" (III.iii.203-4). This prodigality of Jack's, which profits others more than himself, is what seems to infuriate his father most, as the following outburst indicates:

SIR DAVY DAPPER
    ... your Sebastian
Doats but on one drab, mine on a thousand,
A noise of fiddlers, tobacco, wine, and a whore,
A mercer that will let him take up more,
Dice, and a water-spaniel with a duck: oh,
Bring him abed with these, when his purse jingles,
Roaring boys follow at's tail, fencers and ningles

---

³ All references to the text of *The Roaring Girl* are to the New Mermaids edition edited by Elizabeth Cook.

⁴ See also Stephen Orgel, who terms Moll "at heart a good bourgeoise" (24), or Anthony B. Dawson, who remarks that "As a social critic, Moll remains rather more ambivalent than those searching for protofeminist sentiment might wish" (394). For a reading of Moll as "perpetuating the status quo" (78), see Deborah Jacobs.

⁵ Viviana Comensoli calls Jack Dapper "Moll's double" (261), as neither of them repents their actions and Moll is also called "Jack" by her companions. However, this interpretation disregards Jack Dapper's naivety and vanity, which are clearly mocked in the play and also commented on by Moll, who compares him "to a nobleman's bedpost" on account of his "spangled feathers" (II.i.294-295).

(Beasts Adam ne'er gave name to), these horse-leeches suck
My son: he being drawn dry, they all live on smoke. (III.iii.57-64)

While Sir Davy Dapper clearly disapproves of his son's pastimes, the most sexualised accusations alluding to sodomy and oral sex are reserved for the circumstance that Jack lets himself be used by others. These allusions to homosexuality arguably express Sir Davy's disgust at what he perceives as unnatural and emasculating economic behaviour. The portrait of Jack is followed in the same scene by a no less damning portrait of Sir Davy Dapper, unwittingly addressed to Sir Davy himself by the Sergeant hired to arrest Jack:

SIR DAVY
And you know his father too, Sir Davy Dapper?
[Sergeant] CURTILAX
As damned a usurer as ever was among Jews; if he were sure his father's skin would yield him any money, he would when he dies flay it off, and sell it to cover drums for children at Bartholomew Fair. (III.iii.154-158)

The Sergeant's description casts Sir Davy as a "grasping usurer," a commonly stigmatised figure in early modern theatre, as Peter Grav notes (13). Hence, although the play holds up the simpleton and spendthrift Jack Dapper for mockery, his shortcomings, which are accompanied by liberal companionship and which profit the national economy, are clearly presented as more forgivable than Sir Davy's avarice.[6] Moreover, Sir Davy's scheme of having his son arrested seems an extreme and even counterproductive measure. As Muldrew remarks, public arrest constituted an ignominy in early modern society that had serious repercussions on the creditworthiness of both the arrested individual and her or his entire household and was therefore used as a last resort to collect outstanding debts (*Economy* 275-276, 279). Nonetheless, when Sir Davy shares his plan with Sir Alexander, he is encouraged by him (III.iii.55-111). The subplot of Jack's failed arrest thus expressly aligns

---

[6] The play seems to share the period's general attitude towards prodigality and avarice based on Aristotle's *Politics*: "prodigality . . . was still better than illiberality because through his spending the prodigal still benefited others as well as himself, whereas meanness benefited no one, because it was at root anti-social and concerned only with gain and not with giving and taking as reciprocal or generous acts" (Muldrew, *Economy* 159).

the two father figures and reflects on Sir Alexander's meanness.[7] Both fathers put their own present financial profit above their son's welfare and, consequently, their household's future potential for success. Moll's interventions on behalf of the sons on both plot levels reinforce the play's condemnation of such fathers. Even if prodigal sons use their inheritance like Jack for outings "to that nappy land of spice-cakes" (V.i.54), this is nevertheless more acceptable, it seems, than fathers trying to stymie their sons by withholding financial support.

In contrast to filial inheritance, other money transactions in the play do not find Moll's sanction. This becomes most obvious in two instances when Moll short-circuits the flow of money. In the first instance, the gallant Laxton tries to seduce Moll. He gives her ten angels that he has himself received from the apothecary's wife, Mistress Gallipot, for amorous services that he continually defers. Moll takes the money and agrees to a rendez-vous with Laxton. Instead of spending the money, however, she adds ten angels of her own to the sum and transforms the bribe into prize money for the winner of the duel to which she challenges Laxton at their meeting. Thus, Moll actively gains the money with which Laxton thought to transform her into a prostitute.[8] Furthermore, she criticises the use of bribes for seduction not only through her actions but also her speech, famously observing that

> Distressed needlewomen and trade-fallen wives,
> Fish that must needs bite or themselves be bitten,
> Such hungry things as these may soon be took
> With a worm fastened on a golden Hook:
> Those are the lecher's food, his prey[.] (III.i.94-98)

The second instance in which Moll interrupts the circulation of money is when Sir Alexander pretends not to see through her disguise as a musician. He gives his son four hollow-hearted angels to pay for her musical entertainment in order to get her into trouble for possessing spoiled

---

[7] For an analysis of the relations between the different plotlines in *The Roaring Girl* see Comensoli's article, which insists especially on how the citizen-plot's "realistic treatment of conjugal malaise" (251) undermines the romantic comedy ending.

[8] Valerie Forman notes that "Prostitutes were often referred to ironically and punningly as 'angels'" (1549) due to the cost of their services. Jean Howard foregrounds the "punning association" of angels with Jack's "ningles" or ingles, that is, boy-favourites or catamites, and argues that the text suggests the possibility that "Laxton may want from her [Moll] a variety of sexual pleasures, those associated with the ingle as well as with the woman as vessel of reproduction" ("Sex" 182).

or marked coins. Sebastian's and Moll's reactions indicate that neither of them is aware of the trick:

> SEBASTIAN
> Faith thou shalt have 'em [the hollow-hearted angels], 'tis my father's gift,
> Never was man beguiled with better shift.
> MOLL
> He that can take me for a male musician,
> I cannot choose but make him my instrument
> And play upon him. (IV.i.209-13)

Again Moll does not try to spend the money and can thus return the four hollow-hearted angels when Sir Alexander confesses to his treachery at the end of the play. Hence, in both instances Moll actively interrupts the circulation of money. She thereby gains control and avoids being put into a position of dependence,[9] enabling her to thwart plots motivated by self-interest.

This interpretation is again supported by what happens in the citizen plot, in which Mistress Gallipot functions as a foil for Moll. Unlike Moll, Mistress Gallipot is seduced by Laxton's advances and actively participates in the circulation of money, smuggling sums of her husband's money to Laxton. After the ten angels, which she disguises as tobacco (II.i.94-95), she receives another plea for money from Laxton, this time for thirty pounds. To satisfy his demand she invents a *de praesenti* marriage contract to Laxton that allegedly precedes her marriage to Master Gallipot. Thus she manipulates her doting husband into paying Laxton to make him abandon his supposedly prior claims on her (III.ii.115-152). Moreover, Mistress Gallipot comments, "Thirty pound?/'Tis thirty sure, a 3 before an 0,/I know his threes too well" (III.ii.65-67), which suggests that this is not merely the second time Laxton has asked for money. In contrast to Moll, Mistress Gallipot finds herself trapped by her expenses on Laxton's behalf, as she realises when musing on how to procure the thirty pounds:

> My childbed linen?
> Shall I pawn that for him? Then if my mark
> Be known I am undone; it may be thought
> My husband's bankrupt: which way shall I turn?

---

[9] Howard touches on this point when commenting that "both Laxton and old Wengrave try to control the subversiveness of Moll, to subordinate her to them, by economic means" ("Sex" 182).

> Laxton, what with my own fears, and thy wants,
> I'm like a needle 'twixt two adamants. (III.ii.67-72)

In contrast to her earlier admonition to Laxton, "Be not forgetful; respect my credit, seem strange: . . . pray be wary" (II.i.50-52), Mistress Gallipot here does not explicitly dwell on the danger to her personal reputation but focuses on the possible financial repercussions of being known to pawn her linen. Laxton, however, is perfectly aware of the hold he has over Mistress Gallipot's marital reputation thanks to the sums already received from her.[10] Thus, when Mistress Gallipot tries to put him off because she has realised that Laxton is only interested in money (IV.ii.40-41), he gets back at her with the extravagant demand of upping the thirty to a hundred pounds in front of her husband – knowing full well that she can only deny him the money by damaging her own reputation. This is spelt out when Mistress Gallipot finally makes her confession after a bout of haggling, during which she asks Laxton, "Do you seek my undoing?" (IV.ii.257), and pleads with him to be content with "threescore" (IV.ii.256) or "fourscore" (IV.ii.259) instead of "a hundred pound" (IV.ii.249). When Laxton denies her request – "I'll not bate one sixpence, –/I'll maul you, puss, for spitting" (IV.ii.257-258) – Mistress Gallipot makes a clean breast of it in order to stop her husband from paying:

>   Husband, I plucked–
> When he had tempted me to think well of him–
> Got feathers from thy wings, to make him fly
> More lofty.
>   . . .
> He having wasted them, comes now for more,
> Using me as a ruffian doth his whore,
> Whose sin keeps him in breath: by heaven I vow
> Thy bed he never wronged, more than he does now. (IV.ii.274-281)

---

[10] Mistress Gallipot fears that pawning her linen might have disastrous consequences for her husband's business. This bears out Muldrew's observation that "The reputation of all members of households became so important because it was what determined whether a household could obtain credit, and a business could not prosper nor a household increase its level of consumption without it" (*Economy* 149). Hence, as Muldrew puts it, "making a distinction between economically rational transactions and other social transactions, such as courtship, sex, patronage or parenthood, does not make sense" (*Economy* 149). This conflation between the social reputation of an individual and the economic reputation of the household is also signified by Mistress Gallipot's use of the words "undone" and "credit," which can be understood both socially and economically.

Interrupting the flow of money is Mistress Gallipot's only option to regain some control over Laxton and the situation, but this comes at the price of losing the trust of her doting husband and tarnishing her reputation.[11] Hence, Mistress Gallipot finds herself transformed into a "whore" through the circulation of money that she encouraged, even though her adulterous desires remain unsatisfied. This, in turn, underlines the integrity of Moll, whose reputation follows an inverted trajectory compared to Mistress Gallipot's: from seeming looseness to an assertion of chastity.

The use of money by Laxton, Sir Alexander and also Mistress Gallipot – who attempt to reach their ends through money without regard for others or even with the express intention of harming others – is governed by what is commonly termed self-interest.[12] As Amelia Zurcher puts it:

> According to the conventional humanist ideology of the late sixteenth century, self-interest was a form of passion, perhaps even the primary passion, manifested in a simple, self-serving urge to possess that in civil societies was curbed by the more communally oriented calculus of reason. (19-20)

The potential conflict between individual self-interest and the common good that Zurcher's definition implies is, for example, discussed by Montaigne, who, in his *Essays*, regards "the unbridled pursuit of individual self-interest" as "the cause of civil war" (Force 141). The view that "reason dictates that the public interest must take precedence over a private interest" (140) continued to be current in the seventeenth century, Pierre Force observes, as both Thomas Hobbes and John Locke "mention private interest as a destructive force because the content of private interest is defined by private passions" (141). Commenting on the discussion of enclosure practices to increase profit in the treatise *A Discourse of the Common Weal of this Realm of England* (c. 1549), Leslie Clarkson claims that self-interest "was firmly entrenched as a guide to economic behavior even though it was sometimes questioned" (21) in the early modern period. This description of early modern economy as

---

[11] The act ends with Master Gallipot admonishing his wife and forgiving Laxton, which Howard describes as a final male bonding, whereas the citizen wives are "shunted aside" ("Sex" 178).

[12] In the early modern period the term used to refer to this notion would have been self-love rather than self-interest. Pierre Force's study *Self-Interest before Adam Smith* traces the "philosophical and literary tradition" of the concept back to Epicurean and Augustinian writings as well as to Virgil and explains that the term "*self-love*" is "the translation of a technical term used by Renaissance humanists, *philautia*" (2).

driven by self-interest has been rejected in more recent studies by Muldrew. He argues that "the language of utilitarian motivation" which "arose after [Adam] Smith to interpret marketing has in time come to incorporate in itself the notion that the type of marketing it defined grew up in Europe from the sixteenth to the seventeenth centuries" ("Interpreting" 168). Instead, Muldrew's findings suggest that the early modern economy continued to be characterised by moral notions of "trust [and] obligation" ("Interpreting" 163). However, Muldrew admits that the "expansion of market transactions certainly put strains on trust" ("Interpreting" 169), as evidenced by "the huge number of court cases concerning failed credit relations" ("Interpreting" 172). He concludes that

> Structural change leading to a more utilitarian marketing culture, where self-interest could have come to be seen as a more reasonably coherent and believable explanation of behaviour than that provided by the language of trust, must have been slow and piecemeal[.] ("Interpreting" 180)

Nonetheless, the emphasis on trust and trustworthiness in the early modern period betrays an awareness of the danger which self-interest presents for an economy based on pervasive local, national and international credit and debt networks. In such an economy, individual households simultaneously act as both creditors and debtors ("Interpreting" 178). Indeed, early modern households were, on the one hand, competing with each other for a share in the market and, on the other, had to trust in each other's credit for their own solvency. Therefore, as Muldrew observes, "Many began to worry that they might end up paying for the purchase of luxury goods or the good living of their socially ambitious neighbours, if the latter overestimated the profits of their business or labour and were eventually unable to meet their obligation" (*Economy* 4). As a consequence, although profit in itself was not regarded as condemnable if it was the result of thrift and labour (*Economy* 4, 124), "Almost all contemporary references to self-interest . . . were negative in character before the end of the eighteenth century" and "self-love was equated with prodigality and poor housekeeping" (*Economy* 126) – a view which the play seems to share.

Considering this historical economic context of ubiquitous lending and borrowing, the figure of Moll in the play is curiously independent with respect to money. She uses money, but in opposition to the "common belief" stipulated by Grav, "that money had become *the* controlling influence over Renaissance societal values" (1), Moll's character and actions cannot be circumscribed by money. She seems to have money without getting or earning it – witness the ten angels with which she matches Laxton's bribe. Yet, she does not seem to need money to shape events, relying instead on her accomplishments, her superior knowledge of society and her intimate relations to people of all classes. Indeed, linking the main marriage plot with the subplot of the shopkeepers, Moll is a socially exceptional character, who converses familiarly with representatives of all social classes from criminals to noblemen. This characteristic is also underlined by Craig Rustici, who stresses "her ability to evade boundaries and to mediate between disparate communities" (171).[13] As a result, she is not only able to defeat Laxton, but can also disarm vagabonds and pickpockets and command thieves to return stolen money to a friend of hers. Sir Alexander, Laxton and Mistress Gallipot employ money to secure services but ultimately fail and lose their self-interested investments. None of them sees their money again and none of them gets what they try to buy. Moll's relations to others, by contrast, are based on exchanges of favours rather than money. Moll describes the friend whose money is to be returned as "a knight to whom I'm bound for many favours" (V.i.288).[14] She considers saving Jack Dapper from arrest as "one good work today" (III.iii.220) and offers to do the same for other "gentlemen" (III.iii.221). Moreover, she presents her sharing of knowledge about the criminal underworld as a friendly favour (V.i.322-5). Hence, when Moll twice points out her part in bringing about the happy ending, saying, "thank me for't, I'd a forefinger in't (V.ii.168-9) and "Father and son, I ha' done you simple service here" (V.ii.206),[15] she is not asking for money, I would argue. She rather reminds Sir Alexander and Sebastian of their moral obligation towards her, asking them to acknowledge her generosity.[16]

---

[13] See also Coppélia Kahn's introduction to her edition of *The Roaring Girl* in *Thomas Middleton: The Collected Works* (721).

[14] Korda points out that Moll here acts like a so-called "thief-taker," that is, someone with connections to criminals who helps victims of theft recover their belongings in return for a fee (77-78). Korda thus reads this incident as a gesture towards the real material circumstances of the historical Mary Frith (77-79) and as "valuable publicity" for her business ventures (83). Korda does not, however, comment on the circumstance that Moll in the play does not charge any fee for her service.

[15] Marjorie Garber draws attention to the sexual innuendo of "I'd a forefinger in't" given "*The Roaring Girl*'s omnipresent references to castration, emasculation, penises and testicles worn (like clothing . . .) by women rather than men" (225).

[16] Jacobs offers an alternative interpretation of Moll's line "Father and son, I ha' done you simple service here" (V.ii.206), arguing that she thus "summarizes her role as one of 'service' to the existing order" and that the following lines constitute Sebastian and Sir

The notion that "one good turn deserves another" – as opposed to the self-interest of Laxton, Sir Alexander, Mistress Gallipot and also the father of Jack Dapper – is emphasised further on the level of the citizen plot: Master Openwork probes the friendship of the gallant Goshawk and theatrically unveils the "bad turn" with which Goshawk requites Openwork's generosity:

> MASTER OPENWORK
> I'll tell you, Master Goshawk, – Ay, in your eye
> I have seen wanton fire, and then to try
> The soundness of my judgment, I told you
> I kept a whore, made you believe 'twas true,
> Only to feel how your pulse beat, but find
> The world can hardly yield a perfect friend.
> Come, come, a trick of youth, and 'tis forgiven.
> This rub put by, our love shall run more even. (IV.ii.211-218)

Master Openwork's emphasis that "nothing is perfect born" (IV.ii.207) presents truly disinterested friendship as an ideal that one should try to live up to rather than as a reality. If Mistress Gallipot functions as a foil for Moll, Master Openwork can be seen as Moll's double on the level of the citizen plot. The play sets up the resemblance between Moll and Master Openwork in the first scene of act two – that is, the only scene where both characters are on stage – when they go off together for a drink after Moll has warned Openwork against Goshawk (II.i.367-368).[17] Like Moll, whom Aaron Kitch describes as an "examiner of character" (413), Openwork tests those who profess loyalty to him, combining perspicacity with generosity, and he forces Goshawk to acknowledge his moral obligation by inviting him back into the house (IV.ii.221).

As has been shown, Moll (and through her the play, one might argue) does not condone money transactions that further one's own interests to somebody else's disadvantage, and she actively prevents or undoes criminal money transactions, that is, swindling or stealing. In contrast, there are two further types of financial transactions in the play that she sanctions, namely the remuneration of artistic performance and the payment of material goods. That Moll considers artistic performance or

---

Alexander's "recognition of that role" (81). For my own reading of Sebastian's reaction to Moll's line, see below.

[17] I am not convinced by Lloyd Edward Kermode's suggestion that Openwork's quibble on the word "bastards" in "We'll have a pint of the same wine, i'faith, Moll" (II.i.368) implies a secret adulterous relationship with Moll (429-430).

entertainment as worthy of payment is not surprising given the context of the theatre. In front of a paying theatre audience it would be rather counterintuitive if Moll did not endorse the remuneration of performance. What is more intriguing is that after Moll's appearance as a disguised male musician in the third act, the second artistic performance is a bout of canting and a canting song in the fifth act, for which the two rogues Trapdoor and Tearcat receive two shillings sixpence from Lord Noland. Apart from pointing to the enduring popularity of cant, this implies that even rogues – or maybe people of an ambiguous social status like players – deserve to be paid for a pleasing performance. Moreover, although Moll in this instance does not interrupt the circulation of money – unlike earlier in the scene when she prevents Sir Beauteous from giving money to the rogues in soldiers' disguise – she again controls the flow of money. Lord Noland does not pay Trapdoor and Tearcat directly, but gives the money to Moll to distribute, thus putting her into the position of a judge who is to decide on the value of the performance. Moll, in this instance, could even be seen as an idealised "middleman," who does not profit from the financial transaction that she oversees – as opposed to the common perception of middlemen, who, though necessary to the expanding early modern trading networks, "were denounced from the pulpit and widely blamed for rising prices" (Grav 10).

As for the payment of material goods, we never actually see Moll buy anything, but there are several lines in the play implying that she spends money on clothes and pays her tailor. For example, when she feigns taking on the scoundrel Trapdoor as her servant, she tells him, "Come follow me to St Thomas Apostle's,/I'll put a livery cloak upon your back/The first thing I do" (III.i.197-99). When she meets Laxton, she observes "if [gallants] would keep their days as well with their mercers as their hours with their harlots, no bankrupt would give seven score pound for a sergeant's place" (III.i.36-39). To enable a meeting between the two young lovers, Moll has her tailor "fit" Mary Fitz-Allard with men's clothes (IV.i.69), and the short scene between Moll and her tailor (II.ii.72-99) indicates that Moll is a good customer, whom the tailor is eager to retain.[18] With this accumulating evidence of Moll's buying and paying habits as a customer, her indignation when Mistress Openwork tells her to leave the shop becomes in retrospect even more comprehen-

---

[18] Critics' references to this scene generally focus on its bawdy innuendos and the sexualisation of Moll's body (see especially Forman 1544-1546). However, even if the tailor is interpreted as making bawdy jokes at Moll's expense, it is clear that Moll is a regular customer of his, whose wishes he seeks to satisfy.

sible. To Mistress Openwork's "Get you from my shop" (II.i.217), Moll objects, "I come to buy" (II.i.218), and becomes properly enraged at Mistress Openwork's reply, "I'll sell thee nothing, I warn ye my house and shop" (II.i.219). Mistress Openwork then not only offends Moll by treating her as an indecent person or even a prostitute, but she also rejects Moll's vision of honest business relations, valuing the feigned creditability of the gallant Goshawk more highly than Moll's hard currency.

Middleton and Dekker's play has been interpreted from various theoretical perspectives, including gender and new economic criticism,[19] and depending on the critic, the character of Moll acquires a different significance. In gender criticism, some of the recurrent questions concern Moll's attitude towards dominant views of marriage and women's social position and rights. Although scholars generally point out Moll's subversive potential in this respect, they disagree over the extent to which Moll's character can be read as a successful critique of early modern society and over Moll's own final status within this society. Thus, whereas Jean Howard interprets Moll as a character that "def[ies] expectations about woman's nature and . . . protest[s] the injustices caused by the sex-gender system" ("Cross-dressing" 40) and Viviana Comensoli sees Moll as "provid[ing] a compelling alternative to the ideal marriage" (251),[20] Baston argues that Moll ultimately turns into something of a hired performer, "adopt[ing] this role for the entertainment of the assembled gentry, and at the expense of her own dignity" (331). Moreover, Baston sees Moll as "gradually contained and incorporated into the prevailing social apparatus of the play" (320). Mary Beth Rose, by contrast, affirms that "[t]he question of her social identity . . . remains unresolved at the end . . . because she has helped to create a society from which she is both excluded and excludes herself" (91).[21] Susan E. Krantz, finally, reads this self-exclusion positively, proposing that the play "privileg[es] the intellectual reading of Moll as symbolic hermaphroditic ideal" (15), which is self-sufficient and transcends sexual binaries (15-16).

New economic readings of the play have also interpreted the figure of Moll in different ways. Rather than analysing the challenge Moll poses for the "sex-gender system," these readings treat Moll as a sym-

---

[19] For a short introduction to new economic criticism and early modern economy, see Grav (1-27).

[20] For an alternative interpretation of Mary Fitz-Allard and Moll as the "acceptable and less acceptable" sides of "the figure of the 'roaring girl'" (229), see Garber.

[21] This position is challenged in turn by Comensoli (250-251).

bolic figure who reflects contemporary economic anxieties. For Valerie Forman, Moll serves "both as a reminder of the loss of legible and reliable material guarantees and as a compensatory fiction for it" (1540), i.e. her function is to "compensate for the increasingly abstract and 'dematerialized' social relations of the play's credit and commodity-driven economy" (1532). According to Kitch, "Moll is the ultimate source of credit" (413) in a society where creditability is hard to ascertain and requires one to judge the character of others to establish their trustworthiness (407).[22] For Harris, finally, the play and its heroine negotiate contemporary economic concerns over the conflict between the necessity and the dangers of (excessive) consumption (181-2, 184). He thereby sees Moll as an ideal consumer who is both "trendsetting" and able to "control herself and her desires" (182).

Moll is certainly an ambivalent figure from a feminist perspective with her simultaneous challenge and acceptance of marriage and the social hierarchies between men and women this implies. I do not agree with Baston, however, that the play "thoroughly stages Moll's recuperation" (320) and that "Moll's role as translator in act V shows her capitulation to the dominant practices of class and gender" (331). Instead, I see some of these actions, like Moll's support of the young couple, her canting performance or her final appearance in female dress, which Baston interprets as indicating Moll's submission (328, 331-2), as linked to her idealistic character in an economic and social sense. Indeed, Moll's criticism of female oppression may not offer a vision of a society that transcends patriarchal order, but her numerous interventions in the play sketch a code of conduct that points towards an ideal society where, presumably, the relations between men and women would be based on mutual favours. While I would question the weight that Howard accords to Moll's feminist agenda, I generally agree with her claim that Moll's description of an ideal world in which she would consider marrying (V.ii.217-24) "is clear in its utopian aspirations, clear in making the ending of women's oppression a central part of a more encompassing utopian vision of social reform" ("Cross-dressing" 41).

This "utopian vision" of reform also extends to economic concerns. *The Roaring Girl* clearly "registers and addresses economic pressures" (1532), as Forman puts it. Thus, Kitch's argument that the play dramatises the unreliability of credit and the anxieties related to this economic

---

[22] See also Muldrew's remark that "The linguistic distinction between economic and social credit had not yet arisen, and to be a creditor in an economic sense still had a strong ethical meaning" ("Interpreting" 177).

development (407) appears on the whole convincing. What is striking, however, and not sufficiently developed in Kitch's analysis is that, considering her behaviour, Moll as a character seems to operate outside an economy of credit – both in a literal and a figurative sense. Not only does Moll avoid financial indebtedness and seem unconcerned by scarcity of coin, she is and acts according to her principles regardless of the "credit" she is accorded by other characters or the outfit that she wears. In other words, her actions repeatedly do not conform to the various (and often negative) expectations of her voiced in the play and provoked for the most part by her transgressive clothing. This failure to conform to expectations is epitomised, one might say, by the incongruity between the play's subtitle *Moll Cutpurse* and the consistently honourable behaviour of Moll in the play. Moll therefore appears as an independent agent and a genuine entity beyond pre-set opinions or her changing exterior,[23] meaning that "Sebastian can bank on her character" (413), as Kitch formulates it. This impression of genuineness is further reinforced by the metaleptic gestures towards the historical Mary Frith in the play's prologue and epilogue, as both Forman (1541) and Kitch (414) have noted. I am not suggesting that Moll's character should be described as "real" (1541) or "lifelike" (1540) – a critical "trend," which Forman traces back to T.S. Eliot (1541).[24] Rather, I agree with Kitch's characterisation of Moll's authenticity in terms of "credibility," meaning that she represents an "alternative to the false world of credit relationships" (413).[25] In this sense, Moll's genuineness is not so much "lifelike"

---

[23] See also Kitch's claim that Moll's "authenticity derives from her transgression against cultural norms, especially those of clothing" (414). Moll's occasional and sometimes partial cross-dressing has been interpreted in a variety of ways. Patrick Cheney, for instance, proposes a symbolic reading of Moll as a hermaphrodite symbolising married love and the union of two souls (124, 125). Critics like Krantz, Garber, Howard and Baston discuss cross-dressing as challenging gender prerogatives or categories as such. Rustici suggests a medical reading of cross-dressing as the outward manifestation of Moll's mixed male and female nature induced by smoking according to Galenic theory (171-179), and Korda provides a material analysis with Moll's changing clothes pointing to women's investment in the second-hand clothes trade (84-85).

[24] See for instance Comensoli, who comments on "Moll's fullness and complexity" (259) – as opposed to Howard, who thinks that the "competing ideological strands" that constitute Moll's character "prevent her from being read as an entirely unified subjectivity" ("Sex" 179).

[25] In contrast to Kitch, Forman reads Moll as simultaneously representing the wish for and the illusory nature of "material guarantees" (1540) and hence authenticity. However, focusing primarily on the projection of Sir Alexander's "anxious fantasies" (1544) on Moll, Forman disregards Moll's own economic interactions and the criticism of certain financial transactions expressed through her interventions in the circulation of money.

as nostalgic idealisation, harking back to the utopian economic order in works like Thomas Deloney's *Jack of Newbury* (cf. Grav 14). Hence, in accordance with Forman's suggestion that Moll "embodies . . . cultural fantasies" (1541), I would contend that Moll's character represents a more straightforward society and economy where interpersonal relations are forged by mutual favours that are independent of financial transactions and where material goods are paid for without fail – as opposed to the complex credit and debt relations that shaped early modern society in England.[26]

With regard to Moll's final status, the question is therefore not so much whether she appears in a dress in the closing scene or whether her last rejection of marriage is formulaic, as Baston thinks (331-2),[27] but rather whether she is assimilated into a society where, as Sebastian at some point formulates it, "Plain dealing . . . takes no effect" (III.i.194). This, I would argue, is ultimately left open by the play and can be staged either way, depending on how the character of Moll reacts to Sir Alexander's final speech.[28] Already Sebastian's reply to Moll's reminder, "Father and son, I ha' done you simple service here" (V.ii.206), is problematic because by saying, "For which thou shalt not part, Moll, unrequited" (V.ii.207), Sebastian seems to imply that Moll's "simple," that is, disinterested, intervention on his behalf can be recompensed financially. Put differently, he recognises his obligation towards Moll but does not seem inclined to remain bound to her in a system based on exchanging favours. More blatantly, Sir Alexander tries to make up for his trickery with the hollow-hearted angels by paying Moll off, stating, "So far I'm sorry, I'll thrice double 'em/To make thy wrongs amends" (V.ii.256-

---

[26] In his analysis of Middleton's contribution to *Timon of Athens*, John Jowett identifies a similar combination of satiric criticism and sentimentalism with regard to the representation of social relationships and credit- and debt-based economy in the passages presumably authored by Middleton (220-221). This might suggest that Middleton rather than Dekker was ultimately responsible for the ideological perspective of *The Roaring Girl*. This cannot be further supported on the basis of textual indications, however, since, as Mulholland details in his introduction to the play, "Few scenes point conclusively to either dramatist as the main writer" (11) and "Each writer may . . . have revised the other's work, and that perhaps more than once" (12).

[27] In their 2014 production of the play, the RSC offered a controversial reading of Moll's final refusal of marriage by "suggesting that she resists marriage because she's a lesbian," as Rachel Ellen Clark remarks in her performance review.

[28] See also Kitch's argument that Middleton "leaves the audience to make final moral and epistemological judgments" with regard to "credibility of character" (420).

7).²⁹ Since this is the final speech before the epilogue and there are no stage directions, the text gives no clue as to how Moll reacts to this offer and whether Sir Alexander literally tries to give her money at this instant. Acceptance of such a recompense on Moll's part would, it seems to me, severely compromise her financial independence and signal the corruption of her idealistic figure and the utopian society she stands for. A gesture of refusal on the other hand,³⁰ confirms Moll's exceptional status as a generous figure untainted by the lure of self-interest and independent of credit and debt relations – a figure who can command the circulation of money rather than being subject to it.

Acknowledgements
I would like to thank the anonymous readers, Martin Leer and especially Pascal Romann for their helpful feedback on this essay.

---

²⁹ Forman likewise sees the ending of the play as "Sir Alexander's attempt to reintegrate Moll . . . by making her a subject of his forgiveness, an act that would nonetheless keep his position of authority relatively intact" (1551). Forman notes that "Moll undermines his attempt to make her the subject of his authority" (1551), but she does not comment on Sir Alexander's final offer of money.

³⁰ In the 1983 RSC production, Moll is presented as "incorruptible" (288), as Chi-fang Sophia Li notes, and "rejects all monetary temptations as well as rewards" (private communication with Chi-fang Sophia Li of 25 May 2015). The 2014 RSC production of *The Roaring Girl* also seems to have gone in this direction since Peter Buckroyd writes in his review that "Moll spits at the departing Sir Alexander" – an action that he found slightly discordant in the context of the production.

References

Baston, Jane. "Rehabilitating Moll's Subversion in *The Roaring Girl*." *Studies in English Literature, 1500-1900* 37.2 (Spring 1997): 317-335.
Buckroyd, Peter. "*The Roaring Girl*." RSC Review. *Moss Cottage*. 23 April 2014. Web. Accessed 18 May 2015. http://www.mosscottage.org/the-roaring-girl.
Cheney, Patrick. "Moll Cutpurse as Hermaphrodite in Dekker and Middleton's *The Roaring Girl*." *Renaissance and Reformation / Renaissance et Réforme* 7.2 (Spring 1983): 120-134.
Clark, Rachel Ellen. "Victorian Drag King: Jo Davies's *The Roaring Girl*." *Early Modern Studies Journal* 6 (2014). Web. Accessed 18 May 2015. http://www.earlymodernstudiesjournal.org/book_reviews/performance-review-moll-cutpurse-victorian-drag-king-jo-daviess-roaring-gir/.
Clarkson, Leslie A. *The Pre-Industrial Economy in England 1500-1750*. London: B. T. Batsford Ltd., 1971.
Comensoli, Viviana. "Play-Making, Domestic Conduct, and the Multiple Plot in *The Roaring Girl*." *Studies in English Literature, 1500-1900* 27.2 (Spring 1987): 249-266.
Dawson, Anthony B. "Hic and Haec: Representations of Moll Frith." *Studies in English Literature, 1500-1900* 33.2 (Spring 1993): 385-404.
Force, Pierre. *Self-Interest before Adam Smith*. Cambridge: Cambridge University Press, 2003.
Forman, Valerie. "Marked Angels: Counterfeits, Commodities, and *The Roaring Girl*." *Renaissance Quarterly* 54.4 (Winter 2001): 1531-1560.
Garber, Marjorie. "The Logic of the Transvestite: *The Roaring Girl* (1608)." *Staging the Renaissance: Essays on Elizabethan and Jacobean Drama*. Ed. David Scott Kastan and Peter Stallybrass. New York: Routledge, 1991. 221-234.
Grav, Peter F. *Shakespeare and the Economic Imperative: 'What's aught but as 'tis valued?'*. New York: Routledge, 2008.
Harris, Jonathan Gil. *Sick Economies: Drama, Mercantilism, and Disease in Shakespeare's England*. Philadelphia: University of Pennsylvania Press, 2004.
Howard, Jean E. "Cross-dressing, the Theatre, and Gender Struggle in Early Modern England." *Crossing the Stage: Controversies on Cross-Dressing*. Ed. Lesley Ferris. London: Routledge, 1993. 20-47.
———. "Sex and Social Conflict: The Erotics of *The Roaring Girl*." *Erotic Politics: Desire on the Renaissance Stage*. Ed. Susan Zimmermann. London: Routledge, 1992. 170-190.

Jacobs, Deborah. "Critical Imperialism and Renaissance Drama: The Case of *The Roaring Girl*." *Feminism, Bakhtin, and the Dialogic*. Ed. Dale M. Bauer and Susan Jaret McKinstry. Albany: State University of New York Press, 1991. 73-84.

Jowett, John. "Middleton and Debt in *Timon of Athens*." *Money and the Age of Shakespeare: Essays in New Economic Criticism*. Ed. Linda Woodbridge. New York: Palgrave Macmillan, 2003. 219-235.

Kermode, Lloyd Edward. "Destination Doomsday: Desires for Change and Changeable Desires in *The Roaring Girl*." *English Literary Renaissance* 27 (1997): 421-442.

Kitch, Aaron. "The Character of Credit and the Problem of Belief in Middleton's City Comedies." *Studies in English Literature, 1500-1900* 47.2 (Spring 2007): 403-426.

Korda, Natasha. "The Case of Moll Frith: Women's Work and the 'All-Male Stage'." *Women Players in England, 1500-1660: Beyond the All-Male Stage*. Aldershot: Ashgate, 2005. 71-87.

Krantz, Susan E. "The Sexual Identities of Moll Cutpurse in Dekker and Middleton's *The Roaring Girl* and in London." *Renaissance and Reformation / Renaissance et Réforme* 19.1 (1995): 5-20.

Li, Chi-Fang Sophia. "*The Roaring Girl* in Retrospect: the RSC Production of 1983." *New Theatre Quarterly* 30.3 (2014): 274-297.

Middleton, Thomas and Thomas Dekker. *The Roaring Girl*. Ed. Coppélia Kahn. *Thomas Middleton: The Collected Works*. Eds. Gary Taylor and John Lavagnino. Oxford: Clarendon Press, 2007. 721-778.

———. *The Roaring Girl*. New Mermaids. Ed. Elizabeth Cook. 2nd ed. London: Methuen Drama, 1997.

———. *The Roaring Girl*. Ed. Paul A. Mulholland. Revels Plays. Manchester: Manchester University Press, 1987.

Muldrew, Craig. *The Economy of Obligation: The Culture of Credit and Social Relations in Early Modern England*. Basingstoke: Macmillan, 1998.

———. "Interpreting the Market: The Ethics of Credit and Community Relations in Early Modern England." *Social History* 18.2 (May 1993): 163-183.

Orgel, Stephen. "The Subtexts of *The Roaring Girl*." *Erotic Politics: Desire on the Renaissance Stage*. Ed. Susan Zimmermann. London: Routledge, 1992. 12-26.

Rose, Mary Beth. *The Expense of Spirit: Love and Sexuality in English Renaissance Drama*. Ithaca: Cornell University Press, 1991.

Waswo, Richard. "Crises of Credit: Monetary and Erotic Economies in the Jacobean Theatre." *Plotting Early Modern London: New Essays on Jacobean City Comedy*. Ed. Dieter Mehl, Angela Stock and Anne-Julia Zwierlein. Aldershot: Ashgate, 2004. 55-73.

Zurcher, Amelia A. *Seventeenth-Century English Romance*. New York: Palgrave Macmillan, 2007.

"How to Live Well on Nothing a Year": Money, Credit and Debt in William Makepeace Thackeray's *Vanity Fair*

Barbara Straumann

The following contribution explores the debt and credit economy developed in William Makepeace Thackeray's *Vanity Fair* (1848). Thackeray's novel offers a satirical panorama of a society obsessed with wealth and status. Seeing through the vanities of others, the protagonist Rebecca Sharp appropriates and subversively performs their social and economic system. It is thanks to her smart social performance that she gains both social and financial credit – without ever repaying her debts. The credulousness of her creditors can be read as an effect of what Jochen Hörisch ("Geld") calls the "autopoiesis" of money, that is the idea that money is covered by the belief in money. Rebecca can be seen to embody this monetary autopoiesis since she succeeds in making her creditors (falsely) believe that she actually possesses sufficient assets to secure her debts. Thackeray's text uses the figure of the equally sharp and dazzling social climber in order to expose a snobbish society that is duped by her self-fashioning because of its very own obsession with money and status and is thus made to pay for its vanities. Rebecca, on the other hand, not only remains unrepentant but – unusual for a female literary character of the period – gets away unpunished.

William Makepeace Thackeray's novel *Vanity Fair* is named after John Bunyan's Vanity Fair in *The Pilgrim's Progress*, where nearly everything is offered for sale. This includes:

> [. . .] Houses, Lands, Trades, Places, Honours, Preferments, Titles, Countreys, Kingdoms, Lusts, Pleasures, and Delights of all sorts, as Whores, Bauds, Wives, Husbands, Children, Masters, Servants, Lives, Blood, Bodies, Souls, Silver, Gold, Pearls, Precious Stones, and what not. (Bunyan 73)

Thackeray takes his cue from Bunyan's representation of Vanity Fair so as to present a satirical panorama of a society driven by social and financial ambitions. Thackeray's best-known novel, written at a time when modern capitalism and consumer society were already firmly established, depicts a world full of vices and follies, sins and evils. However, in contrast to Bunyan's Puritan allegory, which juxtaposes vices with virtues so as to show the proper way to spiritual salvation, Thackeray's Victorian satire does not replace the corrupt world of Vanity Fair with a better system. In Bunyan's text, Vanity Fair is just a site of potential temptation in the town of Vanity, but in the world of Thackeray's novel, Vanity Fair is everywhere; there are no figures and no areas of social life that are not affected by its logic. Human relationships are determined by economic motives and money literally forms the only value. Characters rate one another based on their social rank and alleged spending power alone. As a result, the narrator points out, "[. . .] Vanity Fair is a very vain, wicked, foolish place, full of all sorts of humbugs and falsenesses and pretensions" (89). Indeed, there is a lot of vain and empty show displayed by the characters in their competition for wealth and status. Thackeray's satire is clearly underpinned by his moral imagination; the text confronts readers with various moral perspectives and invites them to judge the characters. Yet, in contrast to Bunyan's allegory, in which virtuous conduct is represented by means of allegorical personifications, Thackeray's novel never spells out the moral norms against which the society of Vanity Fair and its various members are to be measured. Instead the text offers detailed descriptions of the behaviour of individual characters making up the social world of Vanity Fair, which more often than not proves to be vain and foolish in its fixation on materialistic values.

With his portrayal of a highly acquisitive world, Thackeray offers a comment on the effects that the prevalence of money has on Victorian society.[1] Money is revealed to be an indifferent medium: In order to create equivalences between different things, goods and services, which facilitates their exchange, money allows people to treat all objects in the same way and reduce them to the exchange value they have as commodities.[2] Predating the first volume of Karl Marx's *Capital* (1867) by

---

[1] *Vanity Fair* is set in the Regency era but written and published in the late 1840s, the novel can be seen to reflect on the culture of the mid-Victorian period.

[2] On the indifference and abstraction of money, see the following passage by Jochen Hörisch:

two decades, the fictional world of Vanity Fair illustrates how social relationships between persons come to resemble the relationship between things. The cold abstraction that characterizes the exchange value of commodities also shapes social interactions, which are stripped of any emotional and sentimental value. "Ours is a ready-money society" (229), one character observes explaining to his bride-to-be why his sisters do not show any love towards her as a person of lesser means.

In the 1830s and the so-called Hungry Forties, Great Britain was faced with economic and social difficulties. The mid-Victorian period, however, was perceived by many contemporaries as an era of great prosperity and economic expansion. Britain's industrialization and the concomitant rise of modern capitalism meant that social influence began to shift from traditional structures of wealth based on landownership to new forms of accumulation based on "the liquidities of manufacturing, commerce, speculation, and credit" (Herbert 188). Christopher Herbert emphasizes that the crux of this and related socio-economic developments in Victorian Britain was not so much "the ascendancy of newly monied classes" but "the emergence of a new imaginary" and "new psychological structures" (188). "Observers at the time constantly noted [. . .] what seemed to them to be an all-consuming idolatry of money among their contemporaries [. . .]" (188). As one of several examples, Herbert quotes Friedrich Engels, who in 1845 observes that having become "the slaves of the money they worship," the middle classes in England

> really believe that all human beings [. . .] and indeed all living things and inanimate objects have a real existence only if they make money or help to make it. Their sole happiness is derived from gaining a quick profit. They feel pain only if they suffer a financial loss. (Engels, quoted in Herbert 188)

Money-making is the all-important goal in the society described by Engels; everything else only counts if it can be made to serve this purpose. Engel's comment on the English middle classes would equally fit the characters of *Vanity Fair*. Driven by their desire for money and so-

---

If we buy a commodity with money or sell commodities (including our labour) for money, we do something remarkably abstract: we produce equivalences between things, goods, values and services which are plainly not identical and not even compatible but which are put on a level and equated by virtue of the exchange mediated by money. The translation of "equivalence" back into German throws the problems at stake into sharp relief: equivalence means cold indifference. ("Geld" 111; my translation)

cial status, they not only represent exaggerated versions of the individual self-interest advocated by Adam Smith as part of his *laissez-faire* theory, but they also embody the money-worship described by Engels. A few years before Thackeray published his novel, Thomas Carlyle famously attacked the dominant role of the cash nexus and the materialist spirit of the age in his book *Past and Present* (1843). In the chapter "Gospel of Mammonism," for example, he argues, "We have profoundly forgotten everywhere that *Cash-payment* is not the sole relation of human beings; we think, nothing doubting, that *it* absolves and liquidates all engagements of man" (152). Almost two decades later, John Ruskin was to offer a similar critique of Victorian notions and beliefs in his four articles that appeared in the *Cornhill Magazine*, the very journal which was edited by Thackeray. These articles, which were harshly criticized and which Ruskin went on to publish in his book *Unto This Last* (1862), challenge political economy, notably its doctrine of *laissez-faire* and its argument that economic individuals are motivated by material gain alone. Political economy, according to Ruskin, disregards human affections and instead conceives of the individual as "a covetous machine" (167).

The aspects that Engels, Carlyle and Ruskin criticize in Victorian culture – the pervasiveness of money-worship and individual self-interest, the commodification of people and their relationships – are at the very centre of Thackeray's *Vanity Fair*. Like these thinkers, Thackeray foregrounds the capacity of money to flatten out different aspects of human life through its cold abstraction. Yet, adopting the genre of the novel instead of the critical essay, *Vanity Fair* exposes the materialism of the age through its satirical portrait of a vain fictional world. In contrast to Carlyle and Ruskin, who develop heroic and noble counter-models, Thackeray's subtitle "A Novel without a Hero" underlines that his characters are without exception all subject to the materialistic obsession of Vanity Fair.[3]

---

[3] See Ruskin's call for "a kind of commerce that is not exclusively selfish" and for merchants who act according to a (paternalistic) code of honour (177, 178-179). Similarly Carlyle envisions "Leaders of Industry" who are "virtually the Captains of the World" (278). Once Mammon ceases to be the deity of Victorian society, a more benign way of doing business will become effective:

> Competition, at railway-speed, in all branches of commerce and work will then abate: [. . .] Bubble-periods with their panics and commercial crises will again become infrequent; steady modest industry will take the place of gambling speculation. To be a noble Master, among noble Workers, will again be the first ambition with some few; to be a rich Master only the second. [. . .] By degrees, we shall again have a Society with something of Heroism in it [. . .]. (277).

A crucial role in Thackeray's social satire is played by the figure of Rebecca Sharp. Rebecca represents no doubt the shrewdest and most ruthless character in the world of *Vanity Fair*. Thackeray's protagonist is not only an astute analyzer of the social economy surrounding her but also its most masterful manipulator. In what follows, I will explore the significance of money including credit and debt in Thackeray's *Vanity Fair* by focusing on Rebecca Sharp. As suggested by her name, the sharp Rebecca sees through the vanities of her social surroundings. Likewise she also both appropriates and subverts the social and economic system of Vanity Fair by means of her smart self-fashioning. My discussion of Thackeray's novel is divided into three parts. I will begin by exploring Rebecca's social performance in the credit economy of *Vanity Fair*. As we shall see, it is her self-fashioning that compels other characters to give credit to her – and that also allows her to get away without ever repaying her debts. In the second part, I will offer a theoretical reflection on money, notably the notion that money represents value because people believe in it. This idea allows us to draw a parallel between the autopoietic dimension of money and the self-fashioning of Rebecca. The third and last part, finally, will be devoted to the ways in which Thackeray deploys the roguish character of Rebecca in his social satire of self-interested greed.

What renders Rebecca Sharp such a radical character is her self-fashioning that allows her to move up the social ladder of the English class system. At the beginning of the text, the daughter of a French "opera-girl" (17) and a debt-ridden artist starts out as a destitute orphan. Yet rather than revealing her humble background, she presents people with a self-fabricated family history of noble descent. A relative of her employer, the Baronet Sir Pitt Crawley, finds several of her stories in one of the dictionaries in his library. Ironically, it is the very source that Rebecca must have consulted and used for her narrative self-fictionalization that "strengthened his belief in their truth, and in the high breeding of Rebecca" (103). Gaining the trust of the Crawley family forms an important element of Rebecca's calculated strategy. As the narrator mentions, "it became naturally Rebecca's duty to make herself, as she said, agreeable to her benefactors, and to gain their confidence to the utmost of her power" (100). According to his ironic understatement, "there entered some degree of selfishness into her calculations" (100). But in actual fact, it is for purely selfish reasons, namely her wish for social advancement, that she ingratiates herself with the family. Rebecca is initially hired as a governess for the children, but winning Sir Pitt Crawley's confidence, she becomes his secretary and "almost mistress of the house" (103). With her intelligence and brilliance, she also dazzles Miss Crawley, the baronet's snobbish half-sister, who tells Rebecca, "My dear, you are a perfect *trouvaille* [. . .] a little paragon – positively a little jewel [. . .] my equal in every respect [. . .]" (118-119). The considerable wealth of Miss Crawley is what everyone in the Crawley family is after, and Rebecca becomes her cherished companion thanks to her sparkling self-performance.[4]

Knowing that she has to go husband-hunting without the help of a mother, Rebecca secretly marries Rawdon, the son of Sir Pitt Crawley. When his family discovers the secret marriage, the not so noble Miss Sharp is no longer considered "a perfect *trouvaille*" and Rawdon finds himself disinherited by Miss Crawley, his rich aunt. Nevertheless, the couple do manage to sustain an extravagant lifestyle, because thanks to her irresistible charm and wit, Rebecca is always able to find creditors who are more than willing to extend credit to her. The text describes Rebecca's clever managing of her financial household affairs as follows:

> [. . .] there was no woman in Europe who could talk a creditor over as she could. Almost immediately after their marriage, her practice had begun, and her husband found the immense value of such a wife. They had credit in plenty, but they had bills also in abundance, and laboured under a scarcity of ready-money. Did these debt-difficulties affect Rawdon's good spirits? No. Everybody in Vanity Fair must have remarked how well those live who are comfortably and thoroughly in debt: how they deny themselves nothing; how jolly and easy they are in their minds. (249)

Rebecca's powers of persuasion mean that the couple have "credit in plenty."[5] They live a carefree life of ease precisely because they are "comfortably and thoroughly in debt."

Furthermore, Rebecca's charismatic sex appeal attracts the attention and admiration of Lord Steyne, who showers her with expensive gifts in exchange for sexual favours. Examining the novel's "linkages between

---

[4] For a reading of *Vanity Fair* that focuses on the performed identities of both Rebecca Sharp and Amelia Sedley, see Dobson.

[5] The text suggests that Rebecca has honed her persuasive skills from an early age. Because of her father's debts and the deprived circumstances of her childhood, she frequently had to enter into negotiations with creditors and debt-collectors. "[. . .] she had the precocity of poverty. Many a dun had she talked to, and turned away from her father's door; many a tradesman had she coaxed and wheedled into good humour, and into the granting of one meal more [. . .]" (18). Also see Lisa Jadwin, who reads *Vanity Fair* as an unorthodox *Künstlerroman* with Rebecca perfecting her techniques in order to conquer the social world of Vanity Fair (665).

women's adulterous sexuality and their extravagant economic expenditure," Margot Finn describes Rebecca's illicit romance both as "a pragmatic strategy [. . .] to obtain luxurious goods for her home" and as "a fundamental threat to domestic life" (49). Despite her adultery, Rebecca's association with Lord Steyne enhances her social standing and reputation in the eyes of others. Local tradesmen grant her extended credit precisely because of her affair with the aristocratic patron. Having previously been ostracized by the ladies of genteel society, her social connection with the Lord, ironically enough, gives her access to the most fashionable circles:

> After Becky's appearance at my Lord Steyne's private and select parties, the claims of that estimable woman as regards fashion were settled: and some of the very greatest and tallest doors in the metropolis were speedily opened to her [. . .]. (585)

As Lord Steyne's favourite, Rebecca thus gains access to London's high society and, at the very height of her social success, the once poor and penniless orphan is even admitted to the royal court.

What is crucial to Rebecca's spectacular ascent through society is her entirely calculated social performance. As an arch-performer, Thackeray's protagonist plays to the desires and fantasies of others; she knows when to appear "exceedingly modest and affable" (104), and when to appear witty, brilliant, and seductive. She exchanges and adapts her masks because she understands that in the world of Vanity Fair, you are what others perceive and believe you to be. The great significance of the perception and belief of others is particularly palpable in the credit system of Vanity Fair and the way in which Rebecca uses it to her own personal advantage. Because of her brilliant self-fashioning as a lady of ample means, Rebecca invariably finds herself at the centre of society's attention. Moreover, because people not only succumb to her charms but also believe in her seemingly eminent social position, creditors will willingly be persuaded to grant credit to her and her husband. This in turn fuels their luxurious lifestyle and hence their creditworthiness in the eyes of others.[6]

---

[6] In fact, Rebecca's credit economy functions according to "the parasitic relationship between character and credit" which Margot Finn describes in her study of personal debt and credit in the long nineteenth century. "An assumed identity sustained by the very commodities which it allowed consumers to purchase on credit," Finn argues, "character was constituted in significant part by tradesmen's continuous valuation and revaluation of their customers' status and social connections" (47).

The most detailed description of Rebecca's method of dazzling her creditors can be found in the two key chapters entitled "How to live well on Nothing a Year" and "The Subject continued" (418-443). After their excursion to the Battle of Waterloo, Rebecca and Rawdon live in Paris, where soon after their arrival, her wit and brilliance propel her into a leading position of the capital's society. Believing that she has financial means proportionate to her elevated social position, a great number of people allow her to use their goods and services on credit – only to find out after the couple's sudden departure that they have been cheated:

> It was not for some weeks after the Crawleys' departure that the landlord of the hotel which they had occupied during their residence at Paris, found out the losses which he had sustained: not until Madame Morabou, the milliner, made repeated visits with her little bill for articles supplied to Madame Crawley; not until Monsieur Didelot from Boule d'Or in the Palais Royal had asked half-a-dozen times whether *cette charmante* Miladi who had bought watches and bracelets was *de retour*. It is a fact that even the poor gardener's wife, who had nursed Madame's child, was never paid after the first six months for that supply of the milk of human kindness with which she had furnished the lusty and healthy little Rawdon. No, not even the nurse was paid – the Crawleys were in too great a hurry to remember their trifling debts to her. (425)

What this list of goods and services underlines is the cold abstraction of money in general and Rebecca's calculations in particular. By providing this catalogue, the text demonstrates how the individual items – the hotel accommodation, the clothes, the jewels and the breast milk – all appear on the same plane of monetary equivalence. Behind each of the allegedly "trifling debts", there is a human being. The fact that the debts are not paid simultaneously effaces and emphasizes the humanity of the cheated creditors. Rebecca has consumed the goods and engaged the services of a series of persons without paying a single one of them, banking both literally and figuratively on her social performance as a wealthy lady.

Back in London, Thackeray's protagonist continues to use her self-fashioning in order to keep up her lavish lifestyle. Again she promptly attains social prominence and finds herself recognized by illustrious people:

> Rebecca's wit, cleverness and flippancy made her speedily the vogue in London among a certain class. You saw demure chariots at her door, out of

which stepped very great people. You beheld her carriage in the Park, surrounded by dandies of note. (432)

Once again Rebecca and Rawdon use their social appearance for their own material gain. Because he adores the Crawley family as the source of his own prosperity, Raggles, the former family butler, lets a house on desirable Curzon Street in Mayfair to Rebecca and her husband. Raggles owns the property because he has carefully managed his finances all his life. However, together with numerous purveyors, tradesmen and servants, Raggles is taken in and never paid by the couple. While they continue to consume his goods and services on credit, he can no longer pay his taxes, the interest on his mortgage, his life insurance, his children's tuition fees, the groceries for his own family as well as the food and drink consumed by Rebecca and Rawdon. As a result, "the poor wretch was utterly ruined by the transaction, his children being flung on the streets, and himself driven into the Fleet Prison: yet," as the narrator adds in his satirical tone, "somebody must pay even for gentlemen who live on nothing a year [. . .]" (430). Raggles is never paid but made to pay for his belief and trust in Rebecca and her husband, his reckless tenants. He is even sent to debtors' prison, while the couple continue to lead a carefree life as there are plenty of other people willing to give them credit.

The word "credit" is derived from the Latin verb *credere*, "to believe, put trust in," and it refers to the belief in the good reputation of someone's character (see the *Oxford English Dictionary*). Indeed, in personal credit relationships, which were still very much present in the nineteenth century, any credit hinges on the creditor's trust or confidence in the debtor's character and, related to this, his or her intention and ability to pay him or her at some future time. Only because he believes in the creditworthiness of the debtor does the creditor allow money, goods or services to be used without immediate payment.[7] However, belief, confidence and trust are crucial not only in the case of credit but also in the case of money, which is also underpinned by a dimension of belief. Literary scholars such as Marc Shell and Jochen Hörisch have drawn attention to the close relationship between finance and fiction as well as between money and belief. As Hörisch points out, money is backed by the belief in money ("Geld" 111). In contrast to coins made out of precious metal, which suggest that the value they represent is identical with their

---

[7] On the personal dimension of many financial transactions in the Victorian period, see Finn and Hunt.

intrinsic (material) value, paper money and checks are mere promises to pay ("Geld" 110). The de-materialization of money (that is, the separation of intrinsic and extrinsic value) leads to a fictionalization of money. Money becomes a social and symbolic fiction – a sign system that is both arbitrary and conventional. While credit presupposes trust in the character of the individual person, money depends on a systemic belief.

It is at this point that we can invoke Hörisch's notion of the "autopoiesis" of money: Money produces and reproduces itself as a self-referential system and, at the same time, requires our belief in order to work. Unless we believe in it, money loses its validity. Hörisch formulates this autopoietic structure in the following way: "Money is backed by (the belief in) money – just as laws are 'backed' or not backed by laws, belief by belief, love by love, fiction by fiction" ("Geld" 111; my translation).[8] Returning to Thackeray, we can find illuminating analogies between money and fiction in his text. Here I do not just mean that like for a number of other Victorian novelists, an important function of Thackeray's writing was to literally write himself out of financial difficulties; it was because of his shortage of money caused by an Indian banking crisis on the one hand and his idleness and gambling on the other that Thackeray decided to embark on his writing career (see Kohl 575; Rosdeitcher 410).[9] However, on a more fundamental level, both money and art, as Marc Shell points out, form representational systems that use the same mechanisms in order to produce belief:

> Credit, or belief, involves the ground of aesthetic experience, and the same medium that confers belief in fiduciary money (bank notes) and in scriptural money (accounting records and money of account, created by the process of bookkeeping) also seems to confer it in art. (53-54)

Similar to money, fiction requires our suspension of disbelief. Thackeray frames his text with a preface entitled "Before the Curtain," in which the narrator introduces himself as "the Manager of the Performance" (5). Indeed, by describing the novel as a theatrical puppet show, he high-

---

[8] The German original reads as follows: "Geld ist durch (den Glauben an) Geld gedeckt – so wie Gesetze durch Gesetze, Glaube durch Glaube, Liebe durch Liebe und Poesie durch Poesie 'gedeckt' oder eben nicht gedeckt sind" ("Geld" 111). For a further development of Hörisch's exploration of belief in the economic domain, see his recent book *Man muss dran glauben*.

[9] Also note Andrew Miller, who emphasizes the economic basis of the novel and who argues that Thackeray is implicated in the economic system which he criticizes (1,042, 1,052).

lights its status as a piece of artifice that calls on readers to accept it as an aesthetic representation.[10]

However, turning to the actual narrative, we note an even more specific parallel between finance and fiction if we consider the analogy between the fictional and virtual aspects of money and Rebecca Sharp's self-fashioning. Similar to the monetary system, which depends on our collective belief, Rebecca depends on her creditors' belief in her creditworthiness. Because of her autopoiesis, Rebecca mirrors and even embodies the economic system of Vanity Fair. Her figure can be called autopoietic because she fashions herself as a quasi-fictional persona and also because her self-fashioning requires the belief of others. In fact, blinded by their ambition for wealth and status, which affects everyone living in the world of Vanity Fair, they trust her because they believe in her self-fashioning as a seemingly wealthy person. As we have already seen, her family stories are pure self-fiction and her self-fashioning sheer semblance, unsupported by any material assets her creditors believe her to have. Raggles and all her other creditors have confidence in her. Yet, they are all conned by the confidence trick she plays on their gullibility.

Various characters in the novel refer to Rebecca's artifice by calling her a "little artful creature," "an artful hussey" and "an artful little minx" (37, 109, 590). The text refers to her as a "little schemer" and a "consummate little tragedian" (610, 776) and it also repeatedly links her to duplicitous figures such as the devil, Circe and the sirens (34, 167, 611, 747-748, 770, 778). When she rejects Sir Pitt Crawley's marriage proposal by explaining that she cannot be his wife but (having secretly married Rawdon, his son) would like to be his daughter, her former employer is amused by her cleverness: "'Vamous,' said Sir Pitt. 'Who'd ha' thought of it! what a sly little devil! what a little fox it waws!' he muttered to himself, chuckling with pleasure" (167). Similarly, Lord Steyne, on discovering one of Rebecca's clever financial schemes, finds that her duplicity adds to her feminine charm:[11]

> "What an accomplished little devil it is!" thought he. "What a splendid actress and manager! She had almost got a second supply out of me the other day, with her coaxing ways. [. . .] I am [. . .] a fool in her hand – an old fool.

---

[10] A range of different approaches discussing the close links between finance and fiction can be found in the interdisciplinary collection of essays edited by Christine Künzel and Dirk Hempel.

[11] See Lisa Jadwin's article on *Vanity Fair* for a detailed discussion of the cultural discourse in which feminine duplicity is regarded as "both socially sanctioned and commonplace" (663).

She is unsurpassable in lies." His Lordship's admiration for Becky rose immeasurably at this proof of her cleverness. Getting the money was nothing – but getting double the sum she wanted, and paying nobody – it was a magnificent stroke. (611)

Even though Sir Pitt and Lord Steyne appear to relish being taken in by Rebecca's clever wiles, she is fully aware that she has to hide the duplicity that underpins her social performance.[12] Indeed, Thackeray's protagonist seeks to hide the artifice of her self-fashioning because she understands that her performance is successful only as long as others perceive her as genuine and authentic.[13] However, despite her accomplished acting, Rebecca is repeatedly unmasked, and other characters reveal her actual background to one another. As a result, her artfulness is exposed and her performance becomes visible so that the resilient adventuress has to start all over again in another place. Yet her unmasking only goes to underline her satirical role in the text, where time and again other characters are made to realize that they have let themselves be duped as a result of their own vain obsession with wealth and status.

---

[12] Note that invoking the figure of the siren, the text refers to its own dialectical showing and hiding of the monstrous aspects of Rebecca's behaviour:

> I defy any one to say that our Becky, who has certainly some vices, has not been presented to the public in a perfectly genteel and inoffensive manner. In describing this siren, singing and smiling, coaxing and cajoling, the author, with modest pride, asks his readers all round, has he once forgotten the laws of politeness, and showed the monster's hideous tail above water? No! Those who like may peep down under the waves that are pretty transparent, and see it writhing and twirling, diabolically hideous and slimy, flapping amongst bones, or curling around corpses; but above the water-line, I ask, has not everything been proper, agreeable, and decorous [. . .]? When, however, the siren disappears and dives below, down among the dead men, the water of course grows turbid over her, and it is labour lost to look into it ever so curiously. (747-748)

[13] Focusing on performed identities, Dobson notes that

> in the gossiping world that makes up *Vanity Fair*, the characters who attempt to perform what they perceive as an acceptable identity are undercut by others who recognize and denounce their performances as such, and thereby negate their supposed naturalness. The circulation of information and gossip is thus invested with the power to make or unmake characters' social standing. (1)

This is particularly pertinent to the social performance of Rebecca. "The role that Rebecca enacts only succeeds as long as others see her acts as genuine," Dobson writes and goes on to suggest: "This realization in turn prompts her to aspire to genuineness in her performance" (12). Her performance can, however, work "only as long as her artifice and duplicity are not publicly recognized" (14).

Economic aspects such as credit, debt, poverty, extreme wealth and economic extravagance feature prominently in nineteenth-century fiction. However, what renders Thackeray's *Vanity Fair* unusual compared with other Victorian novels is not just the fact that it is a woman who is clearly the most intelligent character in the text, but also the fact that novel depicts Rebecca as an autonomous and independent economic agent at a time when the economic individual was usually pictured as masculine. In nineteenth-century culture, the type of individualism characterizing economic man was seen to run counter to feminine gender norms. As Lana Dalley and Jill Rappoport emphasize in the introduction to their volume *Economic Women*, "'individualism' itself was a concept at odds with dominant notions of women's place within domestic ideology" (2). According to the middle-class ideology of the so-called separate spheres, woman was relegated to the domain of the home and family, where she was expected to define herself in relation to others, notably her husband and children. Dalley and Rappoport further point out that

> [e]ven such economically significant efforts as her household management and reproduction were most frequently detached from the market and characterized as modes of service that privileged the needs of others over the individual economic agent. (2)

Women may have been in charge of the economic management of their households but, in so doing, were expected to efface themselves as individual subjects with financial interests of their own.

Given the gender ideology prevalent in the nineteenth century, it is all the more remarkable that *Vanity Fair* should put a lot of emphasis on female economic agency. The novel does so not just in the figure of Miss Crawley, the maiden aunt in the Crawley family whose considerable wealth gives her great power over her relatives, but first and foremost in the figure of Rebecca, who undermines conventional gender roles through her independent economic actions. Although women in the nineteenth century were generally not perceived and treated as economic individuals, modern consumer culture simultaneously provided them with a certain degree of agency, notably in the cultural imaginary surrounding feminine economic extravagance. The ideal image of the thrifty housewife had a counterpart in the extravagant spender who ran up debts in her retail credit transactions and who might even turn herself into an erotic spectacle and object in order to finance her economic excesses.[14]

It is precisely in this transgressive form that Rebecca possesses economic agency. In her affair with Lord Steyne, she turns herself into an object (and even a commodity), but the gifts, money and credit which she attracts as his favourite simultaneously enable her to act as an independent economic agent.[15] While traditional gift theory argues that in pre-modern societies, the exchange of gifts between individuals from different classes tends to reinforce social hierarchies, the presents from Lord Steyne facilitate Rebecca's social climbing in the context of a more fluid modern consumer credit economy.[16] Her financial operations not only subvert sexual propriety, but they also destabilize the social class system. At the same time, Rebecca's financial dealings also entail a reversal of conventional gender roles in her household: Standing in the public limelight, Rebecca provides for the family by virtue of her smart social performance and her clever financial schemes, while Rawdon is the sole parent who looks after little Rawdon, their son. Indeed, showing none of the emotions traditionally expected from a wife and mother, Rebecca appears to take no interest in her child and uses her husband as

---

[14] See Krista Lysack, who discusses both conduct books promoting the ideal of the economizing housewife and the figure of "the extravagant domestic spender" in connection with George Eliot's *Middlemarch*, and Margot Finn (47-49), who in her analysis of the relationship between gender and consumer credit refers to Thackeray's Rebecca Sharp as her prime example.

[15] Note, for example, that when Lord Steyne and Rebecca meet her for the first time, she presents herself in a carefully staged *mise-en-scène*:

> The great Lord Steyne was standing by the fire sipping coffee. [. . .] There was a score of candles sparkling round the mantelpiece [. . .]. They lighted up Rebecca's figure to admiration, as she sate on a sofa covered with the pattern of gaudy flowers. She was in a pink dress, that looked as fresh as a rose; her dazzling white arms and shoulders were half-covered with a thin hazy scarf through which they sparkled; her hair hung in curls round her neck; one of her little feet peeped out from the fresh crisp folds of the silk: the prettiest foot in the prettiest little sandal in the finest silk stocking in the world. (437)

Rebecca's self-presentation clearly underlines her status as an object and spectacle, but the passage also illustrates her skills as a consummate performer and stage director.

[16] See Marcel Mauss's classic anthropological study *The Gift*, David Graeber's more recent discussion of hierarchical gift exchanges (109-113) as well as Margot Finn's distinction between the hierarchical social order that goes hand in hand with "credit born out of gift relations" and their attendant mutual obligations on the one hand and the social instability that can be observed as a result of "the retail credit that catalysed commodity exchange in consumer markets" on the other (51).

a mere instrument for her self-advancement. Her selfishness is underlined by the fact that she hides some of her money so as not to have to share it with Rawdon; she even neglects his appeal to her to make a deal with the creditor who has imprisoned him for debt in a so-called spunging-house.[17] She would have plenty of money to pay the creditor and free her husband but instead, with Rawdon out of the way, she enjoys a *tête-à-tête* with Lord Steyne. By emphasizing her social and economic success as an individual who only looks out for herself without caring for anyone else, Thackeray positions Rebecca as a figure that is exceptional in Victorian writing, namely as an economic woman who is motivated solely by self-interest.

Rebecca's economic individualism is indeed remarkable because it violates feminine gender norms but also because it disregards moral principles with impunity. Indeed, Thackeray's protagonist not only lacks emotional warmth, but she is equally devoid of any moral responsibility. Living almost exclusively on credit, Rebecca never pays her creditors. "Nobody in fact was paid" (431), notes the narrator in describing her arrangement of "How to live well on Nothing a Year." In the moral imagination of Victorian culture, debt usually creates a sense of moral obligation on the part of debtors to repay their debts. Rebecca, however, sees herself under no debt obligation, let alone under any moral obligation. Given the severity with which supposedly deviant behaviour in female characters is usually punished in Victorian fiction, it is indeed astonishing that as a female protagonist who is guided by her unfeminine self-interest alone, who acts in unscrupulous and even immoral ways, Thackeray's Rebecca Sharp gets away without being punished for her unprincipled actions.

In fact, rather than morally condemning Rebecca, the text uses her ruthlessness in order to expose an entire social system. In the world of Vanity Fair, everyone performs his or her identity in pursuit of his or her personal interest. Rebecca goes certainly further than any other character, but in Thackeray's satire, her extreme self-fashioning only reveals the vain notions and ideas of everyone else in society. The social rise of Rebecca Sharp is possible only because the people of Vanity Fair set great stock upon the appearance of social status and material wealth. Indeed, she is so successful because her performances tally with their

---

[17] A spunging-house (also "sponging-house") was a house kept by a bailiff as a place of confinement for debtors unable to settle their debts (see the *Oxford English Dictionary*). In Great Britain, insolvent debtors were also imprisoned in special debtors' prisons up until the Debtor's Act of 1869 abolished imprisonment for debt. For a detailed discussion of this practice, see Finn (109-193).

mercenary values. Rather than portraying Rebecca as a psychological subject with a complex inner life, the text presents her as a personification of the economic system of Vanity Fair. As readers, we do not know what her individual wishes and predilections are. As Sandy Morey Norton puts it, "[i]t is never clear exactly what Becky wants, except that, like any true capitalist, she always wants more" (134). Since she is driven by social ambition and personal gain alone and, in the end, cares neither for her far less intelligent husband nor their child, little Rawdon, Rebecca Sharp can be said to epitomize the frivolous but also vain and empty world of Vanity Fair. Her ruthless behaviour – notably her practice of using and discarding other people as suits her personal advantage – mirrors the completely self-interested society surrounding her.

Taking this a step further, we can say that Rebecca is a rogue who operates within the existing social system, takes it to its extreme and, in so doing, undermines it. That is, as well as mirroring the world of Vanity Fair, her line of action also carries a subversive dimension. With the exception of the wealthy and independent Miss Crawley, the society of *Vanity Fair* is patriarchal, and women depend on the status and wealth of their fathers and husbands. The fact that as a female social outsider, Rebecca Sharp manages to move from the social margins to the very centre of society makes her a subversive figure.[18] The fact that as a disadvantaged orphan, she gets a lot for nothing in a snobbish class society adds to her power of subversion. The symbolic fiction of money has real social consequences, and it is true that the characters who literally have to pay dearly for their blindness are chiefly from the middle class and thus not from the upper echelons of society. However, in the end, everyone turns out to be duped because they all believe in the system of Vanity Fair, regardless of their social and financial position. In the subtitle, Thackeray calls his text "A Novel without a Hero." At one point, however, the narrator notes that "[i]f this is a novel without a hero, at least let us lay claim to a heroine" (340). After all, Rebecca Sharp figures indeed as the heroine of the text as she performs and, at the same time, exposes the vices of Vanity Fair.

---

[18] For readings that emphasize Rebecca's outsider status, see Lisa Jadwin and Andrew Miller (1,052). Both critics also discuss how Thackeray's protagonist deploys the type of imitation that Luce Irigaray defines as an empowering strategy available to those who occupy a marginal position.

References

Bunyan, John. *The Pilgrim's Progress.* Ed. N. H. Keeble. Oxford and New York: Oxford University Press, 1998.
Carlyle, Thomas. *Past and Present.* 1843. Oxford: Oxford University Press, 1944.
Dalley, Lana L. and Jill Rappoport, eds. *Economic Women: Essays on Desire and Dispossession in Nineteenth-Century British Culture.* Columbus: Ohio State University Press, 2013.
Dobson, Kit. "'An Insuperable Repugnance to Hearing Vice Called by Its Proper Name': Englishness, Gender, and the Performed Identities of Rebecca and Amelia in Thackeray's *Vanity Fair.*" *Victorian Review* 32.2 (2006): 1-25.
Finn, Margot C. *The Character of Credit: Personal Debt in English Culture, 1740-1914.* Cambridge: Cambridge University Press, 2003.
Graeber, David. *Debt: The First 5,000 Years.* New York: Melville, 2012.
Herbert, Christopher. "Filthy Lucre: Victorian Ideas of Money." *Victorian Studies* 44.2 (2002): 185-213.
Hörisch, Jochen. "Geld – Ein Handbuchartikel." *Gott, Geld, Medien: Studien zu den Medien, die die Welt im Innersten zusammenhalten.* Frankfurt am Main: Suhrkamp, 2004. 108-118.
———. *Man muss dran glauben: Die Theologie der Märkte.* Munich: Fink, 2013.
Hunt, Aeron. *Personal Business: Character and Commerce in Victorian Literature and Culture.* Charlottesville: University of Virginia Press, 2014.
Jadwin, Lisa. "The Seductiveness of Female Duplicity in *Vanity Fair.*" *Studies in English Literature, 1500-1900* 32.4 (1992): 663-687.
Kohl, Stephan. "Thackeray, William Makepeace." *Metzler Lexikon Englischsprachiger Autorinnen und Autoren.* Ed. Eberhard Kreutzer and Ansgar Nünning. Stuttgart and Weimar: Metzler, 2006. 575-577.
Künzel, Christine and Dirk Hempel, eds. *Finanzen und Fiktionen: Grenzgänge zwischen Literatur und Wirtschaft.* Frankfurt and New York: Campus, 2011.
Lysack, Krista. "*Middlemarch* and the Extravagant Domestic Spender." *Come Buy, Come Buy: Shopping and the Culture of Consumption in Victorian Women's Writing.* Athens: Ohio University Press, 2008. 80-108.
Mauss, Marcel. *The Gift: The Form and Reason for Exchange in Archaic Societies.* 1950. Trans. W. D. Halls. New York and London: Norton, 2000.
Miller, Andrew. "*Vanity Fair* through Glass Plate." *PMLA* 105.5 (1990): 1041-1054.
Norton, Sandy Morey. "The Ex-Collector of Boggly-Wollah: Colonialism in the Empire of *Vanity Fair.*" *Narrative* 1.2 (1993): 124-137.

Oxford English Dictionary. Web. Accessed 6 September 2015.

Rosdeitcher, Elizabeth. "Empires at Stake: Gambling and the Economic Unconscious in Thackeray." *Genre* 29.4 (1996): 407-426.

Ruskin, John. *Unto This Last and Other Writings.* Ed. Clive Wilmer. London: Penguin, 1997.

Shell, Marc. "The Issue of Representation." *The New Economic Criticism: Studies at the Intersection of Literature and Economics.* Ed. Martha Woodmansee and Mark Osteen. London, New York: Routledge, 1999. 53-74.

Thackeray, William Makepeace. *Vanity Fair: A Novel without a Hero.* 1848. Ed. John Carey. London: Penguin, 2003.

"Scrupulous Meanness," Joyce's Gift, and the Symbolic Economy of *Dubliners*

Sangam MacDuff

In 1906 Joyce informed his publisher that he intended to write "a chapter of the moral history" of Ireland "in a style of scrupulous meanness" with "Dublin for the scene." *Dubliners* is famously economical, if not miserly, and Joyce treats his subjects somewhat harshly, but the sparseness of the stories is complemented by richly symbolic passages in which Joyce's poetic gifts shine through. This lyrical-symbolic mode would seem to run counter to the "scrupulous meanness" of *Dubliners*, but Mark Osteen argues that Joyce reconciles spendthrift habits with bourgeois thrift to create an aesthetic economy of the gift, where loss is gain. This analysis suggests that Joyce's poetic gifts are compensated, both artistically and financially, by putting literary language into circulation. Osteen, Ellmann and others have demonstrated the importance of Joyce's circulating systems, but I will argue that breaks in circulation are equally significant, and that, paradoxically, it is the gaps where language breaks down that put the signifying system into motion. Analysing "Two Gallants," I will suggest that this paradox provides the key to Joyce's symbolic economy, where the withholdings of textual lacunae become portals of unlimited growth, while the riches of symbolic proliferation always contain a Midas touch of loss.

He was too scrupulous always

In December 1905 James Joyce sent a collection of twelve stories to the Dublin publisher Grant Richards. No doubt surprised at receiving a manuscript entitled *Dubliners* from Trieste, Richards was nevertheless impressed, and accepted *Dubliners* on 17 February 1906, signing a contract in March. Meanwhile, however, Joyce had sent Richards an addi-

Economies of English. SPELL: Swiss Papers in English Language and Literature 33. Ed. Martin Leer and Genoveva Puskás. Tübingen: Narr, 2016. 181-197.

tional story, "Two Gallants," which precipitated a protracted dispute, delaying publication for eight years. Despite the difficulties this caused Joyce, the delay was in some ways felicitous, for in the interval he added "A Little Cloud" and "The Dead," substantially revised his earlier stories, and in a lengthy correspondence with Richards, Joyce formulated some of the key aesthetic principles which would govern his later work.

Perhaps the most famous of these statements occurs in a letter dated 5 May 1906:

> My intention was to write a chapter of the moral history of my country and I chose Dublin for the scene because that city seemed to me the centre of paralysis. I have tried to present it to the indifferent public under four of its aspects: childhood, adolescence, maturity and public life. The stories are arranged in this order. I have written it for the most part in a style of scrupulous meanness and with the conviction that he is a very bold man who dares to alter in the presentment, still more to deform, whatever he has seen and heard. (*Letters* II 134)

The idea that Dublin represents "the centre of paralysis" echoes Joyce's explanation to Constantine Curran: "I call the series *Dubliners* to betray the soul of that hemiplegia or paralysis which many consider a city" (*Letters* I 55), and I will come back to this notion of paralysis in the symbolic economy of *Dubliners*. Likewise, there is more to be said about Joyce's moral history and the structure of *Dubliners*, but first I want to focus on his "style of scrupulous meanness."

The *OED* defines "scrupulous" as "[t]roubled with doubts or scruples of conscience; over-nice or meticulous in matters of right and wrong" (1a), which would appear to be the sense Eliza has in mind when she says that her late brother, Father Flynn, was "too scrupulous always" in "The Sisters" (*Dubliners* 9). But the word has several meanings, including "[m]inutely exact or careful, [. . .] strictly attentive even to the smallest details" (*OED* 5), which tallies well with Joyce's "conviction that he is a very bold man who dares to alter [. . .] whatever he has seen and heard," and would thus seem to be the predominant sense in the letter, defining Joyce's style as one of scrupulous realism. The word can also mean "characterised by doubt or distrust" (1b), which fits *Dubliners* perfectly, while Joyce's stories had a nasty habit of "causing or raising scruples" and to this day they remain "liable to give offence" (2a), so that the phrase suggests several key aspects of *Dubliners*: social realism as an aesthetic and moral concern; the unsettling nature of a text characterised by doubt and distrust; and the propensity of these uncertainties to raise readers' scruples.

"Meanness" is similarly ambivalent, hovering between miserliness and nastiness. Any reader of *Dubliners* knows that Joyce's stories are highly economical; many would complain they are downright stingy, withholding key facts which would enable interpretation. As I intend to show, though, this apparent incompleteness is only one side of the coin, the flip side of the endless interest they generate. Similarly, although Joyce's early reviewers frequently condemned *Dubliners* for insisting on "the sordid and baser aspects" of life, full of "such scenes and details as can only shock,"[1] and Joyce himself admitted that "the odour of ashpits and old weeds and offal hangs round my stories" (*Letters* I 64), conceding that at first glance the book is "somewhat bitter and sordid" (*Letters* I 70), he also told Richards of his belief that "in composing my chapter of moral history in exactly the way I have composed it I have taken the first step towards the spiritual liberation of my country" (*Letters* I 62-3).

It is no accident that the furor over *Dubliners'* publication was ignited by "Two Gallants," nor that the letter in which Joyce describes his "style of scrupulous meanness" begins with a question about that story:

> Dear Mr Grant Richards, I am sorry you do not tell me why the printer, who seems to be the barometer of English opinion, refuses to print *Two Gallants* and makes marks in the margin of *Counterparts*. Is it the small gold coin in the former story or the code of honour which the two gallants live by which shocks him? I see nothing which should shock him in either of these things. (*Letters* II 132-33)

Despite Joyce's protestations, even today, when virtually every taboo has been broken, the story still has the power to shock readers, and it is interesting to consider why.

Like all of Joyce's stories, the tale is deceptively simple. Two men, Lenehan and Corley, conspire to extract a gold sovereign from a young slavey, or maid of all work. The apparition of this coin at the end of the story offers an enigmatic epiphany, but one which is just as likely to provoke outrage as wonder, for it would appear that the young woman, perhaps duped by the promise of marriage, has been defrauded of approximately two months' wages by the unscrupulous young "gallants,"

---

[1] Anonymous review, *Athenaeum*, 20 June 1914, 875 (qtd in Deming 61-62). See also the unsigned review of *Dubliners* in *Everyman* (3 July 1914, xc, 380): "'Two Gallants' reveals the shuddering depths of human meanness" (qtd in Deming 64; compare Deming 58-65).

who, it goes without saying, are anything but chivalrous.[2] With some justice, "Two Gallants," has been called "the nastiest story" in *Dubliners* (Reizbaum and Ellmann 126), as can be seen from the range of critical interpretations: Corley has been viewed as a pimp, a prostitute and a perambulating phallus, with Lenehan the leech as his homosexual hanger-on; the slavey has been likened to a prostitute, a slattern and a slave; while the entire story has been read, with good reason, as an allegory of Ireland's servitude and submission to her colonial masters.[3] Yet Joyce considered it "one of the most important stories in the book," the story, after "Ivy Day," which pleased him most (*Letters* I 62) and it remains a favourite among readers – a kind of ugly duckling in the collection. The source of this fascination, and its capacity to shock, is not that the story says all, or even any, of these things directly, but rather that Joyce is scrupulously mean in withholding information, while simultaneously sowing seeds of doubt, so that as Reizbaum and Ellmann put it, "the story confronts us with our own dirty minds, mirrored in Joyce's 'nicely polished looking-glass'" (128).[4]

Several features contribute to make "Two Gallants" a scrupulously mean text. First, the story has a double-blind structure. It begins *in medias res*, just as Corley is "bringing a long monologue to a close." We soon realise that this monologue foretold how Corley would obtain the gold coin, so that the story we read in "Two Gallants" is presented as

---

[2] According to Joyce, "the code of honour which the two gallants live by" is based on Guglielmo Ferrero's "moral code of the soldier and [. . .] gallant" (*Letters* II 134-35), possibly referring to a passage in *Il Militarismo* which describes how "officers, being short of money to pay for the dissolute lives they were leading, tried [. . .] to become the lovers of rich middle-class ladies, getting money out of them as a recompense for the honour conferred upon those ladies by condescending to make them their mistresses" (qtd in Reizbaum and Ellmann 132 n5). But Stanislaus Joyce reports that "the idea for 'Two Gallants' came from [. . .] the relations between Porthos and the wife of a tradesman in *The Three Musketeers*, which my brother found in Ferrero's *Europa Giovane*" (*Letters* II 212), and this source suggests that the young men's "gallantry" is tied (ironically, perhaps) to the motto "all for one and one for all," pointing to a third aspect of the homosocial code which governs Lenehan and Corley's behaviour: the unspoken promise of loyalty, solidarity, and secrecy, as well as material aid (through the precarious liquidity provided by such customs as the standing of drinks or the offer and repayment of small loans in a debt-ridden economy), all of which take precedence over the relations between men and women (see Norris 40-42).

[3] See Boyle; Epstein; Walzl; Torchiana; Leonard; Norris; Reizbaum and Ellmann.

[4] The reference is to another of Joyce's well-known letters to Richards: "I seriously believe that you will retard the course of civilisation in Ireland by preventing the Irish people from having one good look at themselves in my nicely polished looking-glass" (*Letters* I 64).

the reenactment of a tale concluded at its opening, the very tale which would explain its significance. Moreover, at the key point in the reenactment, when Corley heads off with the slavey, the narrative switches to Lenehan, and the second half of the story is focalised through him, although he does little more than eat peas and drink ginger beer,[5] which explains why the dazzling coin itself becomes a kind of narrative blind at the end, occluding the enigmatic nature of Lenehan's hold over Corley. The mystery surrounding what Corley does with the woman, and more precisely, how he gets the coin out of her, is accentuated by Lenehan's vague, but increasingly insistent questions: "I suppose you'll be able to pull *it* off all right, eh?, [. . .] Is she game for *that*? [. . .] are you sure you can bring *it* off all right? [. . .] Did you try her?" (*Dubliners* 46-47, 54; my emphasis). Since we are told that Lenehan "had the habit of leaving his flattery open to the interpretation of raillery," and that he begins his interrogation "dubiously" but ends with "a note of menace" in his voice (46, 54), the tone of these exchanges is not easy to gage. In the same way, Corley's braggadocio casts serious doubt over the reliability of his narration, particularly following his characterisation as a police informer,[6] who was "fond of delivering final judgments," though "he spoke without listening to the speech of his companions." Yet this too is rendered problematic when the narrator lets drop that in Corley's solipsistic accounts of "what he had said to such a person and what such a person had said to him and what he had said to settle the matter," he "aspirated the first letter of his name after the manner of the Florentines" (45) – which is to say, (w)Horley – raising doubts about the reliability of Corley and/or the narrator, for it is difficult to know whether the irony of Corley's self-appellation is supposed to be deliberate. Indeed, tonal ambiguity afflicts the story as a whole, leading to diametrically opposed readings, from the perverse pleasure of collusion in the two gallants' success, to shock and outrage at their base exploitation, and this uncertainty is codified by a series of puns and ambiguities in the text.

---

[5] This detail is glossed amusingly by Terence Brown: "Lenehan's repast must be one of the most dismal in all of literature" (*Dubliners* 264 n53). Beneath the grim humour, though, the meagre sum of "twopence halfpenny" Lenehan spends on dinner, having eaten nothing all day except a few biscuits cadged off a bartender, clearly represents his "poverty of purse and spirit" (51-52).

[6] "Corley was the son of an inspector of police [. . .]. He was often to be seen walking with policemen in plain clothes, talking earnestly. He knew the inner side of all affairs" (45).

For instance, Corley first refers to the woman as "a fine young tart," which has led some critics to conclude that she is a prostitute, although "tart" was originally applied, often endearingly, to a young girl or woman, especially a wife or girlfriend (*OED; Dubliners* 44).[7] Similarly, when Corley says she used to "go with a dairyman," presumably he means she went out walking with him, a common Hiberno-English expression, but the phrase is calculated to induce the suspicion that she slept with him, particularly when Corley admits – or feigns – his fear that she would "get in the family way" (44). The full stop which follows this is typical of Joyce's art of insinuation, allowing a short pause to open up a grammatical gap that admits alternative readings – here, the phrase "up to the dodge" suggests not only that she takes contraceptive measures, but also that she willingly participates in Corley's criminal dealings. Indeed, if Corley can be trusted, she has already filched a couple of cigars from her employer (44); and if the narrator can be trusted that Corley is a police informer, this places her in his hands, offering a quite different motive from Lenehan's speculation that she hopes to marry (45).

These examples should suffice to show how Joyce cultivates doubt and distrust in "Two Gallants" through a series of ambiguities which simultaneously withhold certainty and invite speculation; seen in this light, puns like "tart" are both miserly and generous, employing one word to summon up multiple interpretations, and the same principle is amplified through Joyce's textual hiatuses. Just as the boy in "The Sisters" puzzles his head to extract meaning from Old Cotter's unfinished sentences (*Dubliners* 3), Joyce meticulously riddles *Dubliners* with holes, gaps, silences and ellipses for the reader to puzzle over, such as Lenehan's euphemistic references to "it" and "that," the grammatical gap opened by the dodgy full stop, or the narrative blinds in "Two Gallants." As I have tried to show, through the story's ubiquitous tonal ambiguity, which undercuts any certain meaning while opening up the text to multiple interpretations, Joyce creates a work that is scrupulous in its meanness, ready at any moment to dupe the reader.

---

[7] Corley reports the woman as saying she is a slavey in Baggott Street, which seems to be confirmed when, at the end of the story, she goes into a house there, apparently returning with the gold coin. But even this is not straightforward, since she enters by one door and leaves by another, a notable crux, and the moment Corley receives the gold coin is not shown, leaving open the possibility that he does not in fact obtain it from her. Indeed, the woman never speaks directly in the story, remaining both nameless and voiceless, so that her motives remain as inscrutable as Corley's, Lenehan's, and the narrator's.

The gift of easy and graceful verse

Yet, as I have also tried to suggest, there is richness in Joyce's hoarding. Returning to Joyce's letter, it is worth noting that Joyce doesn't say *Dubliners is* written in a style of scrupulous meanness; he says he has written the book "*for the most part* in a style of scrupulous meanness" (*Letters* II 134; my emphasis). The point is so simple that it is usually overlooked, but it is worth considering what that other part might be. Another letter, written to his brother Stanislaus in September 1906, gives an important clue:

> Sometimes thinking of Ireland it seems to me that I have been unnecessarily harsh. I have reproduced (in *Dubliners* at least) none of the attraction of the city [. . .] I have not reproduced its ingenuous insularity and its hospitality. The latter 'virtue' so far as I can see does not exist elsewhere in Europe. I have not been just to its beauty: for it is more beautiful naturally in my opinion than what I have seen of England, Switzerland, France, Austria or Italy [. . .] And after all *Two Gallants* – with the Sunday crowds and the harp in Kildare street and Lenehan – is an Irish landscape. (*Letters* II 166)

Critics generally assume that Joyce sought to redress this harshness in "The Dead," where Gabriel celebrates his aunts' hospitality, humanity and humour (*Dubliners* 204), but Joyce is typically ambivalent about the "virtue" of Irish hospitality, and the last sentence in the quotation shows that he is equally equivocal about his portrayal of Dublin. "Two Gallants" is not unremittingly nasty after all, but an "Irish landscape"; the Sunday crowds Joyce refers to set the scene in the first paragraph of the story:

> The grey warm evening air of August had descended upon the city and a mild warm air, a memory of summer, circulated in the streets. The streets, shuttered for the repose of Sunday, swarmed with a gaily coloured crowd. Like illumined pearls the lamps shone from the summits of their tall poles upon the living texture below which, changing shape and hue unceasingly, sent up into the warm grey air an unchanging unceasing murmur. (43)

The rhythmic rise and fall of Joyce's phrases is audible here, woven together through patterns of repetition and variation like "the grey warm evening air" which becomes "a mild warm air" and then "the warm grey air" at the end of the paragraph, or the runs of alliteration and assonance which link the memory of summer circulating in the streets to the unceasing murmur of the crowd. The simile of the pearly lamps and the living texture of the crowd metaphor advertise themselves as poetic language, yet this doesn't mean they are somehow cheapened, a kind of prose pornography, as Margot Norris argues; nor does it make the passage an epiphany, as Reizbaum and Ellmann suggest, although the style is derived from Joyce's lyrical Epiphanies.[8] Rather, by flaunting its poetry, Joyce exposes the workings of lyrical language, simultaneously inviting cynicism and disarming critical resistance, which allows readers to enjoy Joyce's prose all the more. As Jonathan Culler argues, no matter how hairsplitting the analysis of aural and rhythmical effects, there are visceral *affects* that elude reason, which Culler likens to miniature versions of the sublime (133-85). This irrational, irreducible power of poetic language[9] explains why Joyce's lyricism is actually enhanced by its openness to irony: tonal ambiguity multiplies the possibilities for interpretation, but it does not alter the body of the text. For example, there is rich irony in the "*gift of easy and graceful verse*" Little Chandler imagines a reviewer praising in a book of poems he is yet to write (*D* 69), yet Chandler's poetic reveries in "A Little Cloud" contain some beautiful vignettes of Dublin, so that the ironic distance afforded by Joyce's free indirect discourse enriches the poetry of the narrative. Set pieces such as these, or the Sunday crowd scene in "Two Gallants," are found throughout *Dubliners*, showing that, far from being mean or harsh, there is great pleasure in Joyce's style.[10]

This richness is not only a question of poetic language, but also of allusion and suggestion, as Joyce's second example shows:

---

[8] As A. Walton Litz has observed, the two types of Epiphany, dramatic and lyrical, represent "the twin poles of Joyce's art," which Litz labels "dramatic irony" and "lyric sentiment" (Joyce, *Poems and Shorter Writings* 158). The "scrupulous meanness" of "Two Gallants" represents the first pole while its poetry is an expression of the second.

[9] Jean-Jacques Lecercle calls this the "remainder," arguing that language is not only an abstract system of relations, but also a material product of the body whose sound and shape physically affect the reader (see Attridge 65).

[10] Examples from "A Little Cloud" include the sunset scene (65-66), the street urchins (66), and the vista from Grattan Bridge (68). The more closely one reads *Dubliners*, the more these prose-poetic examples multiply: the collection is replete with alliteration and assonance (e.g., "All the branches of the tall trees which lined the mall were gay with little light green leaves and the sunlight slanted through them on to the water" [13]), rhyme and rhythm (e.g., "Every morning I lay on the floor in the front parlour watching her door" [22]), and the abundant imagery Chandler employs in his vignettes (compare, for instance, the beginning and ending of "Araby").

They [Corley and Lenehan] walked along Nassau Street and then turned into Kildare Street. Not far from the porch of the club a harpist stood in the roadway, playing to a little ring of listeners. He plucked at the wires heedlessly, glancing quickly from time to time at the face of each newcomer and from time to time, wearily also, at the sky. His harp too, heedless that her coverings had fallen about her knees, seemed weary alike of the eyes of strangers and of her master's hands. One hand played in the bass the melody of *Silent, O Moyle*, while the other hand careered in the treble after each group of notes. The notes of the air throbbed deep and full. (48)

As Boyle, Walzl and others have pointed out, the harp symbolises Ireland and its mythical past, popularised by poets like Thomas Moore, whose *Irish Melodies* include "Silent, O Moyle," originally entitled "The Song of Fionnuala." Moore notes that "Fionnuala, daughter of Lir, was by some supernatural power transformed into a swan" (qtd in *Dubliners* 262 n.33), which may recall Zeus's transformation in the Leda myth, strengthening the association between sexual subjugation and colonial domination in "Two Gallants." In any case, the harp, "heedless that her coverings had fallen about her knees" yokes Ireland to the abused women in the story, so that Joyce's prosopopoeia works on three levels: the personified instrument is weary alike of passersby and the harpist; the "girls off the South Circular" Corley "used to go with," at least one of whom is "on the turf" now (46-47), are weary of the prying eyes and hands of pimps and clients; and Ireland is equally tired of the "strangers" in its Isle (a traditional reference to the English) and the rule of the Anglo-Irish Ascendancy. Indeed, as Donald Torchiana has shown, the whole story is a tour through the Ascendancy, beginning at Rutland Square, seat of the Orange Lodge, and here traversing Nassau Street (Lord Henry Nassau fought for William of Orange at the battle of the Boyne) which runs along the south side of Trinity College (which, in the late nineteenth century, was intimately associated with Unionism, Anglicisation and Protestantism), to the Kildare Street Club, an exclusive gentlemen's club restricted to Anglo-Irish Protestants which "epitomized the religious, economic and social callousness" (Torchiana 116) of the Ascendancy.

We can see from this that, far from the pastoral scenes of the Celtic Twilight, Joyce's "Irish landscape" offers a complex, multifaceted portrayal of social, political, historical, cultural and religious conditions at the turn of the century. In one sense it is a scrupulously mean portrayal, both in its unrelentingly bleak vision of Dublin as a "centre of paralysis," and in the economy of its depiction, which only reveals the full depth of its perspective to those who know the background. Yet this too is part of Joyce's gift, a meticulous attention to detail which ensures that every proper noun in *Dubliners* contains a wealth of allusion, a scrupulosity he would later extend to each word in *Finnegans Wake*.

The same combination of obliquity and complexity characterises the apparition of the coin at the end of the story. Pursued by Lenehan, Corley turns down a blind alley and halts under a lamp, recalling the lamps of the opening.[11] Framed under the light, there is a good deal of suspense, even for the savvy reader who suspects success, for Lenehan, at least, is anxiously expecting failure. Thus the scene offers a dramatic tableau which Corley milks for all it is worth:

> Corley halted at the first lamp and stared grimly before him. Then with a grave gesture he extended a hand towards the light and, smiling, opened it slowly to the gaze of his disciple. A small gold coin shone in the palm. (55)

The theatrical quality of the scene makes it seem somewhat unreal, as though Corley had conjured the coin by sleight of hand, adding to the mystery of how he has obtained it, and what it represents. Under Lenehan's gaze, the shining coin both echoes and contrasts the poetic apparition of the moon earlier in the story, first when "Lenehan's gaze was fixed on the large faint moon circled with a double halo," watching "earnestly the passing of the grey web of twilight across its face" (46), and then when Corley "too gazed at the pale disc of the moon, now nearly veiled, and seemed to meditate" (46). In this way, each man's musings on the likely outcome of the meeting is linked to, and prepares for, the manifestation of the coin, contradicting Norris's reading of these scenes as mere trickery. In fact, given Lenehan's power over Corley, "disciple" is a better candidate for deception, as though the narrator had caught Lenehan's habit of irony, allowing "[a] shade of mockery" to "reliev[e] the servility" (46). At the same time, "disciple" clearly suggests religious significance, perhaps as an allusion to the parable of the rich man who entrusts ten servants with a gold coin each in Luke,

---

[11] They may also recall the "swinging lamp" of the boy's dream in "The Sisters" (6), the contrast between the "electric candle-lamps" and daybreak in "After the Race" (38-39, 42), or the gas lamps in "Araby" which both illuminate the object of the boy's desire, like Mangan's sister framed angelically under the light, and veil it ("I was thankful that I could see so little. All my senses seemed to desire to veil themselves. . .": 21-24). Lamps and streetlights constitute an important leitmotif in *Dubliners*, figuring prominently in "A Little Cloud," "Counterparts," "A Painful Case," and "The Dead."

chapter 19 (Reizbaum and Ellmann 135-36).[12] At the same time there is a faint echo of the "two men [. . .] counting money on a salver" at the end of "Araby" (27), which recalls the moneychangers in the temple (Matthew 21: 12-13). Announced on the first page, simony is a central theme in *Dubliners*, most obviously in "Grace," where Father Purdon preaches a sermon on the "Mammon of Iniquity," offering to be his congregants' "spiritual accountant," but it is also at work in "Araby," suggesting that the men in the bazaar are trafficking in the "prayers and praises" of "desire" (23-24, cf. 21-28), and in the same way, there is something simoniacal about the exchanges in "Two Gallants," trafficking in dreams of love and desire, or in the sacred myths of Ireland, like the harpist busking on the steps of the Kildare Street club, both of which Lenehan and Corley would readily sell for a sovereign piece stamped with the seal of an English monarch.[13]

Thus, the gold coin in "Two Gallants" offers rich possibilities for interpretation, but no guarantee that any will be repaid with certainty.[14] Indeed, its richness as a symbol derives from the fact that it is repeatedly hinted at without ever being shown, accruing a good deal of unpaid in-

---

[12] Florence Walzl suggests "an ironic inversion of the agony in the garden, the betrayal of Jesus for thirty pieces of silver, and the kiss of Judas" (78), but the disparity between the single gold coin and the thirty pieces of silver attenuates the connection.

[13] The coin is most likely a half-sovereign or gold sovereign minted during the reign of Queen Victoria or Edward VII. It could also have been a two or five pound gold coin, but only the Jubilee double sovereign of 1887 was minted in sufficient numbers to go into circulation.

[14] For instance, a Marxist interpretation might discount the magical, fetishistic quality of the coin as concealed alienation and exploitation, uncovering its true value as labour-time. Yet Joyce's hints about the two gallants' labour complicate this discourse: Corley, as a police informer, and Lenehan, as a purveyor of betting tips (44), both live off their wits. Hungry and broke, when Lenehan anticipates having "to speak a great deal, to invent and to amuse," merely for a drink, talk is commodified as the fulfilment of desire. And if Corley has convinced the woman to give or lend him a pound, then this is exactly what the gold coin represents: "Frozen Desire," in James Buchan's phrase. This reading of "Two Gallants" can readily be extended from sexual to political power: for instance, Marc Shell traces the connection between the invention of coinage and the development of dialectic in ancient Greece, both concurrent with the rise of tyranny (11-62). However, I am indebted to an anonymous reviewer for pointing out an equally ancient connection between money and the underworld: in Greek mythology, Charon must be paid an *obolus* to ferry the dead to Hades. Given that the opening words of *Dubliners* ("There was no hope": 1) echo *Inferno* 3.9 ("*Lasciate ogne speranza, voi ch'intrate*": "abandon all hope ye who enter"), and that Father Flynn, the late "paralytic" (3), represents a synecdoche of Dublin as "the centre of paralysis" (*Letters* II 134, above), the coin in "Two Gallants" might symbolise passage to the land of the dead, which is to say, a "[portal] into the unknown" (Joyce, *Portrait* 123).

terest as the unseen object of two loaded exchanges: first between Corley and the woman, then between the two gallants. Withheld until the final line, the shiny gold coin provides the climax of the story, a narrative pay-off which is both highly gratifying and utterly empty, for its provenance and significance are never adequately explained. It is precisely this ambiguity that transforms it into a symbol which can, in theory, be exchanged for anything, becoming a symbol of the symbol itself.[15]

He gave me back that sovereign I lent him and I didn't expect it really

In *The Economy of* Ulysses Mark Osteen provides a compelling analysis of monetary circulation and the textual economies of *Ulysses*, arguing that Joyce sought to reconcile spendthrift habits with bourgeois thrift through an aesthetic economy of the gift, where loss is gain; as I have tried to demonstrate, the same holds true for *Dubliners*, whose scrupulous meanness generates endless interest. Similarly, Maud Ellmann shows how "[t]he city in *Ulysses* takes the form of a gigantic body circulating language, commodities, and money, together with the Dubliners whirled round in these economies" (55), and the same could be said for the text she alludes to: consider "the cars careering homeward" in "After the Race," with Jimmy feeling "the machinery of human nerves str[iving] to answer the bounding courses of the swift blue animal" (35, 38), the physical anxiety provoked by Maria's circuitous tram ride in "Clay" (97-99), or Lenehan's circular walk in "Two Gallants."

Although less prominent than the periodicals and throwaways of June 16 1904, *Dubliners* is characterised by the circulation of information, from the card on the Drapery door which convinces the boy in "The Sisters" of Father Flynn's demise to Lenehan's association with racing tissues to Gabriel's reviews in "The Dead." Blood also circulates as a recurrent trope in the collection, linked significantly to language, money and desire: the name of Mangan's sister acts "like a summons to all [the narrator's] foolish blood" in "Araby" (22); the "thin stream of blood trickl[ing] from the corner of [Kernan's] mouth" forms a "dark medal" on the floor in "Grace"; and the rhythmic descriptions of Gabriel's desire pulsate at the end of "The Dead": "the blood went

---

[15] Rereading Freud and Marx, Žižek provides a brilliant account of money as a sublime object of exchange whose "immaterial corporality" gives form to the symbolic order (11-19). See also Jean-Joseph Goux, "Exchange Value and the Symbolic," in *Symbolic Economies* (122-33, esp. 127).

bounding along his veins; and the thoughts went rioting through his brain, proud, joyful, tender, valorous" (214). Indeed, the symbolic economy of the collection as a whole is governed by circulation; it has often been remarked that the titles of the first and last stories, "The Sisters" and "The Dead," could be exchanged, but the circular structure of beginning and ending is more striking still: *Dubliners* begins with a boy looking up at a lighted window for a sign that the old priest had died, and ends with an aging man looking out of a darkened window thinking of a dead youth. Adding to this sense of circularity and closure, just as many of the characters from *Dubliners* (including Lenehan and Corley) are recirculated in *Ulysses*, characters like Kathleen Kearney from "A Mother" circle back into "The Dead," and in the same way, many of the most important themes and motifs from earlier stories return at the end, including Lily's bitter retort to Gabriel's lighthearted marriage banter ("the men that is now is only all palaver and what they can get out of you" [178]), and the pound coin Freddy Malins repays Gabriel which unexpectedly returns the gold sovereign from "Two Gallants" (218).

Yet *Dubliners* is also a collection of discrete short stories, and the breaks between narratives emphasise Joyce's breaks in circulation. This offers an important corrective to Ellmann, Osteen, and others who would make circulation a master trope for *Ulysses*. For instance, "Aeolus," the chapter which is most obviously about circulation, begins "in the heart of the Hibernian metropolis" where trams circulate citizens along Dublin's arteries, "vermilion mailcars" put letters into circulation, and "a great daily organ" pumps (mis)information into the collective bloodstream (M. Ellmann 55); but by the end of the chapter the tramcars stand motionless in their tracks, "becalmed in short circuit" (*Ulysses* 7.1043-7). In the same way, for all the circulating systems in *Dubliners*, the collection begins with the spectre of Father Flynn, whose circulation has literally stopped, and ends with Dublin's public transportation system at a standstill, for "the snow was general all over Ireland" (225). These breaks in circulation, where paralysis leads to literal or symbolic death, draw heightened attention to the encircling system, allowing the material quality of each paralysed element to be examined in isolation, like the eight lines of tramcars and trolleys individually enumerated at the end of "Aeolus" (7.1043-47). In doing so, these breaks reveal the conditions necessary to activate the circuit; or as Lacan puts it, "the hole in the real that results from loss, sets the signifier in motion" (38).

Hence, Joyce's scrupulous meanness consists in the meticulous care he takes to riddle his texts with holes, while at the same time bestowing all his poetic gifts to charge these holes with association, creating *resonant* hiatuses. The gaps and silences in *Dubliners* become portals of imagination, putting symbolic associations into circulation; but no matter how many associations these symbols accrue, they can never be exhausted, because there is always a gap, an incertitude, at the heart of Joyce's gift. To find a figure for this form of exchange, we need look no further than the first paragraph of *Dubliners*, where Joyce's late additions include the famous triad, *paralysis, gnomon*, and *simony*. The "paralytic" priest in "The Sisters" has died of a stroke, and Joyce, we recall, chose Dublin for the scene because it seemed to him "the centre of paralysis" (*Letters* II 134), suggesting that the priest's demise offers a synecdoche of *Dubliners*; but we should not forget that the boy feels "as if [he] had been freed from something by [Father Flynn's] death" (4), and that the Greek root of paralysis means "a loosening aside" (Skeat; see Whittaker 190). The old priest is also labelled a "simoniac," and even in the Catechism, where it is defined as "the buying or selling of spiritual things" (2121), "simony" is derived from Simon Magus, an archetypal heretic traditionally held to be the founder of Gnosticism. Cognate with Gnostic, from the Greek root for *to know*, the strange word "gnomon" is perhaps most interesting of all. Usually it refers to the pointer on a sundial, but the word has many meanings, including a rule or canon of belief, a carpenter's square, and an indicator. The boy in "The Sisters" knows it from Euclid, who defines the figure as a parallelogram with a similar parallelogram missing from one of its corners (i.e., BCDEFG in Figure 1: see Euclid, *Elements* II, Def. 2).

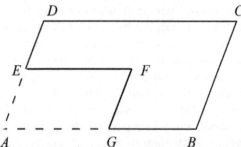

Figure 1: Euclidian gnomon

This figure, like an arrowhead, points towards something absent. As with the gnomon of a sundial, it can reveal hidden truths as intangible as time, but it does so through its shadow, for it is only by tracing back the lines of the gnomon that we can fill in the missing piece. Shaped like the carpenter's square, this sets the rule for the gnomonic repetitions of *Dubliners*: each one points back to a gap, a silence, a missing piece at its origin, yet upon inspection, this missing piece turns out to be a shadow of the whole, supplementing the original figure even as it is the lack which generates it. As such, it provides an infinitely reiterable figure for Joyce's symbolic economy, where language is founded, "like the world, macro and microcosm, upon the void. Upon incertitude" (*Ulysses* 9.841-42), yet this spiralling uncertainty turns out to be a teeming, cornucopian void, capable of yielding endless returns for readers who invest in Joyce.

References

Attridge, Derek. *Joyce Effects: On Language, Theory, and History*. Cambridge: Cambridge University Press, 2001.

Boyle, Robert, S. J. "'Two Gallants' and 'Ivy Day in the Committee Room.'" *James Joyce Quarterly* 1.1 (Fall 1963): 3-9.

Catechism of the Catholic Church. Part 3, §2, ch.1, art.1, 3.2121. Libreria Editrice Vaticana: Citta del Vaticano, 1993, 2003. http://www.vatican.va/archive/ENG0015/_P7E.HTM. Accessed 20 January 2015.

Culler, Jonathan D. *Theory of the Lyric*. Cambridge: Harvard University Press, 2015.

Deming, Robert Howard, ed. *James Joyce: The Critical Heritage*. London: Routledge and Kegan Paul, 1986.

Ellmann, Maud. "*Ulysses*: The Epic of the Human Body." *A Companion to James Joyce*. Ed. Richard Brown. Malden: Blackwell Publishing, 2008. 54-70.

Ellmann, Richard. *James Joyce*. Oxford: Oxford University Press, 1959.

Epstein, E. L. "Hidden Imagery in James Joyce's 'Two Gallants.'" *James Joyce Quarterly* 7.4 (Summer 1970): 369-370.

Goux, Jean-Joseph. *Symbolic Economies: After Marx and Freud*. Trans. Jennifer Curtiss Gage. Ithaca: Cornell University Press, 1990.

Joyce, James. *A Portrait of the Artist as a Young Man*. Ed. Seamus Deane. London: Penguin Books, 1992.

———. *Dubliners*. Ed. Terence Brown. London: Penguin Books, 2000.

———. *Letters of James Joyce*. Ed. Stuart Gilbert and Richard Ellmann. 3 vols. London: Faber and Faber, 1957-1966.

———. *Poems and Shorter Writings*. Ed. Richard Ellmann, A. Walton Litz and John Whittier-Ferguson. London: Faber and Faber, 1991.

———. *Ulysses: The Corrected Text*. Ed. Hans Walter Gabler. London: Random House, 1986.

Lacan, Jacques. "Desire and the Interpretation of Desire in *Hamlet*." *Literature and Psychoanalysis: The Question of Reading: Otherwise*. Ed. Shoshana Felman. Baltimore: Johns Hopkins University Press, 1989. 11-52.

Leonard, Garry Martin. *Reading* Dubliners *Again: A Lacanian Perspective*. Syracuse: Syracuse University Press, 1993.

Norris, Margot. "Gambling with Gambles in 'Two Gallants.'" *NOVEL: A Forum on Fiction* 29.1 (1995): 32–44.

Osteen, Mark. *The Economy of* Ulysses: *Making Both Ends Meet*. Syracuse: Syracuse University Press, 1995.

Reizbaum, Marilyn and Maud Ellmann. "En Garde: 'Two Gallants.'" *Collaborative Dubliners: Joyce in Dialogue*. Ed. Vicki Mahaffey. Syracuse: Syracuse University Press, 2012. 125-143.

Shell, Marc. *The Economy of Literature*. London: Johns Hopkins University Press, 1993.

Skeat, Walter W. *An Etymological Dictionary of the English Language*. 3rd ed. Oxford: Clarendon Press, 1888. https://archive.org/stream/etymologicaldict00skeauoft#page/n7/mode/2up. Accessed 14 June 2013.

The Thirteen Books of Euclid's Elements. Ed. Sir Thomas Heath. Trans. J. L. Heiberg. Cambridge: Cambridge University Press, 1908. https://archive.org/details/thirteenbookseu03heibgoog. Accessed 12 December 2012.

Torchiana, Donald T. "Joyce's 'Two Gallants': A Walk Through the Ascendancy." *James Joyce Quarterly* 6.2 (Winter 1969): 115-127.

Walzl, Florence L. "Symbolism in Joyce's 'Two Gallants.'" *James Joyce Quarterly* 2.2 (Winter 1965): 73-81.

Whittaker, Stephen. "Joyce and Skeat." *James Joyce Quarterly* 24.2 (Winter 1987): 177-192.

Žižek, Slavoj. *The Sublime Object of Ideology*. London: Verso, 1989.

Slippery Subjects: Intersecting Economies of Genre in Gay Male Coming-Out Films, 1995-2015

Martin Mühlheim

This essay documents and explains the frequency of one particular motif – boys or men going swimming – in gay male coming-out films produced between 1995 and 2015. To do so, it develops a methodology (*distant watching*) that allows researchers to arrive at a reasonably accurate estimate of a cinematic motif's frequency within any given genre, without actually having to watch all the films in their corpus. It then explains the frequency of swimming scenes in coming-out films through a set of intersecting reasons – some legal, some economic, and some aesthetic. Finally, the essay demonstrates (a) that a better understanding of generic conventions yields interpretative gains in the discussion of individual cases, and (b) that swimming scenes are particularly frequent in one subgroup of coming-out films: those in which the protagonist is still struggling to establish a non-heterosexual self-identity.

Two casual observations led to the present project. The first was mine, made several years ago, while spending the evening with friends. We were watching a series of short films, many of which revolved around the theme of coming out, and at one point I turned to the others and joked: "If I see one more scene with boys going swimming I'll scream." My friends were perplexed, so I explained that boys or men going for a swim (e.g. Figures 1 and 2) was an oddly frequent motif in gay male coming-out films – including the ones we had just been watching. In early 2015, I repeated the observation during a coffee break at work, to

Figure 1: Though still closeted, Tobi is ready to take the plunge.
(Press still for *Sommersturm*, © X Verleih AG)

Figure 2: For Olivier and Hicham, things are getting wet.
(Screenshot from *Le clan*, © PRO-FUN MEDIA Frankfurt am
Main. Film available on video and in digital form)

a friend and colleague, Sarah Chevalier.[1] It was Sarah who then made a crucial second observation: "What do you mean by 'frequent'? Do you have any figures?" Of course, I did not. A research project was born.[2]

This project consisted of three aims. First, I wanted to develop a methodology for compiling and analyzing a large corpus of films (gay male coming-out films, in this case) – a corpus so large that actually watching all films would be out of the question. The method I eventually adopted – *distant watching* – was inspired by Franco Moretti's concept of *distant reading*, and it can easily be applied to the analysis of other cinematic motifs and genres. Second, I wanted to explain the frequency of one particular motif – boys or men going swimming – in gay male coming-out films. It soon became clear that a mono-causal explanation would not be able to account for the high frequency of "swimming scenes" across the generic corpus. Rather, the frequency of this cinematic motif could best be explained by an intersecting set of reasons – some legal, some economic, and some aesthetic or "artistic." Third, I was hoping to demonstrate that an understanding of the general use of a given motif within a genre would in turn allow one to interpret more precisely what goes on in any individual instance of that motif – in this case, the use of the "swimming scene" in Bavo Defurne's *Noordzee, Texas* (*North Sea, Texas*, 2011). In other words, *distant watching* was not intended to replace the detailed study of individual cases, but rather constituted a means to delineate more clearly the cultural field within which a particular text – here: a gay male coming-out film – needed to be placed.[3]

Before we begin, two comments, or words of caution, are in order concerning the title of this paper. First, the phrase "intersecting economies" should not be misunderstood as an exclusive interest in such issues as marketing and profitability, though these will play a part in the

---

[1] In addition to the invaluable input by the colleagues mentioned in the main text, I would like to acknowledge the crucial feedback provided by Nicole Frey Büchel, Rahel Rivera, Nicole Studer, and the students who attended session 9 of my lecture "Twentieth-Century Genres" (University of Zurich, Spring Semester 2015). I would also like to thank the two anonymous reviewers, one of whom especially alerted me to some important gaps in the argument.

[2] Esther Saxey has noted that many protagonists in coming-out novels "swim or surf" (40). However, in this paper, I'm interested not only in films that feature protagonists who *are* surfers or swimmers, but also in those movies in which the protagonist just *happens* to go swimming. To my knowledge, no previous study of this kind exists.

[3] See Matthew Jockers, who suggests that "by exploring the [. . .] record writ large, we will better understand the context in which individual texts exist and thereby better understand those individual texts" (27). For a similar argument, see Bode (4).

argument that follows. Rather, the discussion of more narrowly economic matters will be complemented by a focus on what could be called the "communicative efficiency" of genre: the highly economical way in which, within a given genre, even the sparsest gesture may evoke a wealth of cultural meanings and resources. It is for this reason that, as Mikhail Bakhtin has emphasized, the study of genre allows us to explore the "basic social tone" of cultural phenomena (259) – including that of gay male coming-out films.

My second caveat regarding the title concerns the label "gay male." Queer theorists and historians of sexuality alike have emphasized how problematic it is to posit a simple binary between straight and gay men (e.g. Sedgwick 8-9; Hekma 137). Arguably, the assumption that the terms *gay* and *straight* denote two stable, clearly separate entities serves to re-enforce the ghettoization of a normalized gay community within a heteronormative society that continues to sanction most forms of "queer" behavior (see Drucker 230). One example of this is that the gay-vs-straight binary often results in the elision of bisexual identities, with bisexuality at best figuring as a "passing phase" on the path to a "true" homosexual identity (e.g. Alexander and Anderlini-D'Onofrio 2-3). Indeed, the "exclusion of any bisexual potential" may, according to Esther Saxey, be one of the key driving forces of the prototypal coming-out story (10). Coming-out stories tend to present gay male subjectivity as a pre-given truth that merely needs to be revealed in the course of the narrative. In doing so, these stories disavow their own textual work of constructing the very identity they purport to reveal. Accordingly, my use of the label "gay male" should be read as a convenient shorthand, but not as an endorsement of the term as unproblematic. Similarly, the exclusion of lesbian coming-out films should neither be read as an implicit value judgment nor as a theoretical claim for the existence of essential differences between representations of male and female same-sex desire. Rather, the decision to exclude lesbian coming-out films constituted an attempt to keep the corpus of films at a manageable size; it was a question of scope, not of identity politics.

Swimming Boys: Compiling a Corpus and Distant Watching

The first problem when studying a genre like gay male coming-out films is to compile a generic corpus that is not merely random or entirely dependent on personal preferences – and the Internet proved invaluable in resolving this problem. Using the Internet Movie Database (IMDb.com),

I compiled a first, "rough" corpus of feature-length, fictional gay male coming-out films (limited, once again for reasons of scope, to films produced between 1995 and July 2015). An IMDb keyword search ("feature film," "coming out," and "1995-2015 Release year or range," conducted on 4 August 2015) yielded a list of 323 titles. However, I realized that that the list contained some films – e.g. documentaries – that did not fit the criteria outlined above.

To eliminate the films that did not belong, I went through IMDb's basic information for each of the 323 films on the list, and deleted any short film collections, documentaries, and lesbian coming-out films. This left me with a corpus comprising 224 films: a "beta version." Next, I re-examined each of these 224 films in more detail, using the plot summary, synopsis, and other information (from IMDb.com and additional Internet sources, e.g. Wikipedia and online reviews) to determine whether or not a movie ought to be classified as "a coming-out film" (i.e. whether coming out constituted a central plotline), or whether the film in question featured the problem of coming out only incidentally, as a marginal element (e.g. films in which only a minor character comes out, as in Stephen Daldry's *Billy Elliot*).[4] If coming out was only a marginal element, I deleted the film from the list. This left me with a list of 145 films, to which, in a final step, I added 16 gay male coming-out films produced between 1995 and 2015 that I own on DVD or Blu-ray, but that were not tagged as such on IMDb.com. This brought the total to 161 films: my "definitive" corpus of gay male coming-out films.[5]

At this point, however, I began to have doubts. Would others agree that the 16 films I had added to the corpus really were coming-out films? And did the films that I had deleted from the "beta version" of the corpus really not belong there? To get at least some sense of whether or not my classification was reliable, I generated a random sample of 27 films from the "beta version" of the corpus. I then asked a colleague, Magdalena Leitner, to classify the films on her own, using the same categories and sources of information that I had used. This would allow me to come up with a very basic measure of inter-annotator agreement: In how many percent of the cases would Magdalena's cate-

---

[4] In terms of plot "logic," *Billy Elliot* (2000) could well be considered a coming-out film, as it tells the story of a working-class boy who has to hide his illicit desire – to become a ballet dancer – from his family. However, in the present context, I am interested only in films that feature coming out in its most common, everyday sense (i.e. coming out as *gay*).

[5] The lists are available on my website: www.es.uzh.ch/en/aboutus/team/mmuehlheim-/bibliography.html.

gorization match mine? It turned out that we agreed in 23 out of 27 – i.e. in 85.2% – of all cases. Given my lack of experience with such procedures, I asked Hans-Martin Lehmann, a corpus linguist working in our department, how this figure was to be interpreted. While Hans-Martin emphasized that my statistical test would not hold up in court, he also conceded that the level of agreement made the classification seem at least reasonably reliable.

However, this still left me with one major problem: How could I find out whether the 161 films in my "definitive" corpus featured a swimming scene, without actually having to watch each film (easily over 250 hours)? The solution was a method I termed *distant watching*, inspired by Franco Moretti's concept of *distant reading*. Moretti explicitly defines distant reading as a way of dealing with corpora that are too vast for in-depth study:

> [C]lose reading (in all of its incarnations, from the new criticism to deconstruction) [. . .] necessarily depends on an extremely small canon. [. . . W]e know how to read texts, now let's learn how not to read them. Distant reading: where distance [. . .] is a condition of knowledge: it allows you to focus on units that are much smaller or much larger than the text: devices, themes, tropes – or genres and systems. (Moretti 48-49)

Small tropes: the swimming scene; and larger generic units: gay male coming-out films. It seemed a perfect match.

But what, more specifically, is distant watching? For each of the 161 films from the "definitive" corpus, I conducted a Google image search and, where available, also watched the official trailer (on Youtube or a similar platform). If the still images or the trailer contained a swimming scene, the film went into group A; if they did not, the film went into group B. Evidently, this meant that some films which in fact do feature swimming scenes would erroneously end up in group B; screenshots and trailers are, after all, only excerpts. At the same time, however, group A would contain only correctly identified films as, in each case, I had actually seen the swimming scene (either as a still image or in the trailer). Distant watching thus allowed me to come up with a figure that would (a) certainly not *over*estimate and (b) possibly *under*estimate the actual number of gay male coming-out films featuring swimming scenes. In short, my estimate would be conservative, but otherwise reliable.[6]

---

[6] A more technical way of putting this is to say that *recall* might be low, but *precision* would be very high.

And so, after only a few hours of distant watching, I was finally in a position to meet Sarah's challenge and provide some figures. Swimming scenes, I found, occur in 54 of the 161 films from my "definitive" corpus (i.e. 33.5%). In other words, one out of three gay male coming-out films featured a swimming scene – according to a conservative estimate! Which begs the question: Why?

Afraid of Drowning: Legal and Economic Pressures

I first considered the – potentially difficult – legal and economic context for gay male coming-out films. Like most filmmakers, presumably, the producers of a coming-out film hope to reach a sizeable audience, partly because they want their film to have some meaningful cultural impact, but also, more prosaically, because a larger audience means that the filmmakers are more likely to break even, perhaps even to make a profit. Filmmakers, in other words, want their product to be appealing – and attractive protagonists, preferably naked at some point during the film, are an easy way of achieving this goal: sex sells, as they say.[7]

Some sex sells, that is, for too much (or the wrong type of) sex can lead to prohibitively high age ratings, which in turn may limit the filmmakers' opportunities for legal distribution – in particular, legal distribution to what is arguably one of the core audiences for coming-out films: adolescents. Of course, in the age of illegal downloading, this does not mean that young people will not have access to the film. However, if teenagers download a film illegally – which is more likely in the case of a high age rating – then this translates into a financial loss for the filmmakers, as illegal downloads, by definition, do not generate profits for the copyright owners.

The threat of high age ratings is, moreover, exacerbated in the case of gay male coming-out films by at least two factors: first, the fact that the protagonists are often young, and that sexually explicit scenes featuring young characters are more likely to receive high age ratings than comparable scenes with adult protagonists; and second, the fact that depictions of gay sex tend, on average, to receive higher age ratings than depictions of straight sex (a point made forcefully in Kirby Dick's 2006 documentary *This Film Is Not Yet Rated*, which in one sequence juxtaposes scenes featuring straight sex to comparable scenes featuring gay sex – with the latter

---

[7] What supports this idea is the fact that swimmers and swimming scenes feature quite prominently on advertising posters, DVD covers, etc.

consistently receiving the higher age rating by the MPAA).[8] A combination of legal and economic considerations thus provides some relatively strong incentives for the makers of a coming-out film to avoid "overly explicit" depictions of gay sex – particularly in films featuring teenage protagonists.[9]

And yet, suppressing sex and eroticism altogether would be counterproductive, given that the pressure to hide one's sexual orientation is precisely what gay liberationists aimed to combat with the strategy of coming out (e.g. Weeks 79). Filmmakers thus find themselves in need of a suitable compromise between, on the one hand, the juridico-economic pressures associated with age ratings, and, on the other, an unapologetic representation of same-sex attraction on the screen. And this is, precisely, where swimming scenes offer an almost perfect solution: they allow filmmakers to show naked, glistening bodies, but at the same time to hide any "indecencies" below the surface; boys undress, go swimming and, possibly, fool around a little – yet what goes on below the waistline remains demurely out of sight (e.g. Figure 3). It is, to be sure, not the only possible solution – but certainly a simple and elegant one.

Figure 3: What goes on below the waistline remains out of sight. (Screenshot from *Jongens*, © Salzgeber & Co. Medien GmbH)

---

[8] The Motion Picture Association of America is responsible for US age ratings. More recently, the MPAA's rating of the film *Pride* (2014) sparked some controversy (Burrell, "Pride").

[9] On the economics of age ratings, see Dolgin 130 and Driscoll 129.

Murky Depths: Unconscious Desire and Symbolical Rebirth

I had thus found a rather neat juridico-economic explanation for the frequency of swimming scenes. However, I also remembered Janet Staiger's caveat concerning historically grounded analyses of film. According to Staiger, one must always take into account how legal and economic factors overlap with cinematic signifying conventions that, in turn, may also intersect with each other: "This prevents a simplistic assertion that such and such economic practice determined such and such signifying practice and makes the historical representation more complex, mediated and non-linear. Locating single causes also becomes impossible" (153). In addition to juridico-economic constraints, I thus also needed to consider more properly aesthetic or artistic reasons for the frequency of swimming scenes.

The most obvious artistic reason I could think of for filmmakers to include such scenes is that water has long been regarded as a symbol of the unconscious (e.g. Cirlot 364-365; Ferber 172). Of course, water potentially has a vast range of subtly different meanings, but when focusing on the coming-out genre as a whole, seen through the lens of distant watching, it seemed best to concentrate on the dominant association (for some "secondary symbolic meanings," see Cirlot 366). Water as a symbol of the unconscious, then: the realm of the drives, providing the impetus for sexual desire. In swimming scenes, filmmakers can, in other words, be said symbolically to immerse their closeted protagonists in the waters of – as of yet – unconscious desires: an image of sexual awakening.

It was time to look at one particular example, to examine the range of symbolic meanings associated with a protagonist's immersion in water in more detail. In many religious and mythological traditions, for example, immersion in water carries strong resonances of annihilation and regeneration – i.e. symbolical death and rebirth (cf. the motif of baptism; e.g. Cirlot 365; Ferber 180-181). This, I suspected, might tie in nicely with the theme of coming out: an old, heterosexual identity is symbolically killed off, and a new, gay identity emerges. Were there any films that brought this kind of symbolism to the fore?

One film that came to my mind was Malgorzata Szumokswa's *W imię. . . (In the Name of. . .)*.[10] Szumokswa's film tells the story of a Catholic priest responsible for a group of youths with behavior prob-

---

[10] Two other films in which the symbolism of death and rebirth is particularly marked are Gaël Morel's *Le clan* (2004) and Marco Kreuzpaintner's *Sommersturm* (2006).

lems. While taking care of the injuries that one of his protégés sustained in a fight, the priest becomes aware of his attraction to youth (Figure 4). From here, the film cuts directly to a scene in which the group of young men take a swim in a lake (Figure 5). The youth whom the priest desires jumps into the water but fails to reemerge, and the priest ultimately has to rescue him from drowning (Figure 6). Back on land, the youth remains unconscious, so that the priest is "forced" to revive him through mouth-to-mouth resuscitation (Figure 7) – a symbolical kiss of life, leading to rebirth. Of course, strictly speaking, the symbolism is off here: after all, the sequence is pivotal for the *priest*, not for the youth (though later in the film we learn that the youth does in fact reciprocate the priest's feelings); it is thus the priest who is "reborn." This, however, need not disconcert us, as symbolism does not follow the strict laws of

Figure 4: A priest becomes aware of his attraction to a youth. (Screenshot from *W imię...*, © Salzgeber & Co. Medien GmbH)

Figure 5: The film then cuts to a typical swimming scene. (Screenshot from *W imię...*, © Salzgeber & Co. Medien GmbH)

Figure 6: The youth almost drowns, but the priest rescues him. (Screenshot from *W imię. . .*, © Salzgeber & Co. Medien GmbH)

Figure 7: Mouth-to-mouth resuscitation: a symbolical kiss, leading to rebirth. (Screenshot from *W imię. . .*, © Salzgeber & Co. Medien GmbH)

reason, but rather the more labyrinthine logic of dreams. The symbolism of death and rebirth thus appears in displaced form in *W imię. . .*, projected away from the priest, onto the object of his desire.

A priest, water, death and rebirth: Szumokswa's film provides a good opportunity for a brief detour on how scenes of "sexual baptism" may relate to the coming-out genre's intriguing structural kinship with Christian narratives of conversion. As Norman W. Jones suggests, "[s]exual desire often plays a similar narrative role in gay and lesbian coming-out stories" as the experience of conversion does in Christian life narratives; just like the non-believer's encounter with Christ, sexual desire in coming-out narratives "impinges on the protagonist's will and helps lead to a personal transformation" (114). In both narrative traditions, those who "receive the call" can try and refuse it, or struggle against it; moreover, in both cases, "converts" retrospectively reassess their previous lives in the light of a startling new truth – new, that is, to their conscious lives, for they now believe that this truth had always been there, unrevealed, just waiting for them to discover it (114-115). The "baptismal" symbolism of immersion in water in films like *W imię*... could thus be said to highlight the parallel between coming out and spiritual conversion, in order to emphasize the emotional profundity of the coming-out experience. (This, however, is not to say that symbolical immersion in water occurs only in films from predominantly Christian cultures – witness the ending of Ryosuke Hashiguchi's *Nagisa no Shindobaddo*, 1995.)

Returning to swimming scenes more generally, when thinking about the coming-out films I had seen I also realized that they took place in two different types of setting. While some swimming scenes are located in an urban environment (e.g. a public pool), quite a few are set in remote, isolated places somewhere "out in nature." Seen from a realist perspective, the latter of course makes perfect sense: the closeted protagonists need to hide their non-normative desires, and so they end up in isolated places, far away from prying glances. Read symbolically, however, the association of swimming scenes with natural surroundings can be read, more specifically, as a neo-pastoral rhetoric of innocence – particularly when it is during this scene that the protagonists' sexual longings first erupt. According to this logic, the boys on the screen are not engaging in sexual corruption, but merely discovering their supposedly natural self: who they really are, and whom society ought to allow them to be. Whether or not one finds such a rhetoric of "natural innocence" convincing, the ease with which pastoral surroundings can be combined with swimming scenes provides us with yet another reason why the latter are an appealing visual trope for the makers of gay male coming-out films.[11]

So far, I have thus isolated five interrelated factors – two "economic" and two "artistic" ones – that, *together*, provide us with a plausible way of explaining the frequency of swimming scenes in gay male coming-out films:

(1) a positive economic incentive: naked skin on the screen is appealing ("sex sells");
(2) a negative economic incentive, arising from the existence of age ratings (leading filmmakers to avoid "overly explicit" sex scenes, particularly in movies aimed at younger audiences and featuring adolescent protagonists);

---

[11] The term *pastoral* has a long and complex history, and it would be misleading to reduce the genre generally to a rhetoric of innocence (see Gifford 1-12; Garrard 33-58).

(3) a general symbolic meaning: the association of water with the unconscious and, therefore, desire;
(4) a more specific symbolic meaning: death and rebirth;
(5) a neo-pastoral rhetoric of innocence aimed at emphasizing that the protagonists' same-sex desires are entirely natural.

In any given individual film, only one, or several, or even all of these factors may – consciously or unconsciously – have prompted filmmakers to include a swimming scene.

And yet, when thinking about this list, it occurred to me that there was at least one additional factor – one I decided to term *intrageneric amplification*. What this means is that, as soon as a particular motif becomes frequent in a given genre, audiences and filmmakers are likely to pick up on it, and ultimately to respond to it: in the case of the audience, to expect, savor, or dread it; in the case of filmmakers, to quote, play with, possibly critique it. In other words, once a particular motif has become a recognizable genre convention – recognizable to connoisseurs, at least – this motif is likely to be used again and again, in an intrageneric dialogue that amplifies the motif's frequency.

Lost at Sea: Lotman's Minus Device, Noordzee, Texas, *and Sex vs. Maturity*

As soon as a generic motif becomes widely recognized, filmmakers can thus start toying with audience expectations: they can include the usual cues, provide the usual set-up – and then refuse to deliver the expected motif. This constitutes what Yuri (a.k.a. Jurji) Lotman has called a *minus device*: "cases where the non-utilization of some element, its meaningful absence," becomes part and parcel of the text's "artistic message" (51). Given that swimming scenes are frequent in gay male coming-out films, they might, therefore, be used by filmmakers as a minus device.

And indeed, against the backdrop of the general genre convention, I was now able to recognize such a minus device – used not once, but twice – in Bavo Defurne's *Noordzee, Texas*, one of the films from my corpus. Pim, Defurne's protagonist, has long had a crush on Gino, and when the latter tells his mother that he would like to spend the night with Pim, in a tent on the beach, savvy audience members can see where this might be going: two boys on a beach, a swimming scene; then, possibly, an erotic adventure. Such expectations will, however, not be fulfilled: the camera cuts directly to the interior of the tent, and the two protagonists evidently do not need a symbolical swimming scene to awaken unconscious desires (Figure 8). Later in the film, we encounter Pim and Gino driving out to the countryside on Gino's motorbike, in what looks like a neo-pastoral escapade; they stop in a suitably remote place, right next to a pond: the prototypical set-up for a swimming scene. Yet, once again, it doesn't happen. Rather than going for a swim, the protagonists start making out right then and there, on the very edge of the pond (Figure 9).

Figure 8: No swimming, Part I – Pim and Gino know exactly what they desire. (Screenshot from *Noordzee, Texas*, © Salzgeber & Co. Medien GmbH)

Figure 9: No swimming, Part II – Pim and Gino make out right on the edge of a pond. (Screenshot from *Noordzee, Texas*, © Salzgeber & Co. Medien GmbH)

What renders this twofold inclusion of the minus device in *Noordzee, Texas* particularly interesting is that Defurne's film does feature a swimming scene later on – one that emphasizes the problematic of maturity or coming-of-age, rather than that of desire and coming out. In this later scene, Pim is disillusioned with life in general and, in particular, with Gino, who pretends that his feelings for Pim were just some sort of adolescent foolishness. Pim decides to burn all the treasured mementoes he has collected since early childhood, including a portrait of Gino he once drew (Figure 10). Pim then undresses, runs toward the sea, and immerses himself in its cold, dark waters (Figure 11). After a while, the camera loses sight of the boy, showing us some rolling waves and then a glimpse of the sky (Figure 12) before cutting away to a funeral procession (Figure 13). There is thus more than a hint that Pim, in his sorrow, may have committed suicide – that it is his funeral we are now watching. This, however, turns out not to be the case, which renders the sequence a perfect example of "merely" symbolical death, followed by spiritual regeneration. In other words, the two sequences in which Pim "acts out" his desire both employ the minus device. By contrast, the swimming scene that does occur is emphatically *not* linked to awakening desire; instead, it focuses on Pim's rejection of "childish illusions."

Figure 10: Pim symbolically burns the illusions that remain from his childhood. (Screenshot from *Noordzee, Texas*, © Salzgeber & Co. Medien GmbH)

Noordzee, Texas may thus implicitly critique the swimming scenes in other coming-out films, which tend to conflate sexual awakening with the achievement of maturity ("coming of age"). Defurne's film, by contrast, suggests that growing up is a more complex phenomenon; it certainly involves understanding the nature of one's desire, but this in itself

Figure 11: Disillusioned, Pim immerses himself in the sea's cold waters. (Screenshot from *Noordzee, Texas*, © Salzgeber & Co. Medien GmbH)

Figure 12: The camera loses sight of Pim and shows us a glimpse of the sky. (Screenshot from *Noordzee, Texas*, © Salzgeber & Co. Medien GmbH)

will not be enough. It also requires the rejection of infantile views as a precondition for mature behavior. In short, having recognized the swimming scene's general importance for the gay male coming-out genre, we can now read *Noordzee, Texas* as strategically modifying the convention in order to express artistic dissent from the ideological implications of a formal device.

Figure 13: The camera then cuts to a funeral – is it Pim's? (Screenshot from *Noordzee, Texas*, © Salzgeber & Co. Medien GmbH)

Parting the Waters: Coming out to Oneself vs. Coming out to Others

At this point, I had completed my initial three tasks: I had developed a methodology that allowed me to document the frequency of swimming scenes in coming-out films; I had provided a set of explanations; and I had found a nice example illustrating the interpretive gains. And yet, in the course of my research, a fourth question occurred to me and refused to go away: What if there were different types of coming-out films – distinct generic subgroups, each with its own, characteristic relation to the swimming scene?

After giving the matter some thought, I settled on a tripartite division. First, there were some films in my corpus – Simon Shore's *Get Real*, for example – in which the focus lies on a protagonist who is only just becoming aware of his same-sex desires: an experience that triggers intense self-scrutiny and, more often than not, an identity crisis. For Esther Saxey, this type of plot is synonymous to the coming-out story *tout court*:

> The coming out story describes *an individual's path to lesbian, gay or bisexual identity*. Its protagonist is most likely to be a troubled teenager whose insistent desires drag him or her through a minefield of social and sexual dramas. *The protagonist gathers clues to make sense of the situation*, but the reader is often sure well in advance where the protagonist is headed. (1; my emphasis)

However, while coming out to oneself is certainly crucial, sociologists tend to regard this as only one of four, frequently interrelated, steps in a longer, more convoluted process: (1) coming out to oneself; (2) meeting and getting to know other lesbian and gay people; (3) telling friends and relatives; and (4) publicly acknowledging that one is lesbian or gay (Zastrow 239-240). The four steps do not necessarily have to occur in this order (e.g. one may tell one's friends first and only then decide to meet other gays and lesbians), and the process may remain incomplete (e.g. one may be hindered from coming out publicly because gay sex is a capital offence in one's country of residence). Nevertheless, the four-part model highlights that coming out is not usually one single event, but a process with various, potentially overlapping phases.

And yet, in the present context, we can simplify the model and note that, in addition to films focusing on coming out *to oneself*, a second subgroup is concerned with the issue of coming out *to others*. Such films – Ivan Silvestrini's *Come non detto* or Harmage Singh Kalirai's *Chicken Tikka Masala*, for example – deal with protagonists who have already established a gay identity when the movie opens, but who have not yet told all their family or friends. If the first subgroup involves the problem of self-scrutiny and the development of a new self-image, in other words, the second revolves around the impact that coming out to others will have on the protagonist's life, while taking his sexual identity as a given.

While these first two subgroups differ in terms of *content* – i.e. the type of coming out involved – there is, moreover, a third subgroup comprising a *structurally* distinct set of movies that I decided to call "episodic/multi-protagonist films." These are films that feature several, equally important plotlines – either as distinct episodes (as in Sergio Tovar Velarde's *Cuatro lunas*), or as important individual plotlines that run parallel to a central "group plotline" (as in Matthew Warchus's *Pride*, which focuses on an activist group supporting a community of striking miners). In the episodic/multi-protagonist films from my corpus, the problem of coming out – to oneself or to others – is thus not *the central* plotline (as in the other two subgroups), but only *central to one* of the various plotlines.

Now, the question was: Would swimming scenes be distributed equally across the subgroups, or would there be any notable differences? I once again went through my "definitive" corpus, using IMDb.com plot summaries and other information from the Internet to re-categorize all 161 films into the three subgroups. The figures I ended up with were:

(1) 94 films about coming out to oneself;
(2) 41 films about coming out to others;
(3) 26 episodic/multi-protagonist films.

Predictably, inter-annotator agreement was lower this time, with Magdalena and myself agreeing in only 19 out of 27, or 70.4% of all cases. This level of agreement was – once again according to Hans-Martin, my expert on such matters – just about acceptable, though evidently no longer particularly impressive. Nevertheless, I couldn't resist calculating the percentage of swimming scenes for each of the three subgroups – and the results were remarkable indeed:

(1) swimming scenes in films about coming out to oneself: 46.8%
(2) in films about coming out to others: 9.8%
(3) in episodic/multi-protagonist films: 23.1%

Leaving aside for the moment the episodic/multi-protagonist subgroup, one thing was readily apparent: swimming scenes were associated especially with the problem of coming out to oneself – they occur in almost half of these films! – but were not exceptionally frequent in films focusing on protagonists who already self-identify as gay and "merely" have to come out to others.

This result, I eventually realized, tied in nicely with the juridico-economic reasons I had provided for the frequency of the motif. For one thing, given that films focusing on coming out to oneself are more likely to feature adolescent protagonists, the problem of age ratings is particularly acute in this subgroup, rendering the compromise solution of swimming scenes – naked skin without "overly explicit" sex – all the more appealing. By contrast, films focusing on coming out to others are more likely to feature characters who are slightly older: protagonists who already know they're gay, and whose problems – re-negotiating their relationships with friends, co-workers, and family – are arguably more appealing to a slightly older audience. This, in turn, means that films from this second subgroup can treat age ratings more cavalierly and be somewhat more daring in depicting gay sex – which renders the need for "euphemistic" swimming scenes much less pressing.

Moreover, the more artistic or symbolical dimensions of swimming scenes that I had identified also worked well to explain the marked difference in frequency between the two first subgroups. First, water as a symbol of unconscious desire is evidently more appropriate for characters who have yet to discover their sexual orientation, as opposed to those who already know. Second, while symbolical death and rebirth are obvious metaphors for the process of coming out to oneself – one emerges, as it were, into a new life – such imagery is not particularly suitable for a character who is already "fully formed." Third, a neo-pastoral rhetoric of innocence is more to the point whenever the sexual identity of a character is still in question: the protagonist is faced with an ethical decision concerning his same-sex desires, and the pastoral scene suggests that these desires are not deviant or abnormal, but perfectly natural. By contrast, if a character has already accepted his sexual orientation, the question of "naturalness" or "innocence" may not exactly be settled, but it is certainly less urgent (i.e. the protagonist has, for better or worse, already made his ethical choice). Finally, if for all these reasons swimming scenes are not particularly frequent in films about coming out to others, then there will also not be any intrageneric amplification in this second subgroup, as such amplification depends on a motif's pre-existing, "base level" frequency. In other words, intrageneric amplification only occurs when a given motif is already frequent – as is the case with swimming scenes in subgroup one, but not in subgroup two.

Which left me with the episodic/multi-protagonist films, where matters were somewhat less clear, and more complex. At 23.1%, swimming scenes are still quite frequent in this group. Could it be that most of the episodes or plotlines concerned with coming out in these films are about the problem of coming out to oneself, rather than about coming out to others only? It is difficult to tell, based solely on distant watching: each of these films features several plotlines, which means that plot summaries, trailers, etc., provide comparatively little information on the individual plotlines. My impression – and it is no more than that – is that the majority of the relevant plotlines indeed deal with coming out to oneself, rather than with coming out to others – which would explain why the percentage in this group is higher than the percentage for films about coming out to others.

But why would the percentage for the episodic/multi-protagonist films be so much lower than for the coming-out-to-oneself subgroup (23.1% vs. 46.8%)? One reason may have to do with narrative economy: several distinct plotlines are crammed into one single feature film, which means that there is only limited time per individual plotline, and hence not enough time to include leisurely swimming scenes. A second factor, moreover, could be that symbolism in episodic/multi-protagonist films is chosen with a view to the entire movie, as a way of providing symbolical coherence across the film's various plotlines. This would mean that the set of "incentives" to include a swimming scene in the coming-out plotline might sometimes be counteracted by the symbolical design envisioned for the film as a whole (i.e. a swimming scene might simply not fit into the overall design). A third factor, finally, might be that distant watching is even more likely than usual to miss some swimming scenes because, in episodic/multi-protagonist films, they only appear in one of several plotlines (i.e. the details of that one plotline may not feature very prominently in trailers or still images).[12] These explanations are tentative, to be sure, and less compelling than the ones for the other two subgroups. Perhaps it would be better to treat episodic/multi-protagonist films as a different genre entirely? At any rate, it was clear that my investigation had reached an end.

Conclusion: Charting the Crosscurrents of Genre

There are some obvious limits to the results I have presented in this essay. For one thing, as noted throughout, none of the figures are absolutely reliable in any strict, statistical sense. Genre categorization will always be, to some extent, subjective, and there are bound to be films in my corpus that, according to others, ought not to be included. Moreover, in addition to contenting myself with very basic statistical tests, I have refrained from even asking some evident follow-up questions: Were swimming scenes equally frequent in coming-out films produced before 1995? Are they becoming less frequent now that images of gay sex are, supposedly, more widely accepted? When in a film do these scenes typically occur (i.e. early, middle, or towards the end)? How frequent are swimming scenes set "in nature" (e.g. in a forest), as opposed to those set in a densely populated area or even indoors (e.g. on a crowded beach, or in a public pool)? Are swimming scenes set indoors more likely to occur in a particular type of coming-out film and, if so, why? In short, it would be possible to analyze the device more carefully, and thus to refine the results of my distant watching.[13]

Finally, my initial decision to exclude lesbian coming-out films makes it impossible to say whether swimming scenes are comparably frequent in this parallel corpus – or, for that matter, in heterosexual coming-of-

---

[12] In other words, *recall* may be lower for subgroup three than for the other two groups.

[13] I would like to thank Franco Moretti, who, in his comments on a late draft of this essay, suggested some of these follow-up questions to emphasize that "there is a trap in the idea that all attentive reading is CR [i.e. close reading]" (e-mail, 21 March 2016). The example of swimming scenes set in different locations (e.g. indoors vs. outdoors) was suggested, in conversation, by Misha Kavka (29 March 2016).

age movies. If I had to venture a guess, I would say that swimming scenes are not *in*frequent in straight coming-of-age films, but perhaps quite a bit *less* frequent than in gay male – and, possibly, lesbian – coming-out films. As we have seen, stories focusing on coming out to oneself have a structural affinity to conversion narratives, thus rendering the symbolism of death and rebirth associated with swimming scenes particularly appropriate. By contrast, while straight coming-of-age tales often do focus on sexual awakening as well, they seem to me far more likely to echo a different Christian narrative, namely, that of a traumatic fall from grace (i.e. not rebirth, but expulsion from the "paradise of childhood innocence"). In addition, euphemistic self-censorship, too, may be somewhat less imperative when depicting straight sexuality, thus lowering the pressure for the compromise solution provided by the swimming scene. But these are speculations.

What I have shown, however, is that swimming scenes are frequent in gay male coming-out films in general, and very frequent in one subgenre in particular: those films that focus mainly on a protagonist's struggle with his emerging awareness of same-sex desires (i.e. coming out to oneself). There are various intersecting reasons for this – legal and economic, symbolic and intertextual – which *together* explain the frequency of swimming scenes *across* the corpus, though not necessarily such scenes' presence in any given individual film. Having shown that the motif is frequent, moreover, I was able to explain why even the absence of swimming scenes can – for a genre aficionado, at least – become a source of meaning: a film like *Noordzee, Texas* may play on generic expectations, and then break or frustrate these expectations in order to engage in a critical dialogue with the established genre convention (Lotman's minus device). More generally speaking, the essay provides insight into how gay male subjectivity is constructed by zooming in on one seemingly incidental motif that turns out to be a surprisingly central component of the "gay male imaginary" – at least in the cinematic field.

Beyond any findings relating to coming-out films and swimming scenes in particular, I would like to highlight the general, methodological implications of my paper: (a) that distant watching allows us to chart at least the outlines of a large corpus of films that would otherwise be almost impossible to navigate; (b) that the findings generated through distant watching (or, in the case of literary texts, distant reading) do not replace, but in fact help us situate more precisely – and thus enhance – the close analysis of individual cases (as I tried to demonstrate with the example of *Noordzee, Texas*, and as Franco Moretti himself has pointed out);[14] and (c) that elements which are frequent across a given genre are likely to be so, not because of one single factor, but due to various interrelated reasons ("likely to be so": it is by no means inconceivable that, every once in a while, a mono-causal explanation happens to be correct). Methods like distant reading/watching, in short, provide us with powerful tools to better understand the construction of even such slippery subjects as boys and men swimming – perhaps even kissing – in the genre of coming-out films.

---

[14] For instance, in a recent talk entitled "Where Is the Humanities in the Digital Humanities?" (Cabaret Voltaire, Zurich, 29 February 2016), Moretti argued that the stylistic uniqueness of Joyce's *Ulysses* could be described with a much greater degree of precision if we had a better understanding of sentence structures across the novelistic corpus.

References

Fiction films

Billy Elliot. Dir. Stephen Daldry. Studio Canal et al., 2000.
Chicken Tikka Masala. Dir. Harmage Singh Kalirai. Medtia Group, 2005.
Come non detto. Dir. Ivan Silvestrini. Mondo Home Entertainment, 2012.
Cuatro lunas. Dir. Sergio Tovar Velarde. ATKO Films, 2014.
Get Real. Dir. Simon Shore. Arts Council of England et al., 1998.
Jongens. Dir. Mischa Kamp. Pubkin Film/NTR, 2014.
Le clan. Dir. Gaël Morel. Sépia Productions, 2004.
Nagisa no Shindobaddo. Dir. Ryosuke Hashiguchi. Toho Company, 1995.
Noordzee, Texas. Dir. Bavo Defurne. Indeed Films, 2011.
Pride. Dir. Matthew Warchus. Pathé et al., 2014.
Sommersturm. Dir. Marco Kreuzpaintner. Claussen & Wöbke, 2004.
W imię. . .. Dir. Małgorzata Szumowska. MD4 et al., 2013.

Secondary sources

(a) Print and web

Alexander, Jonathan and Serena Anderlini-D'Onofrio. "Bisexuality and Queer Theory: An Introduction." *Bisexuality and Queer Theory: Intersections, Connections and Challenges.* Eds. Jonathan Alexander and Serena Anderlini-D'Onofrio. London: Routledge, 2012. 1-19.
Bakhtin, Mikhail. "Discourse in the Novel." 1934-35. *The Dialogic Imagination.* Ed. Michael Holquist. Trans. Caryl Emerson and Michael Holquist. University of Texas Press Slavic Series 1. Austin: University of Texas Press, 1981. 259-422.
Bode, Katherine. *Reading by Numbers: Recalibrating the Literary Field.* 2012. Paperback ed. Anthem Scholarship in the Digital Humanities. New York: Anthem Press, 2014.
Burrell, Ian. "Pride: Are US Film Censors Pandering to Homophobia?" 30 September 2014. *The Independent.* 17 August 2015. www.independent.co.uk/arts-entertainment/films/features/-pride-are-censors-pandering-to-homophobia-9765935.html.
Cirlot, Juan Eduardo. *A Dictionary of Symbols.* Trans. Jack Sage. New York: Dover, 2002.
Dolgin, Alexander. *The Economies of Symbolic Exchange.* Berlin: Springer-Verlag, 2009.

Driscoll, Catherine. *Teen Film: A Critical Introduction*. Berg Film Genres. New York: Berg, 2011.

Drucker, Peter. *Warped: Gay Normality and Queer Anti-Capitalism*. 2015. Historical Materialism 92. Chicago: Haymarket, 2016.

Ferber, Michael. *A Dictionary of Literary Symbols*. 1999. 2nd ed. Cambridge: Cambridge University Press, 2007.

Garrard, Gregg. *Ecocriticism*. New Critical Idiom. London: Routledge, 2004.

Gifford, Terry. *Pastoral*. New Critical Idiom. London: Routledge, 1999.

Jockers, Matthew L. *Macroanalysis: Digital Methods and Literary History*. Topics in the Digital Humanities. Chicago: University of Illinois Press, 2013.

Jones, Norman W. *Gay and Lesbian Historical Fiction: Sexual Mystery and Post-Secular Narrative*. New York: Palgrave Macmillan, 2007.

Lotman, Jurij. *The Structure of the Artistic Text*. 1971. Trans. Gail Lenhoff and Ronald Vroon. Michigan Slavic Contributions 7. Ann Arbor: The University of Michigan Press, 1977.

Moretti, Franco. *Distant Reading*. London: Verso, 2013.

Saxey, Esther. *Homoplot: The Coming-Out Story and Gay, Lesbian and Bisexual Identity*. Gender, Sexuality and Culture 7. New York: Peter Lang, 2008.

Sedgwick, Eve Kosovsky. *Epistemology of the Closet*. Berkeley: University of California Press, 1990.

Staiger, Janet. "Mass-Produced Photoplays: Economic and Signifying Practices in the First Years of Hollywood." 1980. *Movies and Methods*. Ed. Bill Nichols. Vol. 2. Berkeley: University of California Press, 1985. 144–161.

Ulin, Jeff C. *The Business of Media Distribution: Monetizing Film, TV and Video Content in an Online World*. 2010. 2nd ed. Burlington: Focal, 2014.

Weeks, Jeffrey. *Making Sexual History*. Cambridge: Polity Press, 2000.

Zastrow, Charles. *Introduction to Social Work and Social Welfare: Empowering People*. 10th ed. Belmont: Brooks/Cole, 2010.

(b) Documentary

This Film Is Not Yet Rated. Dir. Kirby Dick. Independent Film Channel, 2006.

Spillage and Banditry: Anne Carson's Derivatives

Oran McKenzie

This essay argues that traditional notions of literary value cannot account for the work of the contemporary Canadian poet Anne Carson because her poetry needs to be situated in the context of the emergence of a new form of economic value in the age of financial derivatives. This stems not from the poet's superficial wish to keep up with the times, but from a deep engagement, born out of Carson's training as a classical philologist, with how the introduction of coinage in Lydia in the 7th century BC changed – or even created – subsequent ways of thinking in philosophy and poetry: the perception of reality and value, the notions of self, subject and object, the separation of form and matter. In the collection *Decreation* (2005) Carson takes derivation (in both the literary and economic sense) beyond traditional forms of intertextuality, encouraging a "spillage" of sources within the text which she observes already in Longinus' essay *On the Sublime*. Through her own practice of a form of "banditry" trading on this spillage, which makes the relationship between the original and the derivative ever more obscure, Carson explores the possibilities of a poetical order grounded in a different kind of visibility. Such a new poetics, which Carson the classicist in effect traces back to Simonides of Keos at the very beginning of the Greek canon, does not deal in the representations, illusionism and exchange between an estranged self and other, all features of a coinage based culture, but strives for the *"withness"* of a new form of gift economy.

The invention of coinage between 700 and 600 BC in the kingdom of Lydia changed the way humans think about and perceive reality. It also transformed poetry. Bruno Snell argued that ancient Greek lyrics bear the traces of a revolution in human self-awareness that he calls "the discovery of the mind," a consolidation of the self which accounts for "the rise of individualism" (235, 42). Hans Jonas discussed how at the same time sight came to be privileged over the other senses, giving rise to "the concept of objectivity, of the thing as it is in itself as distinct from the thing as it affects me," a distinction from which arises "the whole idea of *theoria* and theoretical truth" (147). Marc Shell introduced the idea that the emergence of this "new logic" is linked to the "development of money," the spread of coinage which transformed both philosophy and literature (11). Richard Seaford built on this insight to argue that the origins of philosophy lie in "the counter-intuitive idea of a single substance underlying the plurality of things manifest to the senses," an idea which, he contends, springs from the nature of coins (175). Contemporary to these transformations, the development of a new alphabetic literacy provoked a shift from the oral to the written and a revolution in the "techniques of literary composition" (Carson, *Eros* 43).

A new measure of value, a new sense of self, a new way of perceiving and relating to objects, a new technology to write poetry: "It is not always easy . . . to trace the subtle map of cause and effect that links such changes," writes the Canadian poet and classicist Anne Carson in her first book, *Eros the Bittersweet* (1986), "[b]ut we should make an effort to do so. There is an important, unanswerable question here" (41). She sustained the effort, discussing how the transition from a traditional gift economy to an economy based on money transformed poetry in *Economy of the Unlost (Reading Simonides of Keos with Paul Celan)* (1999). Building her argument on the juxtaposition of early fragments of Greek poetry with the poems of someone who famously despaired at the possibility of continuing to write verse in the second part of the twentieth century, her discussion seems to imply another, unformulated question: if written poetry is linked to the introduction of coinage, what might it become in the age of financial derivatives?

The American poet Kenneth Goldsmith recently claimed that "poetry as we know it – sonnets or free verse on a printed page – feels akin to throwing pottery or weaving quilts, activities that continue in spite of their cultural marginality" (Goldsmith). His argument is that the information overload brought about by new technologies puts verbal arts in a position similar to that of visual arts after the invention of photography. Beyond the rise of the Internet, though, there is an intrinsic connection between money and the notion of value, including in discourses about literature, so could it be that the marginalisation of coinage in the economy also disqualifies traditional notions of literary value? Goldsmith's own solution for literature in this new age is what he calls *uncreative writing*, a writing of "language hoarders" rather than creative geniuses which abandons traditional poetic practices in favour of activities such as databasing, recycling, appropriation and intentional plagiarism. Inspired by Marcel Duchamp, this is a writing which consists in reframing existing texts rather than creating new, original content; in other words, a writing of derivatives.

Anne Carson is not an uncreative writer, far from it, but she is known for a "heretic form of poetry" (Aitken) which is also highly derivative, blending poetry, essay, criticism and translation in multi-layered and complex juxtapositions of quotes, allusions, echoes and ekphrastic descriptions. In *Decreation* (2005), her seventh collection, she pushes the derivative nature of her poetry even further, confounding most of its reviewers. If the essays in the collection are generally praised, much of its poetry is often ignored or, when discussed, dismissed as "bad poetry," a "cliché-ridden jumble" which "overpowers the limits of the lyric in the name of formal or rhetorical experimentation" (Pollock). But is this simply bad poetry or, as with the texts of uncreative writers, is it poetry for which the traditional notion of literary *value* has been rendered inoperative?

In the same way that Carson argues that the poetry of Simonides of Keos emerges from and illuminates the social changes brought about by the invention of coinage, could her own poems – often described as opaque and experimental – depend on and engage with the rise of a new phase in the history of capitalism? "Every time a poet writes a poem," Carson notes on Paul Celan, "he is asking the question, Do words hold good?" (*Economy* 112). Extending Celan's question from the post-Holocaust era to the beginning of the twenty-first century, this paper intends to question the possibility for poetry to still "hold good" in the age of globalised financial capitalism.

My aim is not to argue that Carson's poems "hold good" by being literary equivalents of financial derivatives, but I am interested in attempting to go beyond the idea that their opacity is the result of gratuitous formal experimentation by reflecting on how it relates to the emergence of a new form of economic value. I will begin by sketching the mental horizon which emerges with the invention of coinage in order to set a background on which to then contrast the dynamics at play in Carson's derivations in *Decreation*. Suggesting that these texts echo the logic of derivatives, I will end by marking their difference. If the development of financial capitalism puts large portions of the world population at risk, there might be another side to the disappearing coin: an opportunity to capture some of the energy unleashed by the collapse of the older order in poems which may help to reinvent a different kind of vision, and a more open future.

Of coins and dualisms

One of the main characteristics of a literate culture, according to Carson, is its emphasis on separation. The argument of *Eros the Bittersweet* is based on the idea that the advent of alphabetic literacy is linked to a "reorientation of perceptual abilities," a shift towards the visual sense which informs the literature of the time (43). "[T]o know words," she writes, is "a matter of perceiving the edges between one entity and another," a fact which has profound consequences: "As separable, controllable units of meaning, each with its own visible boundary, each with its own fixed and independent use, written words project their user into isolation" (*Eros* 51, 50). The development of coinage has a similar effect, she continues in *Economy of the Unlost*, severing social relations that previously remained continuous. If a gift is "personal and reciprocal, and depends on a relationship that endures over time," money, on the opposite, "is an abstraction that passes one way and impersonally between two people whose relationship stops with the transfer of cash" (*Economy* 12). The "moral life of a user of money" thus differs from that of someone enmeshed in a traditional gift economy (*Economy* 10), opening up the age of the "spectacle of *grammata*," an age of separation and edges (*Eros* 58).

There is a connection between money and thought, and it implies visibility. In *The Economy of Literature* (1978), Marc Shell argues that there is a "'constitutional' relationship between the origin of money and the origin of philosophy itself," noting that "[i]t is not easy for us, who have used coinage for some twenty-five hundred years, to imagine the impression it made on the minds of those who first used it" (11, 13). Carson alludes to the same idea through a visual metaphor and a Chinese proverb: "No one who uses money can easily get a look at their own practice. *Ask eye to see its own eyelashes*" (*Economy* 10). For Shell, the most striking characteristic of money is its capacity to "transform visibles into invisibles and invisibles into visibles" (Shell 13), while Carson uses Marx to also note that "[m]oney is something visible and invisible at the same time. A 'real abstraction,' in Marx's terms. You can hold a coin in your hand and yet not touch its value" (*Economy* 45).

This double nature of money is precisely what constitutes its relationship with philosophy, according to Shell, noting that "[i]n the thought of Plato, the Idea (especially that of the Good) [also] plays a role at once visible and invisible, unreal and real" (41). Confronted with a profoundly new type of object, both visible and invisible, Greek thinkers used this new form of visibility to further their investigations. "The Ideas cannot be separated from problems of visibility," Shell adds, since "*Eidē*, in fact, is cognate with *idein* (to see)" (42). Socrates follows the rift which appears between material objects and abstract value and devises a similar separation between things and Ideas: "we say that things are seen (*horasthai*) but not intellected (*noeisthai*), while the Ideas (*eidē*) are intellected but not seen" (*Rep.* 507b, qtd in Shell 42). In the *Timaeus*, Ideas are associated to the notion of *form*:

> we must acknowledge that one kind of being is the form which is always the same, uncreated and indestructible, never receiving anything into itself from without, nor itself going out into any other, but invisible and imperceptible by any sense, and which contemplation is granted to intelligence only. (qtd in Shell 43n)

The visible, material things of the world are separated from the forms from which they emerge and in relation to which they remain secondary: "The reality after which an image is *moulded* does not belong to it," Plato affirms, and Shell adds "any more than the die from which a coin is cast belongs to it" (43n).

The logic of money is thus also at the root of the dualism between matter and form. The anthropologist David Graeber extends Shell's argument and suggests that the advent of coinage is also responsible for the birth of what he calls "Axial Age spirituality" (244):[1]

> The war between Spirit and Flesh, then, between the noble Idea and ugly Reality, the rational intellect versus stubborn corporeal drives and desires that resist it, even the idea that peace and community are not things that emerge spontaneously but that need to be stamped onto our baser material natures like a divine insignia stamped into base metal – all those ideas that came to haunt the religious and philosophical traditions of the Axial Age . . .

---

[1] Graeber borrows the phrase "Axial Age" from Karl Jaspers, who "became fascinated by the fact that figures like Pythagoras (570-495 BC), the Buddha (563-483 BC), and Confucius (551-479) were all alive at exactly the same time, and that Greece, India, and China, in that period, all saw a sudden efflorescence of debate between contending intellectual schools" (223). He extends Jaspers' notion to include the period going from 800 BC to 600 AD, noting that "[t]his makes the Axial Age the period that saw the birth not only of all the world's major philosophical tendencies, but also all of today's major world religions: Zoroastrianism, Prophetic Judaism, Buddhism, Jainism, Hinduism, Confucianism, Taoism, Christianity, and Islam" (224).

can already be seen as inscribed in the nature of this new form of money. (247)

Building on Richard Seaford's argument concerning the origins of philosophy, Graeber proposes that all the major religions and philosophies are "built on a bedrock of materialism," that is to say that they spring from the question inherited from the problems of visibility intrinsic to the use of money: "What substance is the world made of?" (244). The search for some "underlying material behind the physical forms of objects in the world" quickly leads to "some notion of God, Mind, Spirit" as an "active organizing principle that gave form to [but] was not itself substance," he writes, noting the proximity between a notion such as Anaximander's *apeiron* – a "pure abstract substance that could not itself be perceived but was the material basis of everything that could be" – and the properties of gold when it is stamped into a coin (244, 245).[2] As Shell writes, "[g]old has a universal nature that, like the sculptor's metal or the stamper's wax, can become something else and yet still remain itself. Gold minted into a coin . . . is both homogeneous with itself (as gold) and heterogeneous with itself (as numismatic sculpture or as money)" (53-4). Graeber extends this "double-sidedness" of money to the notion of material itself (245):

> What is "material," anyway? Normally, we speak of "materials" when we refer to objects that we wish to make into something else. A tree is a living thing. It only becomes "wood" when we begin to think about all the other things you could carve out of it. And of course you can carve a piece of wood into almost anything. The same is true of clay, or glass, or metal. They're solid and real and tangible, but also abstractions, because they have the potential to turn into almost anything else – or, not precisely that; one can't turn a piece of wood into a lion or an owl, but one can turn it into an image of a lion or an owl – it can take on almost any conceivable form. So already in any materialist philosophy, we are dealing with an opposition between form and content, substance and shape; a clash between the idea, sign, emblem, or model in the creator's mind, and the physical qualities of the materials on which it is to be stamped, built, or imposed, from which it is to be brought into reality. (246)

---

[2] Graeber notes that "the historical connections [between the invention of coinage and the birth of philosophy] are so uncannily close that they are very hard to explain any other way," pointing to the fact that the first coins were minted in Lydia around 600 BC, precisely in the city in which and at the time when Greek philosophy begins with the speculations of Thales, Anaximander and Anaximenes of Miletus "on the nature of the physical substance from which the world ultimately sprang" (244-5).

A material is thus also something both "homogeneous with itself" *and* the potentiality for being something "heterogeneous with itself": a form (54). Confronted with the novelty of an object "whose nature was a profound enigma," Greek thinkers devised a dualistic way to think about reality which implies, at its heart, "a clash" between substance and abstraction, a tension in which the latter is given precedence and thought to have to be "stamped, built, or imposed" on the former (Graeber 246). Money "transform[s] visibles into invisibles and invisibles into visibles" (Shell 13), and the birth of materialism is also the moment when materiality disappears under the forms devised to understand and master it.

As a classicist, though, Carson notes that "[w]hen the ancient Greeks talk of money, adjectives for 'visible' and 'invisible' occur inconsistently," a fact which explains why "[m]odern scholars have been unsuccessful in efforts to abstract a stable definition for these terms from ancient usage" (*Economy* 45). As a poet, inconsistence and instability is precisely where she finds her value, and an entry into Simonides' poetry: "He lived at an interface between two economic systems" and his writing "makes clear that he gave thought to the concept of visible and invisible, was aware of a turmoil in their categorization and had an interest (conditioned perhaps by economic experience) in their valuing" (*Economy* 45). The invention of coinage changed the way humans conceive and thus perceive reality, generating centuries of confusion caught in the unbridgeable separations and edges between appearances and reality, form and matter, subject and object, self and other. But Simonides' interest, like that of Carson, lies not in the birth of stable categories, but on having the "occasion to observe [the movements of thought and money] and to meditate on their relation to the phenomena of perception" (*Economy* 45).

Of derivation and decreation

If the transition from gifts to coins generates turmoil in the categorisation of the visual, does the transition from coins to financial derivatives produce a similar necessity for poets to meditate afresh on the phenomena of perception? The distinctions between different types of derivatives can be complex, but, for the purpose of this essay, I am merely interested in two basic features: first, the idea that value results from a process of derivation between entities rather than from their intrinsic nature or qualities and, second, that this process of derivation is not a *one-off transfer* of value but, rather, the establishment of a relationship that endures over time and space between what is called an *underlying entity* and the *derivative*.

Derivatives are closer to the logic of gifts than to that of coins. If money "ruptures continuity and stalls objects at the borders of themselves," abstracting them "as bits of sealable value" which "become commodities," writes Carson, a gift, on the other hand, "is not a piece broken off from the interior life of the giver and lost into the exchange, but rather an extension of the interior of the giver, both in space and in time, into the interior of the receiver" (*Economy* 18). Extension and continuity instead of separation and edges: the shift towards an economy in which the notion of value becomes a function of financial products such as derivatives seems to reinstate, within the formation of value itself, some of the logic of the sociocultural system which predates the invention of coinage.[3] Transferred to literature, the logic of derivatives thus forces us to go beyond traditional notions of intertextuality, looking for writings which derive their value not only from the incorporation of various sources but from establishing a form of bidirectional relationship which endures over time and space between themselves and their sources.

The highly derivative nature of Carson's poetry in *Decreation*, confounding even some of her most eager critics, makes it a good place to start probing the kind of visibility associated with such relationships. The title of the collection is a neologism coined by the French philosopher and mystic Simone Weil, "a person who," proposes Carson in lieu of a definition, "wanted to get herself out of the way so as to arrive at God" (*Decreation* 167). Decreation stands for Weil's project of "undoing the subject because her presence to the object – God – is too substantial" (Coles 134). The separation between the subject and the object does not, for Weil, grant access to theoretical truth, but, on the contrary, is something that needs to be bridged. Carson's choice of Weil's notion as the title of the collection is already an indication of the kind of dynamics she is interested in establishing between her texts and the various sources they derive from.

Carson addresses this dynamic in one of the essays of the collection by associating it with the notion of the sublime. In "Foam (Essay with Rhapsody): On the Sublime in Longinus and Antonioni," she starts by defining the sublime as a "documentary technique," by which she means

---

[3] Graeber's argument is precisely that virtual money is "the original form of money," existing long before the invention of coinage (18).

the derivation of quotations as the main building blocks of one's own text:

> A quote (cognate with *quota*) is a cut, a section, a slice of someone else's orange. You suck the slice, toss the rind, skate away. Part of what you enjoy in a documentary technique is the sense of banditry. To loot someone else's life or sentences and make off with a point of view, which is called "objective" because you can make anything into an object by treating it this way, is exciting and dangerous. (45)

She introduces the notion of the sublime as a relationship between the writer and her sources by associating it with a form of looting, a "banditry" which suggests that critical distance is achieved at the expense of "someone else's life or sentences" treated as mere objects so as to "make off with a point of view." Typical of her essays, Carson sketches this definition of the sublime as a form of derivation in a few, very condensed sentences, leaving the implications of such a move buried in her text and letting them unfold in the rest of the essay as effects rather than as an overt argument. The point of departure itself, the association of the sublime to the use of quotations, seems to surface only as an off-hand comment on Longinus' treatise *On the Sublime*: "It has muddled arguments, little organization, no paraphrasable conclusion. Its attempts at definition are incoherent or tautological . . . You will come away from reading its (unfinished) forty chapters with no clear idea what the Sublime actually is," she affirms, but "will have been thrilled by its documentation" (45). The slippage from a lack of paraphrasable definition to the quality of the documentation, however, is far from innocent.

The focus of the essay is on the kind of relations Longinus' "aggregation of quotes" establishes with its sources, but the point is made only obliquely through its thematic content (45). It begins with Longinus' quotation of a sentence of the Greek orator Demosthenes uttered in a lawsuit opposing him to another Athenian who had slapped him in public: "By attitude! by look! by voice! the man who hits can do things to the other which the other can't even describe" (45). Carson then moves to Longinus' analysis on that sentence: "With words like these . . . the orator produces the same effect as the man who hits – striking the judges' minds with blow after blow" (45). She then sucks the slice of orange herself, noting that "Longinus' point is that, by brutal juxtaposition of coordinate nouns or noun clauses, Demosthenes transposes violence of fists into violence of syntax" (46). From quotation to quotation, she continues, "[h]is facts spill over the frame of their original context," and she makes them spill some more:

Watch this spillage, which moves from the man who hits, to the words of Demosthenes describing him, to the judges hearing these words, to Longinus analyzing the whole process, to me recalling Longinus' discussion of it and finally to you reading my account. The passionate moment echoes from soul to soul. (46)

From the brutality of the slap to the violence of syntax, Carson then proceeds with the kind of juxtapositions she enjoys in both her prose and poetry and quotes the Italian director Michelangelo Antonioni to reach back to a more literal slapping, this time of the filmmaker's own actress Lucia Bosé:

How many blows Lucia took for the final scene! The film ended with her beaten and sobbing, in a doorway. But she was always happy and it was hard for her to pretend to be desperate. She was not an actress. To obtain the result I wanted I had to use insults, abuse, hard slaps. In the end she broke down and wept like a child. She played her part wonderfully. (46-7)

Carson's own banditry adds up to a handsome little sum in which "the passionate moment" spills first from her sources to her own text, but then also, within her text, between the sources themselves as one occurrence of violence echoes the other.

Both the banditry and the spillage continue in the series of poems "Sublimes" which follows the essay. Akin to the juxtaposition of Longinus and Antonioni, the poem "Kant's Question About Monica Vitti" juxtaposes Kant's musing on the "Thing in Itself" with a description of the opening scene of Antonioni's l'*Eclisse* (1962), alternating one underlying entity with the other in eleven short stanzas. The relation between the two entities remains obscure, the only direct link being established in the title through the theme of questioning and then alluded to by the pronouns of the first line: "It was hidden in her and it gave Kant pleasure" (70). The line injects a degree of ambiguity as to the object being questioned, twice removed as an "it" hidden in a "her," and frames the relation between the act of questioning and its object in a correlation between hiddenness and pleasure. The neuter pronoun may refer to the question mentioned in the title, but it could also refer to the "Thing in Itself" mentioned at the end of line 5, qualified as "unattainable" and "insurmountable," or maybe to the concept of the sublime through an echo with a line from a previous poem of the series which proposes that "she has somehow got the Sublime inside her" (70, 67). After the first line, in any case, the overt relation between the two entities dissolves and the poem itself becomes an opaque derivative which resists efforts to answer the question raised by its title.

Both entities mirror each other as different forms of questioning of an unattainable object. Kant's "Thing in Itself" is doubled, in the lines which describe *l'Eclisse*, by the character played by Monica Vitti who is also, as line 6 puts it, "observed deeply / by a man in an armchair" (70). A connection is thus suggested between the work of the philosopher and the relation between the two characters, but to grasp the effects of Carson's derivation it is necessary to actually watch *l'Eclisse*. The movie opens with a long silent scene in which Monica Vitti is moving in a room, "with her eyes down," as the poem describes, under the gaze of a man sitting in a chair (70). When the dialogues begin, it becomes a scene of separation and questioning. Vittoria, Monica Vitti's character, is breaking up with Riccardo, and the latter wants to know why. The dialogues are sparse and clichéd: "Be good and tell me one last thing," he tells her, "[w]hen did you stop loving me?" (0:11:47-0:12:21). He wants to *understand*: "Is there someone else?", "Are you really sure?", "But there has to be a reason!" The man demands reason while the woman remains unable or unwilling to provide one: "I don't know," she repeats.

Watching this scene with Carson's poem in mind, the effect of her derivation gradually comes into focus as a bidirectional relation is established between the two underlying entities, producing a kind of stereoscopic vision in which the lover's romantic despair aligns itself with the sternness of the philosopher's theorising. Kant merges with Riccardo, and this composite subject, in turn, merges with the Longinus/Antonioni juxtaposition of the essay, associating the separation between subject and object with both the banditry of the literary critic attempting to "make off" with an objective point of view and the filmmaker's aggression of his lead actress to produce the sublime effect he is looking for.

At the heart of both the discourses of the sublime and Weil's notion of decreation is the question of the relation to otherness. In an interview, Carson summarises the "conventional descriptions of the sublime" as "an ambivalent motion" in which "[d]read [is] followed by a recovery of the feeling of mastery," that is to say a confrontation between self and otherness which results in the reinforcement of the edges separating the two in order to maintain or restore the feeling of mastery of the self (Aitken). The theory of the sublime is thus also a form of banditry, and Carson obliquely builds an argument on how relations built on separation and critical distance imply violence rather than open a path towards truth.

As the title of the series of poems suggests, however, there is a plurality of sublimes. In "Mia Moglie (Longinus' Red Desert)," three distinct variations are derived and become underlying entities which extend, confront and complicate each other. The poem's first two lines, "A caught woman is something the movies want to believe in / 'For instance, Sappho,' as Longinus says" (67), weave Antonioni's belief that "women are a finer filter of reality" (qtd in Ricciardi 10) with Longinus' discussion of Sappho's poetry. As the film critic Alessia Ricciardi shows, Longinus' comments quoted in the poem – "For she is terrified," "For she is all but dying" – align themselves with the "misappropriation of Giuliana's story" by both the husband and the lover in the movie (19). But a third entity then disrupts the poem, and the voice of Sappho herself creeps into the cracks of this juxtaposition of potential misappropriations.

Broken down into single words distributed between each stanza, a line from Sappho's fragment 31 gradually appears, precisely the line with which Carson launches her essay on decreation. Sappho's poem is usually read as a disquisition on jealousy in a love triangle between a girl who laughs, a man who listens and the speaker who witnesses the scene. But Carson underlines how from the second stanza onwards, the girl and the man disappear and the poem focuses solely on the speaker's own mind and body, describing the way in which her "perceptual abilities . . . [are] reduced to dysfunction one after the other" (160). The sentence included in Carson's poem, "[g]reener than grass and dead almost I seem to me," is a variation of the end of Sappho's fragment, just before it breaks into silence, a line that Carson reads as "a spiritual event": "predicating of her own Being an attribute observable only from outside her own body," Sappho stands outside herself and achieves a form of "*ekstasis*" (161). Confronted with otherness, Sappho seems to welcome the reduction of "perceptual abilities" and the dysfunction of the self that ensues, rather than attempting to theorise or systematise the encounter in an effort to recover her feeling of mastery.

It has been argued that Carson's engagement with the sublime in *Decreation* inscribes her poetry in the "Romantic tradition . . . stretching back through Longinus to Sappho, Homer, and the Bible" (Pollock), or, on the contrary, that it represents her efforts to break with the tradition and participate in founding a "feminine" and contemporary alternative to it (Disney 26). But to try to establish whether Carson stands within or breaks with and opposes the tradition both imply reducing the strangeness and opacity of the poem's derivations, and thus run the risk of simply reproducing the very kind of misappropriations they stage. In

"L'(Ode to Monica Vitti)", another poem in the series, after a description of Antonioni's *L'Avventura* (1960) in which Monica Vitti's character is again juxtaposed with men who "stand / gazing," the sentence suddenly breaks down:

> – and as
> for the scandal of our abandonment
> in a universe of "sudden trembling love," blondes
> being
> always
> fatally
> reinscribed
> on an old cloth
> faintly,
> interminably
> undone . . . (63)

The notion of *reinscription* provides a clue. This sentence is a derivation of a quote from Jacques Derrida commenting the notion of "epistemological breaks" in an interview: "I do not believe in decisive ruptures," he says, since "[b]reaks are always, and fatally, reinscribed in an old cloth that must continually, interminably be undone" (Positions 24). Resisting his ambition to somehow *access the real* through the finer grain of his female actresses, Antonioni's "blondes" are always, fatally, re-inscribed on the cloth of older theories of the sublime that maintain a distance with the real. Carson's poetry gains its energy not by trying to break with traditional notions, but by deriving and juxtaposing them, establishing complex relations which endure over time and space and cannot be reduced to a dualistic pair of *for* or *against*.

While in her poems she stages the potential for misappropriation implicit in Antonioni's approach, at the same time she also draws on it to build her own poetics. His "obsessive framing and reframing of multiple iterations of the same image," for example, his aesthetics of formal error and his "systematic efforts to violate the rules of commercial cinematic storytelling . . . clearly welcoming the risk of alienating the film's viewers" indeed all resonate deeply with Carson's poetic practice (Ricciardi 15, 6). The relations she establishes with her sources are better described by what she calls *withness*, a notion she derives from "the preposition chosen by John the Evangelist to describe the relationship between God and The Word" which, in Greek, "[w]hen used with the accusative" means "toward, upon, against, with, ready for, face to face, engaging, concerning, touching, in reply to, in respect of, compared with, according to, as accompaniment for" (*Economy* viii). Withness entails a different kind of turmoil of the visual.

A different kind of vision

"If you want to know why you cannot reach your own beautiful ideas," says the speaker of another long ekphrastic poem in *Decreation*, but "reach instead the edge of the thinkable," you may see that it "leaks" (99). When Carson reaches an edge, or when she uses them to build the triangulations of her poems, she is more interested in what happens after and between them than in what stops at them. Her poetry can be said to echo the logic of financial derivatives in the sense that it derives value from juxtaposition and continuity rather than from separation and breaks, but a central difference remains, and it concerns the question of visibility. Problems of money and visibility are as much at stake today as they were in Simonides' time, and it is by working through how his poetics emerged out of these problems that Carson develops her own for this new age of globalised financial capitalism.

The turmoil in the categorisation between the visible and the invisible brought about by the invention of coinage changed the way reality is represented and, through this representation, controlled. Carson argues that Simonides developed his poetics partly by reflecting on a contemporary revolution in painting, the development of illusionism by Polygnotos and other painters who transformed "the two-dimensional picture plane of archaic style and developed a new technology for the representation of three-dimensional reality" (*Economy* 47). The impact of this "new science" of representation on "the Greek popular imagination" was profound, as the vehemence with which Plato denounces painting as a form of sophistry attests (48, 49). Quoting Gorgias' famous opinion that poetry is simply "prose dressed up in meter," that is to say that it is "distinctive by virtue of its surface, not its content," Carson associates the "art of persuasion" of the sophists with illusionism in painting as the two sides of the same coin: "Illusionism, in paint as in words, . . . entails a total investment in the visible surface of the world as reality and a tendency to disavow the reality of anything not visible. Facts are what matters and facts are what you see" (50). "Like the sophist," she concludes, "the illusionist painter defines the world as data and undertakes to enhance our experience of it by perfecting our control of it" (62).

The historical development of financial derivatives also depends on the invention of a new technology of representation to perfect our control of the world. Bundling together and deriving various financial products entails a certain risk, but since the development of the Black-Scholes formula in 1973, the very notion of risk has been transformed. It is now thought to be calculable and can thus be priced appropriately. In other words, the risk inherent in derivatives is considered manageable by being "brought under the regime of value" through what is presented as an "advance . . . in the technological forces of representation" (Heidenreich). Applying this new advance in the science of representation, financiers use various *materials* (underlying entities) to create new *forms* (derivatives), which can be described as opaque since their complexity makes it impossible to perceive what they are constituted of. As the US subprime crisis and the credit crunch of 2007/8 brutally revealed, even financial institutions did not really grasp what they were investing in with these derivatives. This reincorporation of risk within the manageable through "new forms of securitization" (Graeber 15) – i.e. another version of the theorising of the recovery of the feeling of mastery – thus appears akin to a form of illusionism. Like the illusionist painter or writer, the banker indeed also "claims to make his audience see, as it were, what is not there" (*Economy* 62). Carson's poems embrace a different kind of opacity.

Opposed to illusionism in paint as in words, Simonides' "commitment is to a reality beyond 'what is visible to each person'," Carson proposes, aligning him with her own interest in the leakage of edges: "His medium is words positioned so as to lead you to the edge where words stop, pointing beyond themselves toward something no eye can see" (51). For him as for her, the edge of words does not mark an end but the point from which one needs to start looking: "His poems are paintings of a counterworld that lie behind the facts and inside perceived appearances," she writes, merging the visible and the invisible in her own metaphor (60). What matters is not the dichotomy, but the effort to "paint a picture of things that bring visible and invisible together in the mind's eye as one coherent fact," she explains, "a single fact seen from two vanishing points at once, in defiance of the laws of painterly perspective," she adds, echoing her own poetics of juxtaposition (55, 54).

A "different kind of visibility has to be created by the watchful poet," Carson concludes, a visibility that may breach separations and dualisms and in which we may "see matter stumble out of its forms," as she already proposes in one of her early poems (*Economy* 58; *Short Talks* 52). Carson obliquely addresses the duality of matter and form in an essay in which she aligns it with other dualisms such "as the unbounded from the bounded, as content from form, as polluted from pure," oppositions which, she argues, are based on a "mythological groundwork of assumption" which "can be traced to the earliest legends of the Greeks" and also inform the distinction between the female and the male in the texts of the philosophers ("Dirt and Desire" 132, 135, 133). The gender difference in Greek philosophy is linked to the opposition between the wet and the dry, and from Aristotle's characterisation of wetness as "that which is not bounded by any boundary of its own but can readily be bounded," Carson shows that, explicit in the philosophers' texts, is "[t]he image of woman as formless content" (132). Plato, for example, "compares [the] matter of creation to a mother, describing it as a 'receptacle' or 'reservoir' which is 'shapeless, viewless, all-receiving' and which 'takes its form and activation from whatever shapes enter it'," while Aristotle characterises the female as "raw material": "as when a bed (the child) is made by a carpenter (the father) out of wood (the mother). Man determines the form, woman contributes the matter" (132-3, 133).

"Contact is crisis," writes Carson who enrols social anthropology in her discussion, showing how the presence of the unbounded is a constant threat of "violating a fixed boundary, transgressing a closed category" (130). Because of the "pregnability" of their boundaries, porous to both "incursion from without" and "leakage from within," the logic of myth presents women as "awfully adept at confounding the boundaries of others," she writes, and "since woman does not bound herself, she must *be bounded*" (135, 142). This insight is worth keeping in mind when trying to evaluate the *value* of Carson's own blending of genres and derivative poetry. At the heart of the etiology of that conception, she argues, is a "deep and abiding mistrust of 'the wet' in virtue of its ability to transform and deform" (135). This is a dangerous ability, one that prevents the establishment of critical distance between a subject and the otherness of her object of inquiry, producing the risk to reduce perceptual abilities and lead to a dysfunction of the self rather than to help recover its feeling of mastery.

But this ability is also what opens a path for the decreation of the self through the writing and reading of poetry. Poetic language "reenacts the reality of which it speaks," writes Carson, naming this reenactment "radical mimesis" (*Economy* 52). Mimesis is not, for her, the imitation of nature recorded in a work of art, but "an action of the mind captured on a page," "the action that the poem has . . . on the reader" (Aitken). Reading repeats the action, she says, "it is a movement of yourself through a thought, through an activity of thinking, so by the time you get to the end you're different than you were at the beginning." (Aitken). With its "clean machinery of appositions, vanishing points and conceptual shocks," Carson's poetry as much as Simonides' is composed "as a painter may set daubs of pure color next to each other on his canvas in the knowledge that they will mix on the retina of your eye" (*Economy* 55, 54). Words, like daubs of paint, "interdepend," she explains, "the meaning of the sentence happens not outside, not inside the daubs of paint, but *between* them . . . Visible and invisible lock together in a fact composed of their difference" (*Economy* 54). Her derivations work the same way.

While the illusionist painter or writer or banker claims to make his audience see what is *not* there, Carson summarises, Simonides' claim, just like hers, "is more radical, for it comprehends the profoundest of poetic experiences: that of *not* seeing what *is* there" (*Economy* 62). "The properly invisible nature of otherness guarantees the mystery of our encounter with it," she adds, it "pulls out of us the act of attention that may bring 'some difference' to light" (71-2). Blindness is a more radical and profound artistic experience than the clairvoyance of beliefs and ideas, but it is also more threatening. Rather than restoring mastery and allowing control, it implies a crisis of contact, the violation of fixed boundaries and the transgressing of closed categories to make us wake up "just in time to see matter stumble out of its forms" (*Short Talks* 52). It requires us to encourage, rather than restrict, the leakage of matter and its ability to *transform* and *deform*. It demands a mode of attention to the poet's "syntax of defiance" (*Economy* 54) in which we confront ourselves with what usually remains invisible, but *is* nonetheless there, an experience of *withness* in which our very selves may come undone.

References

Aitken, Will. "Anne Carson, The Art of Poetry No. 88." *Paris Review* 171 (2004): http://www.theparisreview.org/interviews/5420/the-art-of-poetry-no-88-anne-carson. Accessed 20 January 2014.

Antonioni, Michelangelo. *L'Eclisse* (1962).

Carson, Anne. *Decreation: Poetry, Essays, Opera*. New York: Knopf, 2005.

——. "Dirt and Desire: Essay on the Phenomenology of Female Pollution in Antiquity." *Men in the Off Hours*. London: Cape Poetry, 2000. 130-157.

——. *Economy of the Unlost: Reading Simonides of Keos with Paul Celan*. Princeton: Princeton University Press, 1999.

——. *Eros the Bittersweet*. Princeton: Princeton University Press, 1986.

——. *Short Talks*. 1992. London and Ontario: Brick Books, 2015.

Coles, Elizabeth. "The Sacred Object: Anne Carson and Simone Weil." *Acta poética* 34.1 (2013): 127-154.

Derrida, Jacques. *Positions*. Chicago: University of Chicago Press, 1982.

Disney, Dan. "Sublime Disembodiment? Self-as-Other in Anne Carson's Decreation." *Orbis Litterarum* 67.1 (2012): 25-38.

Goldsmith, Kenneth. "The Writer as Meme Machine." *The New Yorker*, 22 October 2013. http://www.newyorker.com/books/page-turner/the-writer-as-meme-machine. Accessed 5 April 2015.

Graeber, David. *Debt: The First 5000 Years*. Brooklyn: Melville House Publishing, 2012.

Heidenreich, Stefan. "Freeportism as Style and Ideology: Post-Internet and Speculative Realism, Part I." *e-flux*. http://www-e-flux.com/journal/freeportism-as-style-and-ideology-part-i-post-internet-and-speculative-realism/. Accessed 5 June 2016.

Jonas, Hans. *The Phenomenon of Life: Toward a Philosophical Biology*. New York: Harper and Row, 1966.

Pollock, James. "Anne Carson and the Sublime." Review. *Contemporary Poetry Review*, 2008. http://cprw.com/Pollock/carson.htm. Accessed 11 April 2015.

Seaford, Richard. *Money and the Early Greek Mind: Homer, Philosophy, Tragedy*. Cambridge: Cambridge University Press, 2004.

Shell, Marc. *The Economy of Literature*. Baltimore: Johns Hopkins University Press, 1978.

Snell, Bruno. *The Discovery of the Mind*. Cambridge: Harvard University Press, 1953.

Notes on Contributors

SARAH CHEVALIER is *Privatdozent* for English Linguistics at the University of Zurich. Her research interests focus on the varieties of English, both from a social and a regional perspective, as well as on the question of multilingualism and multilingual families. Her *habilitation*, a study of the acquisition of three languages by young children, explores one of the many facets of the question of Language acquisition and Language attitudes in multilingual families. Her publications include a monograph, *Trilingual Language Acquisition: Factors Influencing Active Trilingualism in Early Childhood* (2015), a co-edited volume, *Building Bridges: Methodology, Corpora, and Globality in English Linguistics* (forthcoming) and numerous articles on multilingualism.

VIRÁG CSILLAGH is an Assistant at the English Department of the University of Geneva. She holds a Masters degree in English Literature and Linguistics from the Eötvös Loránd University in Budapest. She is currently working on her PhD, in the domain of language teaching methodology, research design and cognitive psychology. Her research focuses on the dynamics of language learning motivation as an element of successful acquisition, and its role in the broader framework of language teaching methodology and educational policy making.

CLAIRE FOREL is Professor of English Linguistics at the English Department and at the *Institut Universitaire de Formation des Enseignants* (Teacher Training Institute) of the University of Geneva. Her double affiliation owes to the fact that she started her career in the Genevan secondary school system as a teacher of English as a foreign language and as a teacher trainer for teachers of English. She holds a PhD from the University of Geneva, with a dissertation on Charles Bally who took over the chair in General Linguistics after F. de Saussure's death. Claire Forel's research interests combine General Linguistics (in the Saussurian sense) and language teaching, and she tries to bring together her experience as both a language teacher and a linguist in exploring how learning a foreign language can be an opportunity to learn what language is and how it works. Her publications include a monograph, *Sociologie et sociolinguistique dans les inédits de Charles Bally*, and numerous articles on Linguistics and gender studies, Phonology, Saussurian linguistics as well as in the domain of Language teaching.

INDIRA GHOSE is Professor of English at the University of Fribourg. She taught English as a Foreign Language in Germany for many years before taking her PhD and *Habilitation* at the Free University of Berlin. Her research interests include colonial writing and literature of the early modern period, especially drama and courtesy literature, and the history of the emotions. Her publications include *Women Travellers in Colonial India: The Power of the Female Gaze* (1998) and *Shakespeare and Laughter: A Cultural History* (2008).

JOHN E. JOSEPH is Professor of Applied Linguistics at the University of Edinburgh since 1997. He held several previous positions and visiting posts in universities around the world, among others as a lecturer in Montpellier (1980-81), a visiting research associate at the American University of Beirut (1998) or a Professor of English Language and Literature at the University of Hong Kong (1993-96). He also taught in Summer schools in Singapore, North Carolina and Berlin. His wide research interests include Saussure's linguistic work and its place in modern linguistics, but also questions about linguistic identity, language and politics and, more recently, the connections between language and the body and the exploration of the physical experimentation of cognition. He is the author of the much acclaimed biography of Ferdinand de Saussure, *Saussure*, published in 2012, as well as of several major monographs, *Language and Identity: National, Ethnic, Religious* (2004), *Language and Politics* (2006) and *Language, Mind and Body: A Conceptual History* (2016).

MARTIN LEER is *Maître d'enseignement et de recherche* and Head of the Section for Contemporary Literature at the University of Geneva. He did his undergraduate degree at the University of Copenhagen and his PhD at the University of Queensland, Australia. His research interests are in colonial and postcolonial literatures, literary geography, literature and the environment, the history of reading and poetry and poetics, and he has published widely in these fields and as a literary translator. Over the years he developed an unhealthy, negative obsession with money and economics, especially after 2008. He hopes this book is the end of it.

SANGAM MACDUFF is an Assistant in Modern English Literature at the University of Geneva. He read English at Cambridge before taking a Master's in English Literature and Creative Writing from the University of Edinburgh. His research interests concentrate on the development of the literary epiphany from Wordsworth to Beckett. He has published on "spots of time" in Wordsworth and epiphanies in Joyce and is preparing to defend his doctoral thesis on *Joyce's Epiphanies*.

ORAN MCKENZIE holds degrees in both Economics and English and History from the University of Geneva. His Master's thesis on materiality and vision in the poetry of Anne Carson won the Prix Marcel Compagnon of the Faculté des lettres of the University of Geneva in 2015. He was recently appointed Assistant in American Literature at Geneva.

MARTIN MÜHLHEIM is an Advisor of Studies, grade and course administration and Instructor in English at the University of Zurich. He completed his PhD thesis at Zurich, *Fictions of Home: Narratives of Alienation and Belonging, 1850-2000* in 2013 and is preparing it for publication. His research interests include narrative fiction and narratology, intertextuality and genre, the concepts of collective memory, shame and identity and quantitative formalism (distant reading). He has published on fiction, film and cultural studies.

RAHEL ORGIS holds degrees in English and American literature and French Literature and linguistics from the University of Bern. In 2013 she completed her PhD thesis at the University of Neuchâtel entitled *Structured Proliferation: Readers and the Narrative Art of Lady Mary Wroth's Urania*. She has published on early modern literature and taught at the Universities of Neuchâtel, Geneva and Lausanne as well as in secondary schools.

GENOVEVA PUSKÁS is Associate Professor in English Linguistics at the University of Geneva. Her main research domains are syntax, the syntax-semantics interface and Finno-Ugric languages. More specifically, her research activities include the syntax and semantics of negation and quantification in a comparative approach, the syntax and semantics of left peripheral phenomena in Hungarian, such as Topic, Focus, wh-questions and Contrastive Topic, and more recently, the syntax of subjunctive clauses and the syntax-semantics interface of Modality. Her publications include two monographs, *Word-Order in Hungarian: the Syntax of A'-positions* (2000) and *Initiation au Programme Minimalisme: éléments de syntaxe comparative* (2013), two co-edited volumes (with Louis de Saussure and Jacques Moeschler) on Tense, Aspect and Modality, as well as articles in international journals and book chapters on the syntax of Focus and Topic, the syntax and semantics of negation, of quantification and floating quantifiers and of subjunctive embedded clauses.

BARBARA STRAUMANN is Assistant Professor with tenure track at the English Seminar at the University of Zurich. Her research interests include literary and cultural theory, psychoanalysis, gender, film and visuality. She is the co-author, with Elisabeth Bronfen, of *Die Diva: Eine Geschichte der Bewunderung* (2002) and the author of *Figurations of Exile in Hitchcock and Nabokov* (2008). She completed her *Habilitation* (postdoctoral thesis) entitled *Corinne's Sisters: Female Performers in the Long Nineteenth Century* in 2014 and is currently working on a study on the cultural afterlife of Queen Elizabeth I and on another research project with the working title "IOU: Debt in the Victorian Novel".

EVA WALTERMANN holds an MA in English Linguistics and a PhD In English Linguistics, both from the University of Geneva. Her PhD dissertation, entitled *Représentations du savoir disciplinaire dans l'enseignement des langues étrangères: le cas des enseignants genevois* [Representation of disciplinary knowledge in the teaching of foreign languages: the case of Genevan teachers] explores the importance for language teaching of language awareness and of the teachers' representations and beliefs about language. Eva Waltermann is also a part-time teacher in a secondary school.

RICHARD WASWO is Professor Emeritus of English at the University of Geneva. He studied at Stanford and Harvard and taught at San Francisco and San José Colleges and the University of Virginia before coming to Geneva in 1976. His many publications include notably *Language and Meaning in the Renaissance* (1987) and *The Founding Legend of Western Civilisation* (1997). His major research interest in recent years has been the relationship between words and money as exemplified in the book that was published from the papers given at his retirement conference *Fiction and Economy*, edited by Susan Bruce and Valeria Wagner (2007)

Index of Names

Aitken, Will, 227, 235, 240-241, 242
Alexander, Jonathan, 202, 222
Alexievitch, Svetlana, 36
Amiel, Henri-Frédéric, 41,
Anderlini-D'Onofrio, Serena, 202, 222
Antonioni, Michelangelo, 234-237, 242
Araujo e Sá, Maria Helena, 91, 94
Aristotle, 131, 132, 133n, 134, 140
Asimov, Isaac, 16
Attridge, Derek, 90n, 196
Bain, Alexander, 49, 50-53, 52n, 53n, 55, 57-58, 59
Bakhtin, Mikhail, 202, 222
Bally, Charles, 54, 56, 59, 63n
Barnes Julia, 98, 116
Barron-Hauwaert, Suzanne, 100, 101, 107n, 115
Baskin, Wade, 48, 61
Baston, Jane, 144n, 145, 155-156, 157n, 158, 160
Béguelin, Marie-José, 54n, 59
Bernanke, Ben, 12, 18, 36
Bode, Katherine, 201n3, 222
Böhringer, Heike, 76, 95
Bourdieu, Pierre, 32, 55, 55n, 59, 137, 140
Boyle, Robert, 184n, 189, 196
Braun, Andreas, 100-102, 104n, 115

Bréal, Michel, 55, 59
Breidbach, Stephan, 93, 94
Broca, Paul, 57, 59
Buchan, James, 21, 36, 191n
Buckroyd, Peter, 159n, 160
Bunyan, John, 163-164, 179
Burghley, William Cecil, Baron, 138, 140
Burrell, Ian, 206, 222
Busino, Giovanni, 42, 59
Carlyle, Thomas, 166, 166n, 179
Carson, Anne, 11, 34-35, 36, 225-242
Castellotti, Véronique, 78, 95
Castiglione, Baldassare, 32, 130-131, 136-137, 140
Celan, Paul, 226, 227
Chaucer, Geoffrey, 124
Cheney, Patrick, 157n, 160
Chevalier, Sarah, 102, 115
Cicero, 131, 133, 140
Cirlot, Juan Eduardo, 207, 223
Claparède, Alexandre, 41, 59
Clark, Rachel Ellen, 158n, 160
Clarkson, Leslie, 150, 160
Cline, Tony, 100-102, 104n, 115
Coleridge, Samuel Taylor, 18
Coles, Elizabeth, 232, 242
Collini, Stefan, 16, 29, 36
Comensoli, Viviana, 145, 147n, 155, 155n, 157n, 160
Comte, Auguste, 55, 55n, 59

Index of Names

Constantin, Emile, 54, 61, 64n, 74
Council of Europe (CEFR), 65-68, 74
Crystal, David, 76, 94, 100, 115
Csillagh, Virág, 80, 81-83, 86, 94
Culler, Jonathan, 188, 196
Dalley, Lana, 175, 179
Dameth, Henri, 29, 42-44, 47-48, 59
Davanzi, Bernardo, 121, 127
David, Jean-Elie, 41, 59
Dawson, Anthony, 145n, 160
De Palo, Marina, 55, 59
De Roover, Raymond, 120, 127
De Swaan, Abram, 99-100, 107, 113, 115
Defurne, Bavo, 201, 211, 213, 222
Dekker, Thomas, 143-162
Deming, Robert Howard, 183n, 196
Derrida, Jacques, 237, 242
Disney, Dan, 236, 242
Dobson, Kit, 168n, 174n, 179
Dick, Kirby, 205, 223
Doise, William, 88
Dolgin, Alexander, 206n, 222
Dörnyei, Zoltán, 81, 83, 94
Driscoll, Catherine, 206n, 222
Drucker, Peter, 202, 223
Egger, Victor, 29, 51-53, 55-58, 59
Elias, Norbert, 130, 140
Eling, Paul, 57, 60
Ellmann, Maud, 184, 184n, 188, 191, 192, 193,196
Ellmann, Richard, 196
Elmiger, Daniel, 76, 95
Elyot, Thomas Sir, 32, 130, 140

Engels, Friedrich, 165-166
Epstein, E. L., 184n, 196
Euclid, 194
Ferber, Michael, 207, 223
Ferguson, Charles, 104n, 115
Ferguson, Gibson, 100, 115
Finn, Margot, 169, 169n, 171n, 176n, 177n, 179
Fitzgerald, F. Scott, 129, 139, 140
Force, Pierre, 150, 150n, 160
Forel, Claire-A., 74
Forman, Valérie, 147n, 154n, 156, 157, 157n, 158, 159n, 160
Forster, Simone, 76, 95
Friedman, Milton, 23
Gabelentz, Georg von der, 46, 60
Garber, Marjorie, 152n, 155n, 157n, 160
Garrard, Gregg, 210n, 223
Gifford, Terry, 212n, 223
Goldsmith, Kenneth, 35, 226, 242
Goux, Jean-Joseph, 192n, 196
Graddol, David, 76, 95
Graeber, David, 11, 19, 21-24, 24, 27, 36, 118, 127, 176n, 179, 229, 229n, 230, 230n, 231, 232n, 239, 242
Grav, Peter F., 146, 151, 154, 155n, 158, 160
Greene, Robert, 138, 140
Grin, François, 28, 30, 65, 74, 79-80, 95
Guazzo, Stephano, 131, 141
Hamilton, Sir William, 50, 57, 60
Hansen, Alvin, 13

Index of Names

Harris, Jonathan Gil, 145, 156, 160
Harris, Roy, 48, 54, 61
Hartley, David, 49
Hawkins, Eric, 68, 74
Hayek, Friedrich von, 14, 36
Heidenreich, Stefan, 239, 242
Hemingway, Ernest, 139
Hempel, Dirk, 173n, 179
Henry, Victor, 29, 60
Herbert, Christopher, 165, 179
Herodotus, 25
Hicks, John, 13
Hobbes, Thomas, 49, 150
Holden, J. Milnes, 121, 127
Homer, 124
Hörisch, Jochen, 33, 164n, 171-172, 172n, 179
Houdebine-Gravaud, Anne-Marie, 87, 90, 95
Howard, Jean, 147n, 148n, 150n, 155, 156, 157n, 160
Hülmbauer, Cornelia, 76, 95
Hunt, Aeron, 171n, 179
Jacobs, Deborah, 145n, 152n, 161
Jadwin, Lisa, 168n, 173n, 178n, 179
Jennings, Kate, 20, 36
Jockers, Matthew, 201n, 223
Jodelet, Denise, 78, 95
Jonas, Hans, 226, 242
Jones, Norman W., 219, 223
Joseph, John, 40, 41n, 42, 46, 47, 51, 55, 60
Jowett, John, 158n, 161
Joyce, James, 34, 221n, 181-197
Juselius, Katarina, 14, 36
Kachru, Braj, 100, 116
Kant, Immanuel, 234-235
Kelso, Ruth, 130n, 140

Kermode, Lloyd Edward, 153n, 161
Keynes, John Maynard, 13-14, 16, 20, 23, 36
King, Mervyn Sir, 12-13, 36
Kitch, Aaron, 153, 156-157, 157n, 158n, 161
Kohl, Stephan, 172, 179
Korda, Natasha, 144n, 152n, 156n, 161
Krantz, Susan, 155, 157n, 161
Krugman, Paul, 13, 16, 36
Künzel, Christine, 173n, 179
Lacan, Jacques, 193, 196
Lanchester, John, 14, 15, 19-20
Lecercle, Jean-Jacques, 188n
Leer, Martin, 36
Lehrman, Lewis E., 118, 127
Lemaître, Auguste, 41, 60
Leonard, Garry Martin, 184n, 196
Lewis, Michael, 20-21, 36
Li, Chi-Fang Sophia, 159n, 161
Litz, Walton A., 188n, 196
Locke, John, 23, 26, 49, 58, 150
Lotman, Jurij, 211, 220, 223
Lüdi, Georges, 77, 95
Lysack, Krista, 176n, 179
Martin, Felix, 12, 19, 23-24, 34, 37, 118, 127
Marx, Karl, 118, 127, 164
Mason, Paul, 28, 37
Mauss, Marcel, 34, 176n, 179
Mercado, Thomas de, 121, 127
Middleton, Thomas, 143-162
Mill, John Stuart, 49, 57, 58, 60
Miller, Andrew, 172n, 178n, 179
Moore, Danièle, 78, 95
Moore, Thomas, 189
Moretti, Franco, 34, 201, 204, 219n, 220, 221n, 223

Index of Names

Muldrew, Craig, 33, 143n, 144, 144n, 146, 149n, 151, 156n, 161
Murray, Heather, 85, 86, 95
Nenna, Giovanni Battista, 134, 137, 140
Nixon, Richard, 22, 24, 118, 117
Norris, Margot, 184n, 188, 190, 196
Norton, Sandy Morey, 178, 179
Nussbaum, Martha, 16, 37
Odier, Henri, 30, 55-56, 56n, 60
Orgel, Stephen, 145n
Ormerod, Paul, 13, 14, 37
Osgood, Charles, 88, 95
Osteen, Mark, 34, 192, 193, 196
Peacham, Henry, 138, 140
Peck, Linda Levy, 131, 140
Pennycook, Alastair, 76, 95
Perregaux, Christiane, 68-70, 71, 72, 74
Phillipson, Robert, 76, 96
Pictet, Amé, 42, 60
Piketty, Thomas, 15, 37
Plato, 25-26, 229, 238, 240,
Polanyi, Karl, 14, 37
Pollock, James, 227, 236, 242
Polo, Marco, 117-118, 127
Power, Eileen, 120, 127
Rand, Ayn, 16
Rappoport, Jill, 175, 179
Reinhart, Carmen, 37
Reizbaum, Marilyn, 184, 184n, 188, 191, 197
Ricciardi, Alessia, 236, 237,
Richards, Grant, 181-182, 183, 184n
Rifkin, Jeremy, 28, 37
Rogoff, Kenneth, 37
Romei, Annibale, 131-132, 140

Ronjat, Jules, 112, 116
Rosdeitcher, Elizabeth, 172, 180
Rose, Mary Beth, 144n, 155, 161
Roulet, Eddy, 68, 74
Rumelhart, D. E., 49, 60
Ruskin, John, 166, 166n, 180
Sandel, Michael,16, 37
Sappho, 236
Saul, John Ralston, 16, 37
Saussure, Ferdinand de, 28, 29-30, 39-61, 63n, 64, 64n, 67, 67n, 70-71, 72, 74
Saxey, Esther, 201n, 202, 215, 223
Schmidt, Alexandra, 91, 94
Seaford, Richard, 19, 25, 26-27, 37, 226, 230, 242
Sechehaye, Albert, 54, 63n
Sedlacek, Tomas, 14, 37
Sedgwick, Eve Kosovsky, 202, 223
Seidlhofer, Barbara, 76, 95, 100, 116
Shakespeare, William, 17, 31, 89, 117-127
Shaw, Katy, 14, 37
Shell, Marc, 19, 25-27, 37, 171, 172, 180, 191n, 197, 226, 228-231, 242
Shulman, Lee, 87, 96
Simmel, Georg, 118, 127
Skeat, Walter W., 194, 197
Smith, Adam, 14, 22, 37, 44, 58, 121, 166
Smith, Sir Thomas, 130, 140
Snell, Bruno, 225, 242
Spencer, Herbert, 49, 61
Spolsky, Bernard, 97, 99, 103, 108, 114, 116

Spufford, Peter, 120, 127
Staigerm, Janet, 207, 223
Stelling-Michaud, Sven, 42, 59
Stone, Lawrence, 130, 131, 141
Taine, Hippolyte, 49, 51, 52n, 61
Taleb, Nassim Nicholas, 14, 37
Tawney, R. H., 120, 127
Thackeray, William Makepeace, 33, 163-180
Thatcher, Margaret, 14, 15
Torchiana, Donald, 184n, 189, 197
Ulin, Jeff C., 223
Ushioda, Emma, 81 83, 94
Verchère, Isaac-Antoine, 40, 41, 41n, 42, 43
Walzl, Florence, 184n, 189, 191n, 197
Waswo, Richard, 144, 162
Weeks, Jeffrey, 206, 223
Werlen, Iwar, 77, 95, 96
Whitaker, Harry, 57, 60
Whittaker, Stephen, 194, 197
Zastrow, Charles, 216, 223
Žižek, Slavoj, 192n, 197
Zurcher, Amelie, 150, 162